SOUL AND PSYCHE

SOUL *and* PSYCHE

*On the Relationship of
Psychotherapy and Religion*

EDWARD CADBURY LECTURES, 1958–1959

Victor White, O.P.

CLUNY
Providence, Rhode Island

CLUNY EDITION, 2023

This Cluny edition is a republication of *Soul and Psyche*,
originally published by Collins and Harvill Press in 1960.

For more information regarding this title
or any other Cluny Media publication,
please write to info@clunymedia.com, or to
Cluny Media, P.O. Box 1664, Providence, RI 02901

• VISIT US ONLINE AT WWW.CLUNYMEDIA.COM •

ISBN: 978-1685952488

NIHIL OBSTAT
Thomas Gilby, O.P., S.T.L., PH.D.
Joannes Hislop, O.P., S.T.L., M.A., D.PHIL.
Carolus Davis, S.T.L., *censor deputatus*
WESTMONASTERII, DIE 20A JANUARII 1959

IMPRIMI POTEST
Henricus St. John, O.P., *prior provincialis*
DIE 20A DECEMBRIS 1958

IMPRIMATUR
E. Morrogii Bernard, *vic. gen.*
WESTMONASTERII, DIE 20A JANUARII 1959

Cover design by Clarke *&* Clarke
Cover image: Adrià Gual, *The Dew*,
1897, oil on canvas
Courtesy of Wikimedia Commons

CONTENTS

post-Christians. *The disastrous psychological and social results of the "repression of the shadow" and the need for "the integration of evil." The traditional conception of evil, and Jung's objections to it. An analysis of the ambiguous notions of the "acceptance" and "integration" of evil. Some necessary distinctions between: the evil we do and the evil we undergo; repression and suppression; consciousness of evil in cognition and conation.*

The practical difficulty in correlating health and holiness, sanity and sanctity. The concepts of health in general, and of mental health in particular. Neurosis, psychosis and wholeness. The "solidarity of death in life," and death as the end or completion of life. "Normality" and "individuation" as aims of psychotherapy. Death and wholeness: the fear of death as the fear of incompletion. Early and later Christian attitudes to health, sickness, suffering and death. The Thomistic account of original sin implies that psychological disorder is "normal" for fallen man, though particular disorders are to be attributed directly to other particular causes, themselves consequent upon original sin. The Christian equation of health and holiness ultimately eschatological, a matter of hope, though already revealed in Christ. Psychological disorders are compatible with holiness in this life.

The problem of correlating religious practice and belief with psychological health and maturity. The classical conception of religion. Religion, thus understood, as a factor of psychological integration and differentiation. The psychological function of prayer and ritual sacrifice. The contemporary "failure of religion" as an integrating force in individuals and societies. Religion as integration and compensation. The witness of depth-psychology to the prior importance of images for religion, and to the need for conformity of exterior images with interior images and needs. Psychological troubles attributable to the poverty or inappropriateness of "holy images," especially in childhood and adolescence. The use and abuse of images from the psychological standpoint. The peculiar demands of Biblical and Christian religion and of the central Christian symbols. Stages of religious development: magic, "natural religion," Old and New Testaments. Law and grace.

☙ ☙

◆

AUTHOR'S NOTE

The core of this book consists of the 1958–1959 Edward Cadbury Lectures in the University of Birmingham. My thanks are due to Professor G. W. H. Lampe and the Committee of which he is chairman for their invitation to me to deliver these lectures.

My debt to the hard labours of others, both theologians and psychologists, will be evident to the reader: it is scarcely less than that of a parasite. The debt is all the greater inasmuch as they may hardly recognize their own handiwork when I have finished criticizing and shaping it to fit my own constructions. My grateful acknowledgments to the numerous authors and publishers whose works I have quoted will be found elsewhere.

The personal friends who have helped me, whether directly in fashioning the text or indirectly in providing me with its content, are too numerous to name.

The bulkiness of the notes and appendices is to be explained by my wish to keep the text as free as possible from technicalities which would be of interest only to the specialist, while at the same time providing some explanation of those technicalities which could not be altogether avoided. They also offer some optional excursions from the main itinerary.

I.

THE COMMON GROUND
OF RELIGION AND PSYCHOLOGY

It is reasonable to expect that many readers of this book will find this preliminary chapter superfluous, a tedious labouring of the obvious. Whatever their estimates of religion on the one side or of contemporary psychology on the other, the fact that both share some common ground and are concerned with a common, or at least an overlapping, subject-matter, will be too evident to them to require any argument. It could hardly occur to them that the psyche, the business of the psychologist and the psychotherapist, is something wholly different from the soul, the business of the theologian and the pastor. They will be aware, of course, that the two parties appear to treat the matter very differently, both theoretically and practically, and that sometimes their respective treatments appear to conflict. But if their respective fields of inquiry and operations sometimes become a battlefield, this can only be because they are operating on the same ground. A distinction of mutually exclusive fields or subject-matters, such as we find (let us say) between those of the marine biologist and of the solar physicist or the political economist, is here hardly thinkable, whether we approach the subject from the psychological or from the religious standpoint. The relationship between them would seem more akin to that between the anatomist and surgeon on the one side and the biologist and physician on the other; in the sense that, though the standpoints and methods of each differ widely, both are concerned with the same living organism and (in the case of the surgeon and the physician) its healthy functioning.

Closer examination, whether conducted from the psychological or from the religious angle, confirms this view. Since William James's *Varieties of Religious Experience,* such phenomena as conversion, faith, mystical experiences—regularly ascribed by religion to "the soul"—have in fact, if not also by right, been subjects for psychological investigation. The right, if such it is, would not readily be surrendered by psychologists, or disputed by most theologians. Provided only that what the theologian attributes to the soul is also, directly or indirectly, an observable phenomenon of mental and emotional life, the empirical psychologist cannot exclude it from his own legitimate field of investigation. Still less can the practical psychotherapist. Although on his first appearance he seems generally to have aspired to be no more than a modest technician, who could be as indifferent to the patient's religious beliefs, disbeliefs, practices and values as could the physician, the position soon proved untenable. Psychoneuroses, character, and psychological problems generally, proved to be very much less separable from such "spiritual" matters than were measles and appendicitis. It was soon found difficult, if not impossible, to banish from any adequate clinical picture, let alone from any treatment which must take into account the totality of the personality, the conscious and unconscious motivations of its behaviour. The advent of depth-psychology made this only more evident. However hostile and inadequate was the appraisal of religion in early psychoanalysis, and whatever its pretensions to *weltanschauliche Neutralität,*[1] it could not exclude from its purview the functions which religion had ascribed to the soul, or ignore their vital role in mental health and sickness. It was precisely *in* the psyche that Jung and his followers claimed to discover, if not religion, then the basic raw material of religion and its indispensable function—"religion *in statu nascendi.*[2] So far from dividing soul from psyche, some Jungians will hold that their effectual separation among many people in Western civilization today is at the root not only of the decay of religion as an effective social and psychological force, but also of much of our mental distress. If the personality is to be divided into two separate spheres of influence, a soul which is the business of religion and theology, and a psyche which is the domain of psychology and psychotherapy, each must surrender any claim to deal with the whole human being or any concern with total personal integration. Many who have experienced deep analysis, especially under Jungian auspices, know that the process allows the withholding of nothing—*opus requirit totum hominem* ("this work demands the whole man"), as the alchemists said. And it is precisely in the psyche, and with the aid of psychology, that they have discovered the personal significance to themselves of the Trinity, the Incarnation, of the Virgin Mother, of Conversion, Sacrifice and Sacrament, and of much else that religion claims for the soul.

But religion can no more exclude from the soul what, by general consent, belongs to the psyche than psychology can exclude from the psyche what traditionally is ascribed to the soul. This is implicitly recognized in those textbooks of psychology and psychiatry, usually of Catholic provenance,[3] which employ the same definitions and descriptions of the soul which have been employed by theologians for the subject-matter of psychology and psychiatry also. We have yet to justify this usage from the theological point of view. But, even without theological equipment, it is difficult for religious believers, anyhow for those whose religion is based on the Bible, to think of the soul as excluding the sphere covered also by contemporary psychology. To the extent that, for instance, their religion is formed by, and expressed in, the Psalms (the example is chosen as being common to Jews, Protestants and Catholics), they will know the soul as the subject of very much more than such exclusively religious activities as praise, prayer, trust in God and thanksgiving to him.[4] Explicitly or implicitly, the soul appears in the Psalter as the subject of every manner of love and hate, of elation and depression, of fear and resentment, of phantasy, dream and nightmare: of emotions and experiences which could not be denied to psychology without denying it any legitimate subject-matter at all. We are not yet arguing that so comprehensive a claim for the soul and for religion is legitimate; we are only drawing attention to the fact that it is made, and that those whose religion is in practice formed by such a book as the Psalms cannot easily suppose that religion and psychology function in two separate and distinct fields. To many who approach the matter from the Christian side, it requires no argument to show that religion cannot be departmentalized into one sector only of human life; the "pearl of great price" demands of a man "all that he hath" (Matt. 13:46).

We might leave matters at that were it not that this view of the objective identity of soul and psyche has been vigorously challenged and contradicted. The challenge is sometimes more implied than openly expressed; but sometimes it is quite explicit. The eminence of the opponents, not only in their professional field of psychiatry but also in the Church, commands the greatest respect; and even though we shall find ourselves unable to agree with them, we must be grateful for their challenge which compels us to examine our position more thoroughly, a position which might otherwise prove to be a rash and unexamined assumption.

Perhaps the most frank and categorical opposition to any identification of soul and psyche is that attributed to one of the leading Catholic psychiatrists in the United States. Replying to some criticisms of psychoanalysis from theologians, Dr. Gregory Zilboorg is said to have written:

They fail to observe the major principle of St. Thomas which saved Aristotle from being re-forgotten after he had been re-discovered. This principle represents perhaps the greatest contribution of St. Thomas. He adapted Aristotle to the prevailing apologetics by means of a new postulate: that which is true in philosophy may not be true in theology and *vice versa*. By confusing soul with psyche or psychic apparatus....the opponents of psycho-analysis found themselves unable to apply Thomistic principles to the Freudian studies and unable to comprehend that what is true in psychology may not be true in traditional apologetics, Catholic, Protestant or secular, and *vice versa*—that the psychic apparatus is not the soul and the soul is not the psyche.[5]

Whatever may be thought of this as a theory, it can hardly fail to spread alarm and despondency in concrete practice; while it may shield the analyst from many problems and conflicts, it can only add to those of the patient. The guardian of Tom's soul tells him he should not masturbate, it is a mortal sin and will hurt his soul. The guardian of his psyche tells him (such things are not un-heard of[6]) that he should masturbate, it will relieve the tensions of his psyche. Just what is Tom to do? The theologian tells him that God is his Maker and his last End and has a paramount claim upon his life and his love. The father of psychoanalysis tells him that God is a phantasy product of his wishful-thinking: a neurosis. Just what is Tom to believe?

We may note in passing that the invocation of St. Thomas Aquinas seems singularly inappropriate—unless we are to suppose that what is false in history may be true in psychology. For, according to all the documentary evidence, it was not Aquinas but his arch-opponent Siger de Brabant who was alleged (probably unjustly) to have held the "double truth": that "what is true in

philosophy may not be true in theology and *vice versa*." And it was
Aquinas who maintained, with considerable insistence and perti-
nacity, that truths of faith and of philosophy could *not* contradict
each other: it was precisely by so doing that he may be said to
"have saved Aristotle."[7]

It is more to our present purpose to observe that Aquinas
seems a most unsuitable patron saint for the view that "the psychic
apparatus is not the soul and the soul is not the psyche." "Soul"
is the English of Latin *anima*; and for Aquinas (as for everybody
else[8]) *anima* is the Latin of Greek *psyche*. We cannot of course argue conclusively to an identity of subject-matter from the fact that
modern psychologists use the same word *psyche* for their own field
of investigation, but quite certainly they cannot legitimately claim
that their field is something distinct from that covered by the traditional *anima, psyche* or soul. For Aquinas this "soul" means the
principle of life which differentiates living matter from dead matter:
it is the source of everything in the individual which is alive. Whenever there is any manifestation of life, voluntary or involuntary,
conscious or unconscious, there is a manifestation of soul[9]:

> That whereby the body lives is its soul. And since life is man-
> ifested by different functions on different levels of living be-
> ings, that which primarily operates every one of these activities
> of life is the soul. For the soul is that whereby primarily we are
> nourished and perceive with our senses, and whereby we move
> from place to place; it is also that whereby primarily we under-
> stand. For the primary source of our understanding, whether
> we call it intellect, or the understanding soul, is [also] the form
> of the body.[10]

Against some of his contemporaries who might seem to have
allowed a number of souls, life-principles or forms in one and the

same individual, Aquinas vigorously maintains that there can be only one primary source of all vital activities, from the highest flights of intelligence and imagination to the humblest functions of nutrition and reproduction which man shares not only with the animals but also with the plants.[11] However the "psychic apparatus" may be described and restricted, it cannot possibly lie outside this comprehensive field.

Dr. E. B. Strauss, one of the most eminent of British Catholic psychiatrists, is more cautious—and correspondingly somewhat less emphatic—than his American colleague:

> It is important to assert from the start that the psyche with which the medical psychologist deals is conceptually different from the soul as defined by the theologian. By the psyche we mean the sum total of what we experience both *actually* and *potentially*—actual experience constituting the conscious, latent and potential experience the unconscious... The soul of theology is conceived of in terms of a different kind of discipline. The soul is that part of a man which is unique, individually created, endowed with survival value. It perceives true and real values, not only phenomena, is modified by values, and transformed by Grace. The definition of the soul, just given, can be either accepted or rejected: and it will strike many of you, doubtless, as arrant nonsense. However, the point I wish to make is that the soul is a theological concept, and hence only understandable in theological and ontological terms, whereas the psyche is a psychological construct.[12]

There are undoubtedly very real and weighty considerations which motivate this eagerness to distinguish soul from *psyche*.[13] The psychiatrist or psychologist—who is usually a very busy man—will be saved much labour if he can regard the psyche as a closed system in which there is no need to correlate his findings with those of other disciplines. But also, and more importantly, he is faced with the fact that, as Dr. Strauss has put it elsewhere, "there have been neurotic, psychotic, and even mentally subintelligent saints,"[14] a fact which seems to make it evident that holiness of soul and mental health are not at all the same thing. A Christian practitioner, especially, is often confronted with the necessity of assuring his devout patients that their mental and emotional disorders do not necessarily signify (as they often suppose) that they are damned, cut off from the grace of God or deficient in piety or good will. A clear-cut distinction between soul and psyche is a useful *ad hoc* device to explain this: their *psyche* is disordered, and with this alone the psychologist is concerned; the *soul* is not his business, and may well be in flourishing condition. The device is no less of a convenience to the theologian or pastor who may prefer sublime verities or harmless generalities to too close an acquaintance with the sordid details and complex causes of mental and emotional misery. Whether this device, tending as it may to widen the split between religion and personal life, is either pastorally or therapeutically effective in the longer run is another matter. In a later chapter we shall examine more closely the relation between health and holiness, and see if we can discover a more satisfactory hypothesis to account for these facts and meet these clinical needs. Meanwhile, we must examine this distinction of psyche from soul on its own merits, and ask if theology itself can accept the restrictions assigned to it.

Dr. Strauss, we observe, asserts only a *conceptual* difference between soul and psyche; and this we may readily grant him. The concept of the soul which is reached by philosophical inference and is used in theology is certainly other than the construct or postulate which the empirical psychologist uses to describe the field of his investigations. Each is indeed reached "in terms of a different kind of discipline."[15] But Dr. Strauss's words seem also to imply a real and objective distinction, a division of territories not unlike that of Dr. Zilboorg's. For although "by the psyche we mean the sum total of what we experience both actually and potentially," Dr. Strauss seems to exclude from this the perception of "true values," modification by values, and transformation by grace. Correspondingly he calls the soul only a "part of man," which is to be "*defined*" wholly in terms of these "higher" attributes.

But the statement that "the soul is a theological concept" could be understood in several different ways, some of which are indubitably correct, but others even theologically untenable.

It could mean that "the soul" is a concept which theology uses and with which theologians are concerned. This is of course undoubtedly true, as it is also true of such concepts as those of Body, Blood, Person, Nature, Bread, Wine, Water. But it could be highly misleading to call these "theological concepts," for it would seem to imply that they have some other meaning, or refer to some other realities, when they are so used than they do in ordinary speech or in other disciplines. Worse, it would seem to imply that the realities to which they refer lie outside ordinary human experience and reflection, and are known only through faith in some supernatural revelation, or are "only understandable in theological and ontological terms."

Or it could mean that theology, grounded as it is in such a faith, forms conceptions or makes statements *about* the "soul" which are peculiar to itself, and which cannot be made on other grounds. This is undoubtedly true—it is also true of Body, Blood, Person, Nature, Bread, Wine, Water. "The soul is the abode of the Holy Spirit," "Christ died to save my soul," "the soul is healed and raised by grace," "my soul is called to enjoy the vision of God" or will "go through purgatory" or "to hell': these are theological conceptions which neither philosophical reflection nor empirical observation is competent either to assert or deny. The most that an empirical psychology can do is to observe that such statements are believed or disbelieved, note their statistical regularity, and study the conditions and results of such belief or disbelief. But although in such statements we may find theological conceptions *about* the soul, this is hardly to say that the soul itself is a theological concept.[16] Such statements as "Your bodies are members of Christ" (1 Cor. 6:15), "He will reform the body of our lowness made like the body of his glory" (Phil. 3:21), "The bread which we break, is it not the partaking of the body of the Lord?" (1 Cor. 10:16), "The blood of Jesus Christ cleanseth us from all sin" (1 John 1:7) are similarly theological statements or conceptions, but theology itself will insist that the body, blood and bread to which they refer are not peculiarly theological concepts, but are the body, blood and bread with which we are all familiar.

But while this may be obvious about body, blood, bread—and many other words and concepts used by theology and religion— it is lamentably true that "soul" has increasingly come to have the sense of what D. H. Lawrence called some "fenced off nice comfortable bit" of man[17]—and in particular of some peculiarly religious entity in man's composition, and quite apart from the psyche of the psychologists. We must presently inquire if such a view is tenable in the light of the Hebrew and Christian Scriptures. Meanwhile we may note that Dr. Strauss is no less eager than Dr. Zilboorg to invoke the support of St. Thomas Aquinas, and he shows closer acquaintance with the saint's thought and words. Commenting later on his own statement, which we quoted above, Dr. Strauss writes:

> That kind of formulation will be unfamiliar to those philoso-
> phers whose psychology is rooted in the writings of St. Thom-
> as... Nevertheless, it seems to me that the differentiation, at

the conceptual level, of the body, the psyche and the soul which I have made does not conflict with St. Thomas's views.

In *De Anima* he says that the *mind* (we today might say the psyche), the principle of intellectual activity, is the form of the human body. And he goes on to say: "the body's first animating principle is the soul. And since life is manifested by various activities in the various grades of living things, that which is the first principle of these vital activities is the soul."[18]

The italics are by Dr. Strauss; but he could have noticed that it was *not* just the "mind" which Aquinas defined as the form of the body, but precisely the soul or *anima*. We may also notice that this definition is translated straight from Aristotle's definition of the soul or (in Greek) *psyche,* and that Aristotle was no theologian or had any knowledge of "theological concepts."[19] It is disputed whether Aristotle regarded this "soul" as also the "principle of intellectual activity" (Aquinas strongly maintained that he did—or should have done[20]), but both of them certainly held that it was the first principle of all "the various activities in the various grades of living things," or the primary source or subject of "the sum total of what we experience both actually and potentially"—and they held this on grounds which had nothing to do with faith or theology. But it is important here to note that it is precisely this definition of soul or *anima* (which, it is recognized, we to-day might call the psyche) that St. Thomas employs *also* in his theology, and to which he also attributes individual creation, immortality,[21] the perception of true and real values, modification by values and transformation by grace. Since the time of Aquinas two General Councils have authoritatively defined for Catholics that to deny that the soul is the "form of the body" (and it is clear that it is with the "soul" of faith and theology that they are concerned) is to be accounted heretical.[22] The relevance of this conception to psychotherapy, and the illegitimacy of separating the sphere of psychology from the soul, even "ontologically" understood, was emphasized in the strongest terms by Pope Pius XII in his address to the Fifth International Catholic Congress of Psychotherapy and Clinical Psychology held in Rome in 1953:

> You psychologists and therapists ought to take account of this fact: the very existence of each faculty or psychological function has its warrant in the purpose of the whole. What makes a human being to be such is principally the soul, which is the essential form of his nature. It is from this that flows, in the last analysis, the whole of human life; in it are rooted all psychological processes with their particular structures and organic laws; and it is to the soul that nature entrusts the government of all these energies to the extent that they have not yet attained their final determination. From this datum, which is at once ontological and psychological, it follows that it would be unrealistic to seek, whether in theory or in practice, to assign the function of determining the whole to some particular factor—for example, to one of the elementary psychic processes—and thus to entrust the helm to a subordinate power.... It has been supposed that we should accentuate the opposition between metaphysics and psychology. This is quite wrong. The psychological [realm] itself belongs to the realm of the ontological and the metaphysical.[23]

But those who are unconcerned with the reasonings and pronouncements of medieval thinkers and councils, or of modern Popes, may still inquire if the word "soul" has so comprehensive a meaning in original and traditional Christian documents. Does the word on the lips of Christ and in the writings of the Evangelists, the Apostles and the early Fathers of the Church, include or exclude the "psychic apparatus" which is the field of the psychologist and the psychotherapist? To this the answer of the New Testament is definite and decisive. For here we find that the one Greek word *psyche* does duty for life in its entirety, for the sum total of the manifestations of life, especially (but not only) "the seat of the will, desires and affections"; and that this same *psyche* is "the object of divine grace and eternal salvation."[24] Indeed the equivalence in the New Testament of *psyche* with life in its entirety has been a notorious difficulty for translators, who have often had to use our two words "soul" and "life" to render it idiomatically. The point may best be illustrated by recalling some familiar texts where the original Greek uses the word *psyche*:

> What shall it profit a man if he gain the whole world and lose his own *psyche*? (Mark 8:36)

> Is not the *psyche* more than the meat? (Matt. 6:25; Luke 12:22)

> Is it lawful…to save *psyche*, or to destroy? (Mark 3:4)

> The son of man is come to give his *psyche* a ransom for many. (Mark 10:45)

> The good shepherd giveth his *psyche* for his sheep. (John 10:11)

> He that findeth his *psyche* shall lose it, and he that loseth his *psyche* for me shall find it. (Matt. 10:39)

> Be not troubled for his *psyche* is in him. (Acts 20:10)

> My *psyche* doth magnify the Lord. (Luke 1:46)

How long dost thou hold our *psyche* in suspense? (John 10:24)

My *psyche* is sorrowful even unto death. (Mark 13:34)

Thou shalt love the Lord thy God with thy whole *psyche*. (Mark 12:30)

You shall find rest for your *psychai*. (Matt. 11:29)

Let every *psyche* be subject to the higher powers. (Rom. 13:1)

The first Adam was made into a living *psyche*. (1 Cor 15:45)

Your prelates…watch as being to render an account of your *psychai*. (Heb. 13:17)

The ingrafted word which is able to save your *psychai*. (Jas. 1:21)

Carnal desires which war against the *psyche*. (1 Pet. 2:11)

The end of your faith, the salvation of your *psychai*. (1 Pet. 1:9)

We do not of course find in the Bible precise philosophical definitions reached by way of inference, nor the hypothetical postulates or constructs of empirical scientific method; but we do find that the word *psyche, or* soul, is used in a sense which is, quite literally, as large as life. And this is not accidental or irrelevant to its essential message. The "Good News" of the Gospel is not just for some higher "part" of man, still less for some independent supernatural entity which is revealed only in the Gospel itself. The New Testament, in fact, simply takes over the Old Testament view of man and his soul, according to which man is an ensouled body rather than an embodied soul. As Professor G. W. A. Lampe has well summarized it:

> The body, in Hebrew thought…is neither a tomb nor a pris-on-house for some "spiritual" or "intelligible" man buried or imprisoned within the flesh. Man is essentially a unity. His physical aspect is not to be rigidly separated in thought from his intellectual or spiritual character. It is the whole man who is the object of God's dealings, and salvation is concerned with the relation of the whole man to God, not with any triumph of the human "spirit" over the corrupt and transitory "flesh." It is man as a single whole who was created by God…. It is the whole man who, as a sinner, is alienated from God, at enmity with him and the object of his wrath: and it is the whole man who is the object of God's grace and is redeemed into the fel-lowship of a son with his heavenly Father.[25]

"Grace perfects nature," and this means human nature in its entirety, in its bodily, even visceral, depths, as well as in its spiritual and intellectual heights. "The word of God is living and effec-tual and more piercing than any two-edged sword and reaching unto the division of the *psyche* and the spirit, of the joints also and the marrow; and is a discerner of the thoughts and intents of the heart" (Heb. 4:12).

However important it may be to distinguish theological con-cepts from psychological constructs, it seems even more import-ant to insist that—even from his own theological standpoint—the theologian cannot allow that any sector of human life, conscious or unconscious, lies outside the "soul" or *psyche* with which he is concerned. Theology would have grievously betrayed its own task of elucidating the Scriptural message had it formed its own concept of the "soul," restricting it to any one section of human life. And it is a remarkable fact that, notwithstanding many vicissitudes, the main stream of theology has resisted many powerful enticements to do so.

The New Testament and other early Christian writers had, of course, simply taken over the word *psyche* from current speech. Although the Christian message enabled them to say much *about* the *psyche* that was new, it had not radically changed the meaning of the word. They announced its immortality, its rebirth and sanctification through God's love, the conquest of its final destruction at the death of the body, even its eventual reunion with the body typified and effected through the resurrection of Christ; but it was still the same *psyche* with which their audience was already familiar that they were talking about. They were not talking about something else. And, as is generally agreed by scholars, *psyche* had long meant the life-principle or life-force in its entirety, and the seat of all the signs and manifestations of life, conscious or unconscious.[26]

When Christianity entered the intellectual world of Graeco-Roman civilization it was confronted by the greatest imaginable variety of opinions on the "nature of the soul." At one extreme was the spiritualism of the Platonists who tended to regard the soul as wholly incorporeal and uncontaminated by matter—immortal, invisible, godlike, a transcendent entity temporarily imprisoned in mortal flesh, unbegotten and deathless. At the other extreme was the materialism of the Epicureans for whom the soul was itself material or corporeal, or at most an epiphenomenon of matter and inseparable from it both in its being and its functioning. This diversity of doctrines concerning the nature of the soul was not something new in the first centuries of the Christian era: it is found also among the earlier Greek thinkers. None of them however denied, all of them presupposed, the basic meaning of the word "soul" as the life-principle in man, and also usually in the whole animal and plant kingdoms. The diversity of doctrines was doubtless enhanced by subjective factors: by different philosophical prejudices, by different methods, by the different psychological typology of those who propounded them. But the diversity arises no less from the astonishing diversity, and apparent contradictoriness, of the phenomena which they set out to explain, of the manifestations of human life itself. For at one extreme we find such "humble" activities as breathing, nourishment, growth and reproduction, which are inconceivable except as functions of physical organs, and argue the dependence of the life-principle on the body, and even its own essential materiality. At the other extreme is man's ability to think, to discover the properties of abstract numbers and to conceive general ideas and their attributes apart from material objects: this could not conceivably be the product of any physical organ, and argues the soul's essential immateriality, and therefore its intrinsic independence of the body and of the body's mortality. Between these extremes lie experiences of human life such as phantasy, dreams, intuitions, symbol-formation, even feelings and moods, which already display a certain "spirituality" and independence of bodily space-time limitations, though not so absolute as that of pure intellectual conception and reasoning. Matters are complicated by the further observations that, on the one hand, even the "lowliest" of vital animal activities appear to display adaptation to purpose, and therefore to imply a certain intelligence independent of material limitation; and, on the other hand, that even our most abstract concepts and reasoning presuppose perceptions through bodily organs and a physical basis. It is small wonder that it was—and still is—found extremely difficult to account for all this paradoxical diversity of phenomena in any one general and comprehensive conception of the soul—i.e., of the human life-principle.

A modern Christian might expect that the early Christian writers would have eagerly embraced the more "spiritual," and would have indignantly repudiated the more "materialistic," of the conceptions of the soul which were then current. It is significant that the very contrary was the fact. The earliest among them, the second-century Greek apologists, generally "speak of the soul as material and naturally mortal."[27] For Irenaeus, writing in the latter half of the second century, the soul is indeed "comparatively incorporeal,"[28] but by this he seems to mean, not that it is immaterial, but that it is composed of some more subtle matter than the "gross matter" of the body which it animates. The first extant work by a Christian expressly devoted to the subject is the *De Anima* of Tertullian, written between A.D. 208 and 211. Its "materialism" is quite astonishing, and of all the theories of the soul current in his time, it is the "spiritual" theories of the Platonists and some of the Stoics that he considers the most inimical to the Christian evaluation of the body. It is noteworthy that although Tertullian claims to base his theories on the Bible, "referring the problems to the letters of God," he expressly regards the soul as a legitimate subject not only for philosophical but also for medical investigation,[29] and his work is "full of impressions gained from his study of physicians, as well as of philosophers, with the most materialistic tendencies."[30] But for Tertullian the soul was also, among other things, the seat or source of what we should now call archetypal images and patterns, and in them he saw a common ground between believers and unbelievers.[31]

Doubtless most of these early Christian theories about the soul were crass, muddled and philosophically negligible. But they are of importance insofar as they show how far were early Christians from supposing that the soul, for which Christ died and which was filled with his Holy Spirit, was some higher entity which had nothing to do with the life of the body, its familiar activities and passions. Soon, these crude theories were to be displaced by more subtle reflections, and the best Christian thinkers were to find a "loving nurse" in the "Platonick Philosophy."[32] These laid far greater emphasis on the soul's spirituality, on its inherent ability to act and to exist independently, and indeed quite separately, from the body. But even for Origen, for whom the soul seemed to be a sort of fallen angel, a pure spirit somehow imprisoned in the body on account of some past misdeeds, and who stresses the conflict between the spirit and the flesh almost to the point of giving them two separate lives and existences, the soul is still the life-principle of the physical organism. Even Gregory of Nyssa, with his sublime doctrines of the God-likeness of the immortal, spiritual soul, also knows it to be the subject and source of the passions that disturb us by day and the dreams that come to us by night.[33] Even Augustine, for whom a man is not a composition of soul and body,[34] a rational animal, but "a rational soul using a mortal and earthly body,"[35] sees also that the soul is the "life whereby we live."[36] For him the *mens,* by which he understands the purely spiritual and immaterial functions of the soul, is not the whole soul, but its "higher part and its chief."[37]

In the Middle Ages also there was a similar divergence of views, though they never reached the extreme "materialism" of Tertullian or the extreme "spiritualism" of Origen. For the Thomist, as we have seen, the soul was one single life-principle, the very perfection, act or form of the body, which produced both purely spiritual acts (and was therefore itself spiritual) and the functions of sensitive and "vegetative" life. It is not, as we know it in this world, a separate substance existing in its own right and having a life of its own: it is our life itself *whereby* we live. The manifestations of life, spiritual and corporeal, conscious and unconscious, are activities of the numerous powers or abilities of this one actuality, which is the very actuality or "form" of the human body. The Thomist conception thus achieved a union of the opposites which had hitherto given rise to such opposed theories.

The so-called Augustinian or Franciscan school generally rejected this. It held, with certain variations, that the soul was "a separate entity, united to the body by means of sensitive and vegetative forms; and although as ruler and mover of the body and its final perfection it desired union with it, nevertheless the connection between them was a hindrance to its true goal, union with God through knowledge and love."[38] But connection with the body there was, and the body was lifeless without it. However, the connection was tenuous, and risked making the soul a separate entity altogether, inimical to, rather than the source of, ordinary human life, sensation and emotion. Such a view, carried to extremes, could gravely imperil the Gospel message of salvation to the whole man, the integrity of the Christian life, and indeed the Incarnation itself. It was doubtless for these reasons that the Council of Vienne took the unusual step of declaring that the denial of a philosophical formula was heretical.[39]

We must return to our own days. There are not, it appears, many writers who have ventured to propound so clear a distinction between soul and psyche as those which we have examined. But other authors, even among those who at least tacitly recognize their identity, propose other divisions of territory between psychology and religion. Thus Father Vanderveldt and Dr. Odenwald, in their often excellent *Psychiatry and Catholicism*, assert that "Religion works on the conscious level; analytical psychology, to a great extent, on the unconscious level."[40] This assertion seems open to the same objections from the theological side, and no more easy to reconcile with the known facts, whether religious or psychological. More often, however, such a division is assumed (though not always consistently) rather than openly declared in much that is written on the fashionable subject of psychology and religion.[41] Especially from France and the United States there has been a considerable output of symposia to which theologians and pastors on the one side, and psychologists and psychiatrists on the other, have contributed excellent and informative essays. Yet each party seems over-eager to protect his own territory from intrusion by the other, and to protest his own determination never to intrude in the other's domain. The result is that, admirable as the individual contributions may be, they seldom appear to get to grips with one another but issue in an amiable but spurious appearance of agreement. As a British medical psychologist has said of one such volume, "if the issues had been brought into relation with the identity of subject-matter, the amicable agreement which is such a feature of the volume could scarcely be maintained."[42]

But it is just this "identity of subject-matter" which the contributors to such volumes generally ignore or expressly repudiate, although the repudiation is seldom supported by any argument either from theological principles or from psychological observation. This is particularly notable in the treatment commonly accorded from both sides to the problem of diabolic action or possession and mental illness. Almost always it is nowadays assumed that a given set of phenomena is to be ascribed either to one *or* the other; never to both. Each, it is supposed, is due to different and mutually exclusive causes ("preternatural" *or* "natural"), and is to be treated by different and mutually exclusive methods (psychiatry *or* exorcism). One has the impression of the devil being driven into an ever narrowing corner before the advance of psychiatric knowledge, and it is hardly surprising if the average reader concludes that science will shortly liquidate him altogether—as of course secularist psychiatry has already done. Père de Tonquédec, for instance, has given us a most informative work on "Nervous or Mental Maladies and Diabolic Manifestations" which even emphasizes their empirical similarities, and allows that the latter are a legitimate subject for psychological investigation.[43] Yet it is his unproven thesis that they are not identical and must be regarded as two different things.[44] This is generally assumed in most modern writings on the subject, though it can be shown that such is not the view of the New Testament nor consistent with the presuppositions of Aquinas on diabolic activity.[45] Nor was it the view of the early Church, for which mental illness was precisely an effect of demonic agency. "Demons," said Lactantius, "secretly work in [men's] inward parts, corrupt the health, hasten diseases, terrify their souls with dreams, harass their minds with frenzies."[46] "Wicked spirits," wrote Origen, "act in two ways: that is, when they either take complete possession of the mind so as to allow their captives the power neither of understanding nor feeling... whom we see to be deprived of reason and insane...or when they fill an intelligent and sentient soul with thoughts of various kinds, persuading it to evil."[47] It is understandable that secularist and positivist psychiatrists have dismissed the idea of diabolic agency entirely, and that psychiatrists generally should regard it as something outside their competence to pronounce either for or against: but it is strange that any psychiatrist can regard the phenomena attributed to it as outside the "psychic apparatus" which is his field of operations, and should be encouraged by theologians and pastors in so doing.[48]

The type of literature to which we have alluded does not, it is true, always make any distinction—explicitly or implicitly—between soul and psyche; but it is fairly littered with descriptions of events as arising *either* from "supernatural" causes *or* from "natural" ones. Just what these terms are intended to convey is seldom made clear, nor is there much evidence that those who use them have stopped to define their terms or to consider whether they have any intelligible meaning in this context at all. But the purpose of the distinction as they use it is clear enough: events which arise from "supernatural" causes are no business of the psychologist or the psychiatrist, but are the exclusive preserve of the priest and the theologian, while events which arise from "natural causes" are no concern of the latter. And this is so however much the said events resemble one another and are empirically indistinguishable from those which are the psychiatrist's daily business. The psychiatrist's position here is a difficult one, for his empiricism precludes him from detecting supernatural causes, and he has only the theologian's (usually very reluctant) say-so to tell him which is which in the concrete instance.

But, employed in this fashion, the distinction is theologically untenable also. As understood in traditional theology, "super-natural" and "natural" causes are not mutually exclusive but supplementary, "natural" being subordinated to "supernatural." If by "supernatural" is understood (as is generally done in theology) that which transcends the powers of any finite being, and by "natural" that which is subject to them, the First Cause of *all* events is always supernatural, and there is no other supernatural cause. But the First Cause can, and commonly does, act in and through "natural" causes which are, very often, subject to human observation. It is however usual and legitimate to call any *effect* "supernatural" if it is something which only the First Cause could produce and which exceeds all finite powers. Thus, revelation is "supernatural" if what is revealed is what only God knows. But this (at least as it was explained by Aquinas) in no way precludes the employment of "natural" psychological faculties, functions and experiences with which the empirical psychologist is familiar.[49] The same must be said of those mystical experiences and graces, spiritual and physical phenomena, which may indeed be, in this sense, "supernatural," but are not on that account to be set on a shelf beyond the psychologist's reach.[50]

It has been the purpose of this chapter to clear the ground for discussion and collaboration between the representatives of Christian religion and psychology and to maintain that there is indeed a common ground between them, whether it is approached from the theological or from the psychological standpoint. We would further repeat that, whatever concepts or constructs they devise, it remains true in therapeutic practice that a psychoneurosis is directly concerned with the patient's mental outlook on life, and with patterns and principles of behaviour, with the whole order of values, motives and duties, in a sense in which it [a purely somatic disease] is not. If psychological treatment does not issue in the change of a man's mentality, his outlook, his manner of conduct, his attitude to the world and his place in the world, it surely fails entirely in its own set purpose. And, however we may choose to define ethics, or for that matter religion, surely we must agree that they are both concerned with these very things. It is therefore hard to see how we can agree with such a distinction between mental and spiritual or moral disorder as is sometimes suggested, or how a responsible and conscientious psychotherapist can disclaim any concern with his patient's religion and morals, and treat these as an untouchable sphere which is no concern of his.[51]

II.

THE PREDICAMENT OF
THE PSYCHOTHERAPIST

Given that, objectively, the soul is the psyche and that the psyche is the soul; given furthermore that the practising psychotherapist cannot exclude in advance any element in the total pattern of the personality with which he has to deal—least of all its dominating beliefs, disbeliefs, values and attitudes; given, finally, the character of many of the phenomena with which the psyche itself presents him, a psychologist is likely to find himself in a serious predicament. The nature of this predicament deserves closer attention than it usually receives.

The views of a theologian on the predicament of the psychologist are unlikely to be unprejudiced, or even disinterested. He also has something to sell; and it may reasonably be assumed that, as a purveyor of the word of salvation, of spiritual consolation, of the opium of the people (call it what you will), other people's predicaments will afford his opportunity. The merchant of eternal verities may be expected to exploit the anguished doubts, questionings and mistakes of dealers in more ephemeral products much as the huckster of patent nostrums will exaggerate and exploit our dyspepsia. And if the victim of predicament be a psychologist the helpfulness of the theologian or pastor may be expected to be all the more eager—and smug. For it is the psychologist who may be supposed to be his successful competitor; it is he who has attracted a large section of tortured humanity, with its depressions and manias, its mental and emotional distress, its guilt and moral

perplexities, away from the church and the rectory to the consulting room. And if, today, the first flush of discovery and triumph
has paled on the faces of many psychiatrists and psychotherapists,
if there is much talk among them now (as on the Continent there
certainly is) of a crisis in their professional domain, of the need for
radical self-criticism and a setting of their house in order, and of
the need for "spiritual values," their competitors from the old firm
may be expected to make the most of it.

We shall, for our part, make no pretence of being unprejudiced or disinterested. But neither do we think it desirable or even
possible to exploit the predicament to the psychologist's discom-
fiture. Our aim will be simply to offer the theologian's own resources in the belief and hope that they may do much to resolve
the psychologist's predicament without trespassing on his own
functions. But first we should appreciate the character of the predicament itself (of which some psychologists themselves seem too
busy to be aware).

This predicament has its roots in what may be called man's
innate metaphysical curiosity: his need for *Weltanschauung,* for
meaning, for some sort of understanding of the universe around
him and his own place within it, of the whence, what, whither and
why of his own existence. Whether or not such questions are answerable, whether or not this need is capable of valid satisfaction,
it is a plain empirical fact that, as Aristotle says in the opening
words of his *Metaphysics:* "All men, by reason of their very nature,
desire to know." Logical and other positivists, who would maintain that such a quest is vain, and such questions meaningless,
are apt to disregard the fact that such positivism itself implies a
world-view, and a conception of man and his capabilities and in-
capabilities; they are commonly spared (as psychologists often are
not) being called upon to deal with the profound emotional disturbances and repressions in the personal lives of their disciples, to

which the limitations of their view give rise. This desire, or need, though it differs vastly from individual to individual, both in intensity and in conscious awareness of its very existence, seems to be as imperious a demand in the psyche as is that in the body for air and food. Truly enough, where this need is satisfied, there is little or no conscious awareness of its existence; just as the well-to-do man with three square meals a day is less acutely aware than the starving man of the imperious demands of hunger, and of the personal and social suffering and disorder which it can engender. The manner in which it is satisfied or not satisfied will also differ widely according to the type of the individual concerned: a thinking type will tend to demand a rational philosophy; an intuitive will prefer an imaginative mythos. Religious beliefs and practices, myths, rituals, philosophies, ideologies, mystiques: all, from the psychological point of view, exist to meet this need to find meaning, significance and direction in life and experience.

The psychologist, and especially the psychoanalyst and the psychotherapist, may urge that Aristotle was altogether too optimistic. The plain fact is, as psychologists see it, that most men do *not* desire to know. Knowledge is too painful for most of them; truth and reality they will at all costs, and with perverse ingenuity, strive to avoid. The vast majority are adepts at self-deception, and will sooner take refuge in any kind of phantasy and wishful thinking rather than face reality. Overwhelming evidence forces us to concede this, even while we may urge that phantasy-formation and reality-substitutes argue a radical and natural desire to know, even when reality is intolerable, much as the making of idols argues a natural desire for God. The observation does not, however, release the psychologist from his own dilemma. It faces him all the more inexorably with the problem: What *is* reality? What *is* truth? Even if his patient has succeeded in meeting the need with a deceptive substitute, that very fact confronts the psychologist himself, and precisely in his professional activities, with the need to know, and with the problem of discriminating the real from the unreal, the true from the false.

But the need is not only for a theory—for a religious belief, a *mythos*, a metaphysic, a world-view, an anthropology in the Continental, more philosophical, sense, of a conception of the what, whence, why and whither of man. There is also the whole realm of ultimate motivation for practical behaviour, of practical moral problems, of "what *A* is to do," of good and bad, right and wrong in given circumstances.

Now it is just these questions which, it seems, the analyst cannot, may not, answer: may not, even if he thinks he can. Let us examine more closely the two horns of his dilemma, and then some of the solutions he has attempted.

In the first place we should notice that these "metaphysical" and "ethical" problems which, as we have said, are the common lot of humanity, press with peculiar urgency on the psychologist's patients and those who have to do with him. Whatever psychology may discover about the genesis and mechanism of mental disorder, however it may classify mental diseases, a psychotic, a madman, is almost always recognizable by his bizarre ideas about the universe, or his own place, or that of his acquaintance, within it. Perhaps he *is* God, or Jesus Christ, or Joan of Arc; or the world is made of cheese, or of something which it is his duty to set on fire. If he is a chronic schizophrenic, he has probably retired into a strange, incommunicable world of phantasy and ideas, which seem nonsense to us, but which to him (it appears) is the only sense, the only reality and truth. The psychiatrist may say that all these things are but symptoms of the disease; not the disease itself. That begs quite a big question, which we need not pursue. There is, anyway, nothing else that the psychiatrist *can* say, short of throwing in the sponge and abandoning his therapeutic task in despair. To say that the ideas make the madness, and not the madness makes the ideas, would be tantamount to pronouncing it incurable. For even if the ideas were amenable to argument and persuasion as to their falsity, and even if the therapist has saner ideas with which to replace them, your really mad patient will not accept them—perhaps not even hear them. Compared with the pressing reality of his own phantasies and convictions, they are—even if he sees their reasonableness—insipid nonsense which will starve his mind of its vitally necessary food, and destroy the world in which he lives. And anyway—and here perhaps is the crux of the whole matter—what is to be the psychologist's own criterion of sane ideas and insane ideas, reality and falsity, even of normality and abnormality? So soon as ever he asks such questions, the psychologist is in danger of being lured away from psychology, and to invoke criteria, whether philosophical or theological or merely of social acceptability, which the psychiatric or psychological technicalities may conceal, but cannot provide.

And even if your madman has no mad theories, at least he has mad morals, mad behaviour-patterns, if he is to be accounted mad at all. These may range from those which society accounts as criminal to those which, while otherwise harmless, are a nuisance to his relations and neighbours, or anyhow to parts of his own personality. It is said that the word "ought" *ought* not to have any place in the psychologist's vocabulary: a seeming paradox which contains an important truth to which we must presently return. But it may be confidently affirmed that, if the word "ought" had no place in human vocabulary generally, there would be no place for the psychiatrist and the psychotherapist in the world at all: he would have no patients.

But the genuine madman, who is the concern of the psychiatrist, seldom if ever is bothered with metaphysical or ethical *questions*. His trouble seems rather that he is incapable of asking such questions; he is so sure of the answers—answers which bring him into conflict with society, with nature or with himself—that he is unable to see any alternative. For him there is no question about them—anyway not for long. Not so the neurotic; not therefore the patient who is more amenable to psychological analysis. Often enough—but by no means always—he may be quite unconscious before he begins analysis that "metaphysical," philosophical or religious problems underlie the conscious problems and troubles that first bring him to analysis at all. But it seems that he can seldom remain that way. We remember C. G. Jung's celebrated declaration in 1932: "During the past thirty years, people from all the civilized countries of the earth have consulted me.... Among my patients in the second half of life—that is to say over thirty-five—there has not been one whose problem in the last resort was not that of finding a religious outlook on life. It is safe to say that every one of them fell ill because he had lost that which the living religions of every age had given to their followers, and none of them has been really healed who did not regain this religious outlook."[1] Here are a few quotations from his address, ten years later, on "Psychotherapy and a Philosophy of Life"[2]:

> The more "psychological" a condition is, the greater its complexity and the more it relates to the whole of life.... If the disturbance lies in a repression then the disturbing factor—that is, the repressive force—belongs to a "higher" psychic order. It is not something elementary and physiologically conditioned, but, as experience shows, a highly complex determinant, as, for example, certain rational, ethical, religious or other traditional ideas which cannot be scientifically proved to have any physiological basis.... As the most complex of psychic structures, a man's philosophy of life forms the counter-pole to the physiologically conditioned psyche, and, as the highest psychic

> dominant, it ultimately determines the latter's fate.... I can
> hardly draw a veil over the fact that we psychotherapists really
> ought to be philosophers or philosophic doctors—or rather
> that we already are so, though we are unwilling to admit it....
> We could also call [our work] religion *in statu nascendi*, for in
> the vast confusion that reigns at the root of life there is no line
> of division between philosophy and religion.... The highest
> dominant always has a religious or a philosophical character.

It is of course open to us to dismiss this interpretation of psychological phenomena as a crank peculiar to Jung and his school. Certainly they have stated it more explicitly and frankly than others—with the possible exception of the post-war "existential analysts" and "logotherapists" in Austria. We have suggested elsewhere that the same findings lurk amid the very repudiations of Freudians and Adlerians, and become quite explicit in many of the experiences of unprejudiced explorers of the unconscious.[3]

There is an objection to trying to substitute "sane" for "insane" ideas which weighs very heavily upon the analyst. He is an empirical scientist, often a medical doctor; his whole training has made him such, and these metaphysical and moral questions are notoriously unanswerable by the methods of empirical science: the methods of observation, experiment, correlation, statistics, hypothesis, law and theory. It has been the aspiration of empirical psychology to model itself on the exact sciences; to transgress their limits and methods would seem to be to surrender its whole claim to serious consideration. The psychologist may of course claim, as others have done, that what is not empirically verifiable by these methods is not knowable; and that consequently the metaphysical and ethical questions of his patients are illusory. Freud seems sometimes to have come close to this position—implicitly if not explicitly; so did Jung in his earlier days. But such an assertion is of course itself not empirically verifiable; and already constitutes a philosophy of man which is incapable of proof or disproof by the methods of the physical sciences. We have only to read such a book as Dr. Edward Glover's *Freud or Jung* to see what a tyrannical idol the word "science" can become. In that book we were presented with "criteria of assessment" in judging between the psychological schools whose own criterion seems to be the tidiness of the doctor's own mind, his rigid adherence to the methods of obsolete physics, rather than the welfare of the patient, or even scrupulous observation of the facts when these fail to conform to a comprehensible sequence of cause and effect. Between this rigid "scientism" and Jung's contention that the patient is there to be treated and not to verify the doctor's theory,[4] no reconciliation seems possible.

Yet Jung also is a determined empiricist; he also, while insisting that the therapist needs a cultural background far beyond the confines of psychology in the narrow sense, declines firmly to become the theologian, the philosophical or moral mentor. The empirical method has proved too successful, departures from it into metaphysical instruction, moral exhortation or moral condemnation have proved too disastrous, to encourage any considerable deflection from the secure, tried paths of the empirical sciences. This is so, because the patient's need—and consequently the analyst's—is to get at the *facts*; theories, hypotheses, let alone beliefs and philosophies, are valuable only insofar as they serve, and do not dominate, this primary task. Intervention of the analyst's own beliefs or morals, however sound they may be in themselves, only introduces a foreign body into the patient's condition; they hinder rather than help him to know and find himself and his own resources and problems. Almost invariably they upset the transference, in ways which the patient's dreams or symptoms will soon make manifest. Either he accepts the analyst's views in virtue of a positive transference, and this will increase his dependence; to the extent that the analyst is unaware of what he is doing—or unwilling to recognize it—this will make immeasurably more difficult the resolution of the transference, and the patient's gaining of independence. Or, the patient will, consciously or unconsciously, resent the introduction of the foreign body, the indoctrination of which he is being made the "captive audience," the advantage which is being taken of his suggestibility in the analytical relationship—from which a negative transference usually ensues which may wreck the whole procedure.

Early, or "classical," psychoanalysis was so well aware of these dangers that it stoutly maintained the necessity, on the part of the analyst, of what is called *weltanschauliche Neutralität*. This meant that the analyst must preserve a strict impartiality, even a lack of interest, in all these ultimate questions of human existence. He must not express his own views on such matters, still less attempt to "suggest" them, or allow them surreptitiously to influence the patient. This programme, it should be clearly understood, was not just a convenient *ad hoc* device to spare the analyst from giving an account of himself and from discussing difficult questions; it was part and parcel of the technique which distinguished psychoanalysis from the methods of suggestion—hypnotic or other—which had preceded it. The analyst was to be a colourless screen on to which the analysant could freely project himself without let or hindrance, and without the inhibitions which must arise from any encounter with the analyst's personality or ideas.

Such at least was the programme; but it may be questioned how far it was, or could be, put into complete effect. Freud himself was certainly not only the pure technician, uninterested in philosophical or religious questions. Indeed, it becomes clear from Dr. Ernest Jones's great biography of Freud that it was precisely these interests which provided the impetus to his investigations, first in

the field of neurology, then in psychoanalysis. In 1896 we find him
calling metapsychology his "ideal and problem child," philosophy
"my original goal...my earliest aim when I did not know what I
was in the world for." Dr. Jones's fascinating book makes clearer
than ever how very definite his views were, and that he never abandoned the deterministic, mechanistic conception of man which
he had taken over from the school of Helmholz. ("Materialistic"
seems hardly the right label for one who freed psychology from
physiology and neurology—after doing pioneer work in both—
and who bravely recognized that ideas could be cured by ideas and
without any physical intervention.) His unceasing interest in, and
hostility to, religion is known to all. This is not the place to examine his position except to remark on the bias which could present
religion as wish-fulfilment, yet be blind to the fact that the assertion of the non-existence of a God to whom men were answerable
for their lives could be explained in precisely the same fashion. All
we need notice here is that works like *The Future of an Illusion*
were certainly not neutral on religious or philosophical issues; and
however successfully Freud may have preserved his neutrality in
the consulting room, he could hardly, without breach of that very
neutrality, have forbidden his patients to read his own books. Igor
Caruso maintains that the claim to *weltanschauliche Neutralität*
was in fact a grotesque self-deception; and he describes a "classical" psychoanalysis as a subtle form of indoctrination into a mechanistic philosophy of life.[5] By the very fact of declining to discuss
religious, ethical or philosophical ideas, by dismissing them as "ra-
tionalizations" and refusing to consider them as relevant, and by
accepting only phenomenal facts and a mechanistic theory of their
causal determinants, an analyst will, whether he wishes it or not,
inculcate a purely positivistic, phenomenalist and mechanistic philosophy. As Mr. Kenneth Walker has said, "This effort to be strictly
impartial makes very little difference in the end, for what happens

is that the patient who has benefited from his treatment takes unto himself the philosophy of the man who has relieved him of his neurosis.... However diffident the analyst declares himself to be about imposing his private philosophy on his individual patient, he does not hesitate to commend it in the most extravagant terms to the world at large."[6] Nor is "classical psychoanalysis" unselective with regard to the phenomenal facts themselves. The analyst, it is alleged, would accept as genuine manifestations of the unconscious only such dream-material or free associations as would square with the Freudian view of man; all else he would dismiss as disguise, resistance, displacement, dream-work, merely "manifest" as opposed to "latent" content.

One can vouch for these allegations only from personal experience of Freudian analysis, but they would certainly seem to be confirmed from much that we find in the Freudian literature. We know that it was this issue of an arbitrary selection and evaluation of the material to fit the theory which was the major factor in the separation of Jung from Freud. Jung took his stand on the principle that "*was wirkt ist wirklich*": what is active is actual. Hence the empirical psychologist has no business to allow his theories to admit one set of factors in his data to be real, to dismiss another set as illusion. From the psychologist's point of view of dynamic function, they may be equally operative, and therefore equally "real" and "true"; and equally entitled, where there is no clear evidence to the contrary, to be taken at their face value. The patently sexual has no prerogative to serious consideration as against the patently "spiritual." In this Jung appears more intransigently empiricist than Freud himself. We must leave to the next chapter a consideration of the "dialectical procedure" which Jung proposes as a method to meet, if not to solve, the predicament of the psychologist and the problems which arise in practice from his patients" "metaphysical hunger."[7]

The "anthropological trend" (*anthropologische Wende*) in Continental psychotherapy since the war, represented by various groups of phenomenologists, existence-analysts, logotherapists, etc., has brought the psychologist's predicament out into the open. Whatever the differences (and they are often radical) between such writers as Boss, Binszwanger, von Gebstattal, Trüb, Frankl, Caruso or von Siebenthal, they are at one in their recognition of the inseparability of psychotherapy from anthropology, understood as some idea of man, his nature, his mode of existence or his destiny. This is so even when it is maintained, in line with Sartre, that "there is no such thing as human nature—*il n'y a pas de nature humaine*"[8]: for, on this account precisely, man is his own maker, and the task of psychotherapy will be precisely to enable him to realize the fact. At the opposite extreme from Sartre's nihilistic and atheistic brand of existentialism, are Frankl's ebullient affirmations of free, spiritual "unconditioned Man" as the goal of therapy,[9] and of our false relations to the "unconscious God" as the root of much of our mental and emotional disorder.[10] For all their efforts to avoid philosophical abstractions and to restrict themselves to "phenomenological" descriptions of human existence, such writings will seem foreign, heady stuff to most harassed and matter-of-fact Anglo-Saxon practitioners. They have nevertheless brought forward many points of the utmost importance in therapeutic practice[11]; and their emphasis on the psyche's powers of self-transcendence, decision and self-creativity (man's power to make or mar his own life and surroundings) is a welcome reaction from the underlying determinism of earlier psychotherapeutic theory. But, whatever may be thought of their respective -ologies and -isms, they do have the merit of insisting that some "anthropology"—some idea of Man, his capacities, destiny and place in the universe—is inseparable from psychotherapy, and that the therapist should himself be conscious of his own norm for mankind. Jung, long ago, showed the impossibility of a purely "objective" psychology, the illusion of the claim to pure *Vorauss-tzungslosigkeit*.[12] The great merit of the "anthropological trend" is to have drawn more explicit attention to the actual "norms" and assumptions about Man that may be employed. The dangers and miseries which may ensue for a patient when his therapist projects his own unconscious philosophy upon him are not inconsiderable, and are all the more probable the more the therapist deludes himself that he does not have one at all. Better a false and foolish one, so long as it is conscious, than an unconscious one however sound. Both parties will at least know where they stand, and be less likely to be entangled in a web of ideological transference and countertransference.

But while such a conscious "anthropology" may help the therapist to be aware of his predicament, and even indicate how it may be resolved, it will seldom directly solve the problem of the patient. In practice, it is of course the patient who is left with the problem rather than the analyst; it is in him that questions and needs have been aroused by analysis to which analysis itself has been unable to respond, even though it may also have activated his resources to deal with them. To tell how in actual practice those who have experienced analysis have solved, or failed to solve, the religious, philosophical or ethical problems which it has stimulated, would start us on a very long story; indeed, as many long stories as there have been analysants. Some have dealt with it in the way in which insoluble or difficult or demanding problems are commonly dealt with—by repression. They simply disregard their religious or metaphysical problems; sometimes they do this with the assistance of psychologists themselves who are eager to explain them away as disguises or displacements of something more tangible and tractable. But repression seldom affords a lasting solution; and for those who have learned of its dangers through analysis itself, the last state is likely to be worse than the first. For still more, the seed is choked by the cares and riches of this world, but with like results. Many more have been driven to work out a technique whereby they can, as it were, work out a *mythos*, a religion, a philosophy of their own in lonely isolation, and on the basis of the experience they have gained in analysis. This they have often done with immense courage and considerable success—at least from some points of view. But from the psychotherapeutic point of view this is not without its dangers—especially for those with schizoid tendencies. The solitary man, as Aristotle remarks, is either a god or a beast; and the dangers of psychological inflation or relapse into identification with the shadow are considerable, and not a few seem to have succumbed to them. The economic obstacles and social objections are obvious. Others find mutual support in so-called psychological "clubs"; institutions which are found to be very much more concerned with religious and philosophical questions than with those commonly associated with academic or scientific psychology, and whose aroma is often very much more that of the conventicle or the temple than that of the laboratory or the lecture-hall.

But others very reasonably look for light from those whose business it is to treat of their newly awakened concerns; the professional philosophers, theologians, ministers of religion—the accredited guardians and investigators of the collective ideas which, they hope, may comprehend and universalize their deep personal experiences and insights, and release them from the oppressive loneliness, the feeling of being the odd man out, which, in the modern world, those experiences and insights can bring with them. A few among them, perhaps, have found not only what they sought, but very much more. But these seem to be the exception. Brought through their psychological experience to appreciate the vital necessity of other functions beside that of intellect for integrated human living, they despair of finding a philosophy of life in the logic and linguistic analyses to which much contemporary philosophy is still confined; they are discouraged at the outset at learning that not only are their metaphysical questions unanswerable but also meaningless. More might be expected of traditional religious faith and practice; but, as Jung has said, "It is certainly a difficult task to find the bridge connecting the standpoint of dogma with the direct experience of psychological archetypes; though the investigation of the natural symbols of the unconscious gives us the necessary building stones." But bridge-building requires not only building-stones, but also some acquaintance with the terrain on both shores; and that—not altogether surprisingly—is not a common attainment.

Most of this volume is concerned with attempts to do some building from the side of dogma and theology. But it is important that bridges should really bridge, and this means that the two sides of the structure should really join. It would be well, then, to take a look at the most significant approach that has appeared on the other—the psychological—bank: that of G. G. Jung and his school.

III.

THE JUNGIAN APPROACH TO RELIGION

My book *God and the Unconscious* was subjected to a good deal of criticism on account of its preoccupation with the Jungian school of psychology, and for its comparative neglect of other schools. An eminent Catholic psychiatrist has complained that Catholic apologists for dynamic psychiatry and psychotherapy have too often been over-enthusiastic partisans of this or that *school* of psychology, and have endeavoured to reconcile their views with Catholic orthodoxy. In my view, this kind of approach in the long run renders a disservice rather than a service to psychiatry in general.[1]

It is certainly not our own intention to be an apologist for any kind of psychiatry or psychotherapy, whether in particular or in general. We must be content only to observe the facts, the postulates and theories alleged to account for them, their beneficial or baneful fruits for humanity, and correlate them as best we can with our Christian faith. We might plead, quite simply, that we cannot each have been to all the schools, and we can speak with any assurance only of those which we have in fact attended.

Although it is regrettably true that there has been altogether too much sectarianism in psychology, it is a mistake to picture the various schools as so many mutually excommunicating factions without influence upon each other. It is a particularly mistaken view of the Jungian school. Jung has, it is true, been severely critical of the *exclusive* claims made for early Freudian theory, and of the appropriateness of the original psychoanalytic technique for *all* cases. But he holds that

> It would be an unpardonable error to overlook the element of truth in both the Freudian and the Adlerian viewpoints, but it would be no less unpardonable to take either of them as the sole truth. Both truths correspond to psychological realities. There are, in fact, some cases which by and large can best be described and explained by the one theory, and some by the other.... It seems hardly necessary to add that I hold the truth of my own deviationist views to be equally relative.[2]

In the same volume, on the *Practice of Psychotherapy*, there are many pages which show the welcome Jung gives to the methods and theories, whether psychiatric or psychotherapeutic, of other schools and individuals; and this precisely in order to deal with the enormous diversity of individual cases and needs. "The more deeply we penetrate the nature of the psyche, the more the conviction grows upon us that the diversity, the multi-dimensionality, of human nature requires the greatest variety of standpoints and methods in order to satisfy the variety of psychic dispositions."[3] While a Jungian's experience will give him certain basic conceptions of psychic structure and therapeutic procedure which will preserve him from hit-or-miss treatments, disguised as "eclectic," he has not only learned much from other schools but will often be glad to refer a suitable patient to specialists in other methods. He will cordially applaud the "principle of multiple aetiology" proclaimed by such genuine eclectics as Dr. E. B. Strauss.[4] Indeed, Jung himself goes much further and insists that the concept of aetiology itself is inadequate for the psychotherapist's purpose, and that he must also employ energic and teleological concepts, and even a more elusive "principle of acausal synchronicity."[5]

The fact however remains that Jung and his colleagues have made a unique and distinctive contribution to depth-psychology, and have made a special field of psychic factors their special study. This field, as is well-known, comprises what Jung at first called the collective, and later the objective, unconscious, and to whose contents and processes he eventually gave the name archetypes. It would not be altogether true to say that Jung discovered them. So soon as there was any methodical exploration of the unconscious, the fact of the presence of non-repressed and non-personal contents and of "religious" and mythological motifs was evident; though their existence and potency were more obvious to Jung, working in a mental hospital with psychotics, than it was at first to Freud treating the bourgeois neurotics of Vienna. But, from quite early days of psychoanalysis, Freud also found himself confronted with resemblances to myths and religious symbols, and with what he considered to be "phylogenetic traces"; and the psychoanalysts have been dealing, in their own way, with such myths and symbols ever since.[6] Jung came to differ from Freud, not about the existence of these psychic facts and experiences, but in taking them seriously at their face-value as effective "symbols of transformation," rather than as worthless phantasy-substitutes for "reality." And the major part of his work ever since has been the study of these archetypal images—as he later called them—and their psychological function: a study which has led him very far and wide from the preoccupations of other schools. And we should notice, lest it be supposed that these archetypes are some exclusively Jungian concoction, that the facts which they label have hardly been disputed by subsequent depth-psychologists. The post-Jungian psychologists of the *anthropologische Wende*, to whom we alluded in the last chapter, mostly take the existence of such archetypes for granted, and have found that their own labours have greatly confirmed the facts which Jung has made his special field of study.

Though many among them have warmly disputed some of Jung's theories, and still more what they suppose (rightly or wrongly) to be his personal views and opinions, their debt to Jung's pioneer work is obviously immense, certainly no less than is that of Jung himself to Freud. In some respects they may claim to have gone beyond Jung, and to have added new viewpoints and dimensions to depth-psychology generally; but they are mostly prepared to accept his empirical findings, and will usually employ the same terms to describe them.[7]

Now it is clear that it is just in this sphere of the archetypes that the contacts and collisions between religion and psychology most manifestly occur. And it is with the specialists in this sphere that such a book as ours must mostly have to do. It may well be true that there are psychologists of other schools who, following in the wake of William James's *Varieties of Religious Experience*, have given more specialized attention to what is called the "psychology of religion." The unique importance of Jung's contribution does not however lie in this restricted field of the psychological interpretation of selected, overtly religious, phenomena, but in the recognition of the religious or potentially religious factors which underlie the structure of the psyche generally, and of their role in mental health and sickness in mankind at large.[8]

The Jungian approach to religion must therefore concern us very particularly, and without further apology. It should be understood that when we speak of Jung's analytical psychology as providing an "approach to religion," we mean not merely that it offers—as do many other psychologies—a psychological language in which so-called religious facts can be more or less adequately described. To many who have undergone analysis under Jungian auspices, or even merely read Jungian books, it has proved to be in actual fact and experience a way (to them, often the only way) to an essentially religious attitude to life. But to others, who view this Jungian approach from other points of view, it presents many difficulties, and it is with these that we must now have more especially to do if we are to bridge the chasm from the religious side.

But, just what is this Jungian approach to religion? As Professor Hostie has shown in his chronological description of Jung's work,[9] it has undergone important developments in the half-century in which Jung has been at work. Moreover we shall not find it neatly summarized in, but scattered here and there throughout, Jung's voluminous writings. But the essential features of it have been well and faithfully summarized in a useful article on "The Psychological Approach to Religion" by Dr. Gerhard Adler.[10] He states the generally accepted Jungian position as follows:

> Both the religious thinker and the psychologist may regard religion and psychology as incompatible, though for diametrically opposite reasons. To the religious thinker it may appear almost sacrilegious to approach the highest content of religion—God—with the "dissecting knife" of psychology. To anyone who holds this view it must, however, be pointed out that religion is most certainly a phenomenon of the human psyche, and a such open to psychological inquiry. It would indeed be a sacrilege if, in the course of its investigation, psychology claimed to be able to make any statement about the absolute existence or non-existence of God, or about any other reality of religious faith. It is not the task of psychology to make such statements, and if it did so it would clearly transcend its competence and possibilities: the realities of faith are, as such, not accessible to psychology. What is, however, the legitimate concern of psychology is the *phenomenon* of religious experience as an activity of the human psyche and as an expression of its inner processes. Psychology is thus not concerned with the question of the reality of God, but with a psychic experience which is understood

to be and formulated as God. This experience may or may not correspond to the existence of an absolute Deity; but in any case it is a *psychic reality* of the utmost importance. On this understanding, psychology does not touch the conceptions of religion and theology which are based on faith in the absolute reality of God. It is only concerned with the appearance that this reality takes on in the human mind. In other words, psychology is concerned with ideas as they manifest themselves in the human psyche. It is thus a "misunderstanding that the psychological treatment or explanation reduced God to nothing but psychology. It is, however, not a matter of God but of ideas of God.... It is man who has such ideas and creates for himself images, and these things belong to psychology..."[11] Psychological study of religious phenomena in the human psyche must obey the rules of psychological exploration. Jung has put this point very clearly in, the following passage: "...the methodological standpoint of the psychology which I represent... is exclusively phenomenological, that is, it is concerned with occurrences, events, experiences, in a word, with facts. Its truth is a fact and not a judgment. Speaking for instance of the virgin birth, psychology is only concerned with the fact that there is such an idea, but it is not concerned with the question whether such an idea is true or false in any other sense. It is psychologically true in as much as it exists.... This point of view is the same as that of natural science...."[12]

Most of this is, from any point of view, eminently reasonable and realistic. Most of it is, from the standpoint of most theologians, eminently satisfactory. Here is no division of territories, but at the same time a definite and clear division of the roles of the psychologist and the theologian within that territory. The modesty of the role claimed by the psychologist should win the theologian's approval; he must cordially agree that the intrinsic truth of religious statements is a matter which lies outside the competence and possibilities of empirical psychology.

But Dr. Adler already introduces us to some ideas, general among Jungians, which may arouse perplexity and misgiving, and produce complications into our task of bridge-building. The conception of "psychological truth" here outlined has aroused uneasiness among psychologists and others besides theologians.[13] The mental patient's conviction that he is Napoleon Bonaparte, or the antics of pink elephants on the bedspread of the sufferer from *delirium tremens*, are also ideas which exist, but it is not commonly considered to be outside the scope of psychology whether they are "true or false in any other sense." A psychiatrist's diagnosis of a "Thurber man," who thinks he hears a seal behind the bed, will not be uninfluenced by observing that there *is* a seal behind the bed! To call any idea "psychologically true" simply on the ground that it exists is at least open to misunderstanding, and we are left guessing what could possibly be "psychologically false." Moreover it is at least unusual to call a "truth" that which is merely "a fact and not a judgment." It has been generally agreed for some millennia that a bare fact or the simple observation of a fact is neither true nor false, and that truth (or falsehood) can be expressed only in a judgment. And, so far as our information goes, the natural sciences, which are here invoked for support, have not departed from this usage. They have become very hesitant to claim the words "true" or "false" at all, but would anyway not claim them except for judgments embodied in statements or equations.[14]

This linguistic idiosyncrasy is not the only difficulty which confronts the would-be bridge-builder in the Jungian literature. Dr. Adler hints at another when he refers to "a psychic experience which is understood to be and formulated as God." We are compelled to ask, *by whom* is any psychic experience understood to *be* and *formulated as* God? No Christian, nor indeed many theists of any sort, can allow for a moment that any psychic experience, which must of its nature be something finite and is, *ex hypothesi*, an observable phenomenon, can possibly *be* God, nor can he conceivably so formulate it. To do so would for us be idolatry, to invest something essentially limited and created with the attributes of divinity. However much we must respect the restrictions which the psychologist sets himself and his methodological refusal "to make any statement about the existence or non-existence of God, or about any other reality of religious faith," we must bring to his earnest attention that it is simply not a *fact* (not therefore, in his own language, "a psychological truth") that we hold that an observable human experience is God, or can formulate it to be God. We recognize his acknowledged incompetence to make statements about divine transcendence, but must protest that the psychological fact is that by "God" we *mean* that which transcends everything finite, and that divine immanence itself can only mean for us the immanence of the Transcendent. These are the psychological facts, the ideas which exist, in us, and which we must ask him, precisely as an empiricist, to observe.

Dr. Adler, throughout the rest of his essay, is careful to distinguish between God and the human experience: the latter he generally calls an archetype or an image *of* God, and he speaks of the "correspondence" between the two. He recalls that Jung himself has pointed out that the very word *archetype* "presupposes an imprinter"[15] and therefore implies a clear distinction between that which imprints and that which is imprinted.[16] But Jung is not always so cautious. He has written that by the word "God," "the theologian will naturally assume that the metaphysical *Ens Absolutum* is meant. The empiricist, on the contrary, does not dream of making such a far-reaching assumption, which strikes him as downright impossible, but when he uses this word he just as naturally

means a mere statement, at most an archetypal motif which pre-
forms such statements."[17] Here again we are confronted by one of
those linguistic oddities which make Jungian literature so baffling
to many outside their own circle, and not only to theologians.[18]
Assuredly Jung is not alone in regarding the affirmation of *Ens Absolutum* "downright impossible," and there are many others who
would hold that any statement about God must be meaningless or
untrue. But it must be doubted whether anyone, even among empiricists and outside his own circle, would call a statement about
God "God," or God "a statement," any more than they would call
a statement about a cat, a "cat." Nor is our difficulty greatly eased
when Jung writes, "When I said that God is a complex, I meant to
say: Whatever he is, he is *at least* a very tangible complex...he is *at
least* a psychological fact. I certainly never intended to say: He is
nothing else but a complex."[19] The simple psychological fact is that
we hold that God is not a complex at all, if by this is understood
anything finite and in any way composite—ready though we must
be to recognize that God is manifested to us through images and
through psychological processes, which may indeed be complexes. This curious usage of the names "God," "Christ," even "Yahweh," to mean human complexes and representations (instead of
what the complex may be about, or what it represents) is sustained
throughout the length of Jung's *Answer to Job*, as that book is
interpreted by Jung himself in its preface. One reader has not surprisingly complained that this fact "makes the reading of this little
book a veritable exercise in aerial acrobatics, even for the reader
who is accustomed to psychological disciplines."[20]

Indeed the usage may seem more rather than less astonishing for coming from psychologists and psychotherapists. For these
commonly (and to this Jungians are certainly no exception) regard
it as an important part of their task to help their patients precisely to distinguish their *imago* or complex from reality: to enable

them to become conscious that, for instance, their father-imago or mother-complex is precisely *not* their "real" father and mother, and so to withdraw the projection and dissolve the identification. Why then, we must ask, do Jung and his followers so consistently confuse God and the God-imago or "archetype of Deity" right from the beginning?

The matter becomes understandable once the Jungians' approach and method is understood. This is summarized by Jung himself when he goes on to explain:

> For him [the empiricist], "God" can just as well mean Jahwe, Allah, Zeus, Shiva or Huizilopochtli. The divine attributes of almightiness, omniscience, eternity, etc., are to him mere statements which, symptomatically or as syndromes, more or less regularly accompany the archetype. He grants the divine image "numinosity," a deeply stirring, emotional effect, which he accepts in the first place as a fact, and sometimes tries to explain rationally in a more or less unsatisfactory way. As a psychiatrist, he is sufficiently hard-boiled to be deeply convinced of the relative character of such statements. As a scientist, his primary interest is the verification of actual psychic facts and their regular occurrence, to which he attaches incomparably greater importance than to abstract possibilities. His *religio* consists in establishing facts which can be observed and proved. He describes and circumscribes these in the same way as the mineralogist his mineral samples and the botanist his plants. He is aware that beyond provable events he can know nothing and at best can only dream, and he considers it immoral to confuse a dream with knowledge.[21]

There can be little doubt that, despite protests to the contrary, certain philosophical and epistemological preconceptions have strongly reinforced this position in Jung's own mind. That mind is altogether too mercurial to be confined to any one "-ism," and it usually slips elusively from the grasp of those critics who attempt to pin it down and label it. But there is abundant evidence in Jung's own writings of the immense influence which Kant's *Kritik* and positivism have had upon him. This means that not only is the empirical method of the observation and verification of facts and their correlation and classification by their regular occurrence his own *religio*: it also leads him to hold that this method is the only real knowledge available to any man, that apart from it he can "know nothing" and all else is dream, faith or opinion.[22] It also means that God is in no way rationally knowable or even approachable; and that so-called rational arguments for the existence of God are "downright impossible."[23] This in its turn means that while the empirical psychologist can check his patient's father-imago or mother-complex against the "real" (i.e., complex-free and empirically knowable and verifiable) father or mother, there is no "real God" in any way knowable and verifiable to which the God-imago or God-complex can be compared. To the psychologist as such, there *is* no God independent of the imago or the complex.[24] Indeed such preconceptions should logically force him to the conclusion that this imago or complex cannot be other than a purely irrational fact: he has no means of ascertaining whether it *is* an imago *of* anything or a complex *about* anything. It just *is.* There are no rational statements about God, no products of directed thinking with which it can be compared. Thus, the very possibility that religion could develop into an adult, rational, voluntary relationship—such as he may hope and expect of his patient's relationship to his parents when the imago has been analyzed—is *a priori* excluded. Such philosophical preconceptions may go some way, not only to explain the bland indifference with which some Jungians use the words "God" and "God-image" (and its variations), but also their preoccupation with what many religious people may consider to be the more childish, primitive, irrational and immature phases of religion.

Our purpose in this book is not to dispute these philosophical preconceptions, still less to criticize the Jungians on philosophical or theological grounds. It would be pardonable if attempts to do so should arouse from their side "vehement diatribes—especially if they seek to minimize or make nothing of the findings of analytical psychology."[25] For while such philosophical preconceptions may be the basis of Jung's denials, they are not the basis of his positive affirmations. This basis is established directly by the empirical method which the Jungians pursue, from the facts which they observe and the generalized correlations which they make of them. And on this, their own chosen and legitimate ground, they should be met and examined.

It is inherent in the empirical method that it involves some preselection of the "facts" or "events" to be observed. It is neither surprising nor reprehensible that the "facts" which have particularly impressed and engaged the attention of the Jungians have been the psychological experiences of "numinosity," a deeply stirring, emotional effect. Deep experiences of this nature are said to have had a profound effect on Jung himself, and led him from a highly sceptical and even antagonistic attitude towards religion to a more positive appreciation of its function in human life. He and his colleagues could not fail to be impressed by the profound therapeutic effects which such experiences had upon their patients—and notably upon those who had been most alienated from a religious standpoint. It is a common feature of these experiences that the subject is purely passive to them: they seize him in spite of his conscious attitudes and volition with feelings of awe and fascination (*mysterium tremendum et fascinans*), and are therefore of a wholly irrational character. It was clear that their source could and should be stated in psychological terms (admittedly "in a more or less unsatisfactory way") as an unconscious complex or *imago*. Very little research into anthropology or the history of religions is required to show that the sources of such experiences had commonly been called "gods" or "God"; and indeed there is evidence which suggests (and indeed is strongly supported by Rudolf Otto's *Idea of the Holy*) that here is the primary "religious experience," the essential religious *Urerfahrung*.[26] Hence, quite apart from Kant or positivistic preconceptions, the Jungians' terminology is quite understandable in the light of their observations, and within their own empiricist frame of reference, however perplexing and confusing it may be to those who approach the subject differently.

There can, we are convinced, be no denying or minimizing of the facts. Nor can we question the validity of the method. But the empiricist, if his science is to advance at all, must always be ready to examine his application of it. And, first of all, he must be ready to examine his preselection of facts. Meteorology could not have made much progress if it had always confined itself to the observation and correlation of *meteora*. Many other facts besides the positions and movements of heavenly bodies are now known to be relevant to the phenomena of weather and atmospheric conditions, which indeed have nothing directly to do with such positions and movements at all. The Copernican could never have displaced the Ptolomean system, the revolution of the Earth could never have been recognized, had not men been prepared to look beyond their perfectly accurate observations that bodies regularly fall down, and do not fall up, or that winds are irregular both in velocity and direction—undoubted empirical facts once honestly considered fatal to the Copernican view. Neither chemistry nor physics, neither biology nor medicine, could have progressed at all had they not considerably enlarged the range of facts which they considered, still less had they assumed that their first observations accounted for all the phenomena within their respective fields and should be the criterion for all the rest. For the empiricist must also beware lest the general hypotheses and laws which he postulates to account for those observations should blind him to other facts which cannot be governed by those hypotheses and laws. Still less may he allow those general hypotheses and laws to be transposed into value-judgments whereby facts which do not fit the law become arbitrarily devaluated as secondary deviations from the norm. The method may not be allowed to distort the observations, nor *a priori* to grade their respective importance.

And it becomes necessary to draw attention to two sets of facts, of which of course the Jungians are well aware, but whose importance to our bridge-building (and perhaps also to their own empirical constructions) they do not seem sufficiently to emphasize. In the first place we must point to that considerable body of evidence which shows that *the experience of "luminosity" is by no means always religious, nor issues in religion.* This is too evident to need any detailed elaboration, and will not be denied. Jung's own works are full of examples which show that this type of experience is the root, not only of religion, but also of much magic, superstition, art, poetry—and also of neurosis and especially of psychosis.

Less considered, but no less important, is the fact that phenomena which are empirically found to be called *religion* (or religious) *are by no means always "numinous,"* or in any way directly connected with the experience of "numinosity." Here again the evidence is overwhelming, though it will naturally be found in the annals of religion itself—in temples, mosques and churches, in theological and devotional literature, in the history of religions and religious biographies—rather than in the consulting room. As Dr. Hans Schaer has said, "religion consists not in merely experiencing the supra-personal forces of the soul as such, but in adopting—psychically—an active attitude."[27] We do not require any *a priori* definition of religion to show that this is so: it is abundantly evident from the empirical study of religious phenomena that, whatever purely passive and indeed overwhelming experience may underlie them, they always consist in some active response. This may be more or less emotional, or more or less rational and voluntary. Jung himself, of course, recognizes that "religion...is voluntary as well as involuntary,"[28] but it is—not unnaturally in view of the experiences to which we have already alluded—the involuntary side that first attracted his interest. In his later work, he has laid much stronger emphasis on the importance of conscious understanding and voluntary decision in religion:

> The *unconscious* conversion of instinctual impulses into religious activity is ethically worthless, and often no more than an hysterical outburst, even though its products may be aesthetically valuable. Ethical decision is possible only when one is conscious of the conflict in all its aspects. The same is true of the religious attitude: it must be fully conscious of itself and of its foundations if it is to signify anything more than unconscious imitation.[29]

Religious activity can be accompanied by complete emotional dryness or aridity; and indeed the mystics, both Christian and non-Christian, tend to prize it the more highly the more "a deeply stirring, emotional effect" is precisely *absent*[30] and it becomes the product of "naked will." Eastern yoga and related techniques seek precisely the cessation of the *vrittis*,[31] St. John of the Cross the transcendence of all images and feelings.[32] For Aquinas and Catholic divines generally religion is a quality or virtue of the soul of a rational and voluntary character, which issues in rational and voluntary acts both interior and exterior.[33] Protestant divines and preachers—from Barth and Tillich to Billy Graham—stress no less emphatically and unanimously the basic need for personal decision in the Christian life.

These are psychological facts which nobody acquainted with the phenomena of religion would deny: they are no less psychological facts than are "numinous experiences." It may be allowed that they possibly represent later developments in the history of religions, and that they do not loom so large or have such efficacy in the psychotherapy of modern patients for whom the reactivation of primitive experiences is often of the most profound personal significance—especially where all religious sense has been lost or is non-existent. But objective empiricism does not permit us to identify the genetically prior with the axiologically prior—what is first in time with what is first in importance. This kind of confusion, which Jung detected in Freud's conception of infantile sexuality, should not be carried over into the empirical study of religious phenomena.

The point needs emphasis here, because recognition of these facts on the part of psychologists seems indispensable, not only if they are to understand what their "religious" patients are talking about and if endless confusion with them is to be avoided, but also because our own task of bridge-building to meet their own structures is difficult, if not impossible, without such recognition. To the extent that they may tend to identify religion with the "numinous experience," or at least to regard it as the criterion by which other religious phenomena are to be evaluated, it is necessary for us to point out that their structure rests on inadequate empirical observation—and that it is hardly possible for us to connect satisfactorily with it—until other facts are recognized, incorporated and allowed due importance.

Much the same must be said—still without departing from empirical facts—about the word "God." Jung has just told us that the empirical psychologist deals with "facts that can be observed and proved," and that "he describes and circumscribes these in the same way as the mineralogist his mineral samples and the botanist his plants." But, as Jung himself has repeatedly stressed, the psychologist's task is very much more difficult—and indeed more problematic. Minerals and plants display a certain constancy and uniformity which render classification comparatively simple. Individual human psyches, on the contrary, display almost infinite variety; so much so that the individual (with whom the practising psychotherapist has to do) cannot be treated as one specimen of a class, nor even as the embodiment of a general category with secondary and unimportant variations, but altogether as unique. General theory must be used in practice for the elucidation of the particular case; never as a category into which the individual must be fitted. The individual variations may be just as important, possibly more important, than the general similarities.[34]

What must be said of human psyches must also be said of their product, human language. This displays variations quite different from the specimens of the mineralogist and the botanist. The word "God," especially, is found to have a variety of meanings and associations which we do not meet in the specimens we choose to call granite or daisy. He would be a very unobservant empiricist who should suppose that the word "God" was the name of a class, or that its meaning was identical to the worshippers of Jahwe, Allah, Zeus, Shiva and Huizilopochtli.[35] The very statements which the psychologist rightly claims as the province of his observations belie it, for it is an evident *fact* that tales are told, and statements made, about Zeus which are not told or made of Allah, that claims are made by Jahwe which are not made by Shiva or Huizilopochtli. The thunder and lightning or the eclipse which may have a profoundly numinous effect on the primitive will leave a modern Christian stone cold; and he will firmly deny to them or to any other natural phenomena, whether physical or psychological, the right to be regarded as God. The rational theist, be he Christian or not, will strenuously deny that what he calls "God" is an irrational fact or an emotionally stirring product of the unconscious. He will often maintain that his affirmation of God can be the logically inevitable consequence of conscious inference about empirical phenomena.[36] That he does maintain this is an empirical fact which the empirical psychologist cannot ignore, whatever Hume, Kant or logical positivists may think about the validity of his procedure; for to him, at least, it is a fact of primary importance which may dominate both his religious activities and his whole psychological orientation. He will be aware that what he calls God transcends rational comprehension, but yet affirm that this incomprehensible mystery and that conscious reasoning itself indicates that inquiry into, and worship of, this mystery can be a perfectly reasonable proceeding.[37] That to this "God" is to be attributed "almightiness, omniscience, eternity" is a statement which follows ineluctably from a conscious and rigorously logical procedure—whether or not such a statement also "more or less regularly accompanies the archetype."[38]

These are easily verifiable psychological facts, which no "abstract possibilities" should allow us to ignore or to minimize. It is certainly not within the professional competence of the empirical psychologist to judge the truth of the relative claims made for Jahwe, Allah, Zeus and the rest. But he can hardly fail to note that, even as phenomena, they are by no means identical, and fidelity to his very empiricism demands that he should observe their differences no less than their seemingly common characteristics. The psychological fact is that to their respective devotees it is the differences rather than the similarities which are of paramount importance: that Jahwe has called and made certain promises to Abraham and his seed, is of indescribably greater influence on the psyche of the believing Jew than any resemblances Jahwe may be found to have to Shiva who makes no such claim. To see these "gods" as specimens of a class, whose variations are secondary and accidental, can only arise from an optical illusion which distorts the facts in the interests of a general hypothesis, however legitimate that hypothesis may be as a means of accounting for a limited selection of facts. The denial of the right to the name "religious" to the imageless and emotionless "Dark Night" of St. John of the Cross, or to the consciously and rationally argued *Deus est* of St. Thomas Aquinas, or the devaluation of their procedures as secondary variations or accidental deviations from the essential religious fact, would argue an arbitrary *a priorism* which is the negation of objective empiricism.

Our plea, then, to psychologists in general, and to Jungians in particular, is not for any departure from empirical methods, but rather for their more rigorous and comprehensive application. It would, quite certainly, be unjust to attribute such consistent misapplication of them, as that which we have just described, to Jung himself. In his later work, especially since his *Psychology and Alchemy*, and most notably in his *Aion* and *Answer to Job*, we find him especially occupied with the distinctive peculiarities of the statements made about the God of the Bible and of the Christian Church: such studies can hardly fail to focus attention on the fact that, even from the phenomenological viewpoint, "God" can by no means "just as well mean Jahwe" as the other "gods."[39] In his *Answer to Job* he acknowledges, and on every page displays, a personal emotional involvement with the God of the Hebrew and Christian Scriptures, and of the Catholic Church, which contrasts sharply with his detached and placid commentaries on Buddhist, Tantric, Taoist and Tibetan scriptures, or on Kerenyi's presentation of the gods of the Greeks.

It must however be acknowledged that in these later works Jung may seem vastly to complicate rather than to facilitate an approach from a Christian standpoint. They contain, besides a wealth of valuable empirical material, a great many interpretations, evaluations, and opinions about ecclesiastical dogmas, philosophical systems and historical events, to say nothing of excursions into Biblical exegesis. He himself repeatedly stresses their difference from, even their opposition to, what he supposes (not always correctly) to be Christian orthodoxy. It may be thought that he has not only raised serious barriers to an approach from that side, but has also tended to depart increasingly from scientific and empiricist rectitude.[40] He makes no secret of his "emotional subjectivity" when thus engaged,[41] and repeatedly glories in what he believes (rightly or wrongly) to be his "heresies."

And it might well be supposed that it was our first task to try to clear up the resultant debris, and to engage in polemics with these interpretations, evaluations and opinions—with many of which we certainly cannot agree. We do not however intend to do so, except incidentally to the more constructive task which we have set ourselves. Jung has explained in the clearest terms why this development in his work—this seeming intrusion into the field of the theologian and the philosopher—has come about:

> There are many well-educated patients who flatly refuse to consult the clergyman. With the philosopher they will have even less to do, for the history of philosophy leaves them cold, and intellectual problems seem to them more barren than the desert.[42]

> I would be only too delighted to leave this anything but easy task to the theologian, were it not that it is just from the theologians that many of my patients come. They ought to have hung on to the community of the Church, but they were shed like dry leaves from the great tree and now find themselves "hanging on" to the treatment.[43]

Jung has commented frequently and at length on this failure
of theologians and philosophers to communicate meaningfully
not only with his own patients but also with their contemporaries
in general.[44] It is a failure of which many theologians and pastors—and perhaps even a few philosophers—are painfully aware.[45]
He has pointed out the burdens which this failure imposes on the
psychotherapist, who necessarily lacks training and authority in
their field, and who also "lacks the Church's means of grace."[46]
He has also drawn attention to the fact that this vacuum brings
about, in therapeutic practice, an inevitable "hanging on" to the
treatment, prolongation of the transference, and complications in
its resolution.[47]

The situation is one which should present a singular challenge
and opportunity to the theologian and the pastor. But he will
hardly meet it by a frontal attack on those of Jung's personal views
and opinions with which he does not agree. His task should be to
meet the same facts (as well as other relevant facts which the Jungians seem to have disregarded or minimized), and so to encounter
basic human needs, rather than indulge in a sterile clash of views
from inevitably divergent viewpoints. As Jung himself has put it:

> As a scientist I must give a wide berth to anything dogmatic
> or metaphysical, since it is not the scientist's task to preach
> the Gospel. But it is precisely what the theologian has to say,
> namely that the dogma is the hitherto most perfect answer
> to, and formulation of, the most relevant items in the objec-
> tive psyche, and that God has worked all these things in man's
> soul.[48]

The next chapters in this volume will attempt a contribution to this task. We shall gratefully accept the "building-stones"
which empirical psychology points out to us, and endeavour to

discover what place they can occupy in our own structure. Although we may sometimes find ourselves obliged to add stones which, though no less "empirical facts," the psychologists seem to reject, and sometimes query their classification and evaluation of those which they have hewn, our criticism will be subordinated to the more constructive task which our common concern imposes upon us.

We may engage upon such a task the more hopefully because Jung himself records that he has found from experience that his Catholic patients are in different case from others, and do not usually lay such burdens of "dialectical discussion" and prolonged transference upon the therapist.

> When I am treating practising Catholics, and am faced with the transference problem, I can, by virtue of my office as a doctor, step aside and lead the problem over to the Church.... The Catholic who has been freed from an excessive personal tie to his parents can return fairly easily to the mysteries of the Church, which he is now in a position to understand better and more deeply.[49]

> In treating devout Catholics, I always refer them to the Church's confessional and its means of grace... A number of my patients...have become Catholics, or at least better Catholics than they were before.[50]

Other therapists have confessed that they have found the treatment of Catholics a far less simple matter than these words had led them to expect, and that their patients' Catholicity had sometimes enhanced rather than eased the difficulties of psychotherapy. But they will generally agree that the case of the Catholic or ex-Catholic patient presents peculiar features which call for peculiar consideration, and that the theologian may be expected to have something to offer to enable them to understand those features.

IV.

THE PSYCHOLOGICAL VIEW
OF SYMBOL AND DOGMA

T he need to correlate Christian beliefs and practices with psychological experience and hypotheses is most obvious to the psychotherapist and his Christian—or would-be Christian—patient.[1] The conscientious therapist or analyst, whatever his own beliefs or disbeliefs, will usually be on his guard against disturbing—let alone opposing—his patient's beliefs, if only in the interests of the treatment itself.[2] Yet they often present him with serious practical problems. They sometimes appear as valuable auxiliaries in the cure, but sometimes also as factors in the illness, or as sources of resistance to the treatment. He cannot fail to notice their beneficial or baneful effects on the patient's health, and that very often their apparent incompatibility with the psychological experiences and understanding gained in analysis may present the patient with further conflicts which neither he nor the patient are equipped to resolve. He seldom has any means of checking whether the patient has rightly understood, or has perhaps distorted, what the beliefs and practices to which he and his Church are committed are really supposed to mean. He is not a theologian, nor can he usually interpret with any authority the beliefs of any denomination. Indeed his own knowledge of Christianity is often more clinical than theological; that is to say, gathered from the often distorted interpretations of his neurotic patients. "Nor does the unrelieved strain of the psychotherapeutic situation, with its host of impressions and emotional disturbances, leave us [psychotherapists] much leisure for the systematization of thought. Thus we have no clear exposition of guiding principles drawn from life to offer either to the philosophers or to the theologians."[3]

This need for correlation presses still more urgently on the Christian patient himself. It may have been doubts and difficulties about his religion, and the seeming inability of his religion itself to resolve them, that have brought him into psychotherapy at all. In other cases, he had not at first suspected any connection between his religion and his complaints, but has discovered some such connection—sometimes of a very radical character—in the course of the treatment. Even when his religion may be healthy and loyal, devout and mature, his religious instruction has often been sketchy. But however excellent his religious education has been, it has seldom been geared to deal with the needs and questions which the new psychological experiences have aroused. However careful his own therapist may be not to disturb his beliefs, he may well be disturbed and perplexed when he reads the works of other psychologists who openly propound "heretical" interpretations and criticism, which he finds himself quite unequipped to counter. To the extent that his psychological experiences have a supra-personal and archetypal character, and that he has himself become acquainted with their "numinosity" and the radical—and often seemingly "religious"—transformations which accompany them, it is simply impossible for him to find a solution by completely separating soul from psyche, and by assigning his religion to the one and his experiences of the unconscious and his reactions to them to the other.[4] Such devices—all theoretical objections to them apart—can hardly be meaningful except to those whose acquaintance with one or the other (or both) is superficial, and who remain blissfully unaware of the total claims which religion and deep analysis both make on the human personality.

It would however be a mistake to suppose that this task of correlation is of interest and importance only to the professional therapist and his professedly Christian patient. Whatever our own present
beliefs or disbeliefs, the near ancestors of the vast majority of us who
live in the territories of Western civilization were professed Christians, and, at least not so many generations ago, Catholics at that.
The overwhelming importance of this fact for understanding our
own present-day psychology and its problems—for the unbeliever
as well as for the believer—is strongly emphasized by Jung:

> We always think that Christianity consists of a certain confes-
> sion of faith and of belonging to a Church. No, Christianity
> is our world. Everything we think is the fruit of the Middle
> Ages and indeed of the Christian Middle Ages. Our whole
> science, everything that passes through our head, has inevi-
> tably gone through this history. The latter lives in us and has
> left its stamp upon us for all time and will always form a vital
> layer of our psyche, just like any phylogenetic traces in our
> body. The whole character of our mentality, the way in which
> we look at things, is also the result of the Christian Middle
> Ages; whether we know it or not is quite immaterial. The age
> of rational enlightenment has eradicated nothing. Even our
> method of rational enlightenment is Christian. The Christian
> *Weltanschauung* is therefore a psychological fact which does
> not allow of any further rationalization; it is something which
> has happened, which is present.[5]

> Our age has a blindness without parallel. We think we have
> only to declare an acknowledged form of faith to be incorrect
> or invalid, to become psychologically free of the Christian or
> Judaic religion. We believe in enlightenment, as if an intel-
> lectual change of opinion had somehow a deeper influence

on emotional processes, or indeed upon the unconscious! We
entirely forget that the religion of the last two thousand years
is a psychological attitude, a definite form of adaptation to
inner and outer experience, which moulds a definite form of
civilization.[6]

What Jung here calls Christianity, we may prefer to call its cultural deposits, but this does not invalidate the point he makes. He
has also drawn attention to the fact that, not only medieval faith
and religious practices, but also medieval scholastic methods have
had an immense influence on our own ways of thinking, even on
our modern science:

> On a historical view, the scholastic spirit in which men of the
> intellectual calibre of St. Thomas Aquinas, Duns Scotus, Abe-
> lard, William of Ockham and others worked is the mother of
> our modern scientific method, and future generations will see
> clearly how far scholasticism still nourishes the science of today
> with living undercurrents.... The great achievement of scho-
> lasticism was that it laid the foundations of a solidly built in-
> tellectual function, the *sine qua non* of modern science and
> technology.[7]

The Christian Middle Ages themselves inherited elements
from many different sources, from Biblical religion, from Greek
and Roman culture, from paganism both Greek and barbarian.
Our very languages, those most potent factors in our psychological formation, have passed through this history. Even those
among us who have no Christian ancestry, but whose origins are
(for instance) purely Jewish, must be in very great measure psychologically conditioned by the type of civilization in which, or up
against which, they find themselves.

Understanding of the symbols and beliefs which have fashioned it may thus be an important factor in understanding ourselves. And to this task the theologian, and perhaps especially the Catholic theologian, should have something uniquely important to contribute. It is a task which should involve no serious deviation from his normal professional business, which is summed up in the traditional formula, *intelligere quod credimus*—the understanding of what we (Christians) believe.[8] He is, or should be, equipped as nobody else can be, to explain to the psychologist (professional or other) just what the symbols and doctrines are, what they mean, what is their rightful place in the general context of the Christian life—and to correct if need be the psychologist's misapprehensions on these points.

Yet it should be understandable (and by nobody better than by the psychologist) if such an undertaking presents the theologian with grave misgivings. Although the material—the symbols and doctrines—which interest both him and the psychologist may coincide, their viewpoints appear to be entirely different. The theologian has been accustomed, and rightly accustomed, to consider them from the standpoint of their intrinsic and objective *truth*; the psychologist, as we have seen, is professionally concerned with them simply as psychological *facts*, and with the manner in which they are observed to *work*. The psychologist's concern with them appears to be wholly *pragmatic* and *functional*. The theologian, on the other hand, will normally claim to be not only the student, but also the guardian of what he believes to be sacred truths, directly or indirectly revealed by God himself; for him they have no other interest or value, and any other concern with them may appear to him to be both impertinent and sacrilegious. Any assistance or encouragement he may give to such a concern may seem like a betrayal of his own sacred trust.

We should, however, observe that the two viewpoints, though certainly not identical, are by no means incompatible; and that the very character of the truth to which the doctrines themselves lay claim—as *verbum salutis,* "saving" or "healing" truth—implies a pragmatic and functional aspect. They are presented not only as "true," but also as somehow "good" for us. We may draw the theologian's attention to his primary concern for the *bonum animarum*—the weal of souls.[9] Whether he likes it or not, the functioning of religious beliefs and symbols is in fact being closely studied and with immense practical consequences, not only to psychologists themselves and to their immediate patients, but also to many who have become acquainted with their work. It must be of some concern to the pastors of souls whether those symbols and beliefs are being correctly or incorrectly interpreted. Moreover, his own "failure of communication" with his contemporaries, and the fact that the truths which are his concern largely fall on deaf ears, should give him pause for reflection before he too abruptly refuses his unique services. For it is an evident fact that those truths are commonly rejected or ignored in the modern world, much less because they are denied, or rejected as untrue, than because they are felt to be irrelevant, and not to "work" or have any relation to life as actually experienced. The fact that psychologists have found it necessary in the interests of their often agnostic patients, and of their own studies, to rediscover their relevance and functioning, cannot leave him indifferent.

Jung's discovery, or rediscovery, of the psychological function of dogmas and creeds is of great interest. He holds that they supply the psychologist with more information about the human psyche than do most varieties of scientific psychology:

> In itself any scientific theory, no matter how subtle, has, I think, less value from the standpoint of psychological truth than the religious dogma, for the simple reason that a theory is necessarily highly abstract and exclusively rational, whereas

the dogma expresses an irrational entity through the image. This method guarantees a much better rendering of an irrational fact, such as the psyche. Moreover, the dogma owes its existence and form, on the one hand, to so-called "revealed" immediate experiences, such as the God-Man, the Cross, the Virgin Birth, the Immaculate Conception, the Trinity and so on, and, on the other hand, to the ceaseless collaboration of many minds and many centuries.... The dogma represents the soul more completely than a scientific theory, for the latter expresses and formulates the conscious mind alone. Furthermore, a theory can do nothing but formulate a living thing in abstract notions. The dogma, on the contrary, expresses aptly the living process of the unconscious in the form of the drama of repentance, sacrifice and redemption.[10]

Such an account of dogma must, of course, seem very odd at first sight to a theologian. To him it is obvious that most dogmas make statements, not about man, or the human psyche, but about God, or at least about God's works in and for men; and it is indeed a manifest fact that they make such statements, whether or not they are held to be true or false, or even meaningful or meaningless. But he must allow that, inasmuch as creeds precisely express what "I believe," they express psychological facts. If he should also have any acquaintance at all with the findings of depth-psychology, of the history of religions, of anthropology—or if he has read any mythology (or even the Old Testament)—he must recognize that, however unique and distinctive their handling of them, the Christian creeds deal with themes which are familiar to many who do not accept them, or have never even heard of them as such. He may prefer to say that the creeds render the super-rational rather than the irrational; but he too must recognize that their formulation, even though divinely guided, is the outcome of the "collaboration of many minds and many centuries" on revealed experiences which, being "acts of God" do not arise from human consciousness or volition, and so may be said, from the empiricist's standpoint, to originate in the unconscious[11]—that is, in that of which we are not, and cannot be, fully conscious.

Jung recognizes that creeds and dogmas originate not only in a "numinous experience," but also in faith or *pistis*, which he understands as "loyalty, trust and confidence towards a definitely numinous effect and the subsequent alteration of consciousness."[12] We shall see in the next chapter that the faith implied in the Christian's *credo* is more than this, but this much the theologian too will usually be ready to allow.

Jung is also much impressed by the age, permanence and stability of dogma, in contrast to the scientific theory which is "soon superseded by another."[13] He observes that dogma has to do with age-old archetypal motifs which may be traced back into the mists of prehistory. And he remarks on its *universality*: "A creed is always the result and fruit of many minds and many centuries, purified from all the oddities, shortcomings and flaws of individual experience."[14]

"But for all that," Jung continues, "the individual experience, with its very poverty, is immediate life, it is the warm red blood pulsating today." Somewhat surprisingly to the Christian reader, Jung sees creeds and dogmas, not only as conscious responses to, and reflections upon, experiences, but as *substitutes* for immediate individual experience, even as *protection against* such experience. Indeed, creeds are a substitute for religion itself:

> The substitution has the obvious purpose of replacing immediate experience by a choice of suitable symbols invested in a solidly organized dogma and ritual. The Catholic church maintains them by her indisputable authority, the Protestant

church (if this term is still applicable) by insistence upon faith and the evangelical message. As long as these two principles work, people are effectively defended and shielded against immediate religious experience. Even if something of the sort should happen to them, they can refer to the church, for it would know whether the experience came from God or from the devil, whether it was to be accepted or rejected.[15]

Jung does not, it should be noted, regard this alleged substitutional and defensive role of dogma with contempt. On the contrary, nobody is more aware than he of the "perils of the soul," of the dangers of the unconscious to an ego too weak or ill-equipped to cope directly with its fascinating power. (We may here recall the devastation wrought by *The Absolute at Large* in Karel Čapek's novel.) But we must still question whether he has correctly understood the normal psychological function of creeds and dogmas, or whether, as Dr. Robert Hobson has put it, he only "describes a possible attitude towards dogmatic formulations."[16] There can be no doubt that this "possible attitude" may at times be a serious clinical reality. Jung's notion of the function of dogma as substitutional and defensive appears to have been influenced to a considerable extent by his experience with at least one of his patients, the young ex-Catholic scientist whose case is referred to in *Psychology and Religion* and *Psychology and Alchemy*. Here undoubtedly occurred a phase which suggested a regressive tendency towards a cosy religiosity in which dogma seemed to offer just such a defence-mechanism. The escape into religious (and also into psychological!) dogmatism is certainly possible, and it describes an attitude towards dogma which can certainly occur, and may be highly deleterious. But abuse should not be confused with use, and it would be a serious mistake to estimate the regular and healthy functioning of an organ from pathological specimens alone.

It must be confessed that, viewed from within the Church, it is not at all "obvious" that creeds normally function in this way. Nor is it easily understandable how this view could arise from observation from outside. There seems to be no statistical evidence whatever that the incidence of immediate, individual experience (however this may be defined) is any lower among Catholics or Evangelicals than anybody else: indeed, there is evidence that among many of them such experiences are both rich and frequent. We shall suggest in the next chapter that creeds and doctrines do indeed provide a criterion of evaluation whereby individual experience can be measured by the standards of the age-long (or Apostolic) and the universal (or Catholic). But it seems that they tend rather to expose the believer to immediate experience than to shield him from it.

Nor is the referring of such experiences to the Church such a simple matter as Jung's words seem to suggest. It is lamentably true that confessors have been known to pronounce dogmatically that this experience is from God and is to be accepted, and that that experience is from the devil and is to be rejected. St. Teresa has related the "deep depression" that such procedure brought into her own life. She tells us movingly how the assurance that certain of her own visions came from the devil taxed her credulity, and how the command to "snap her fingers" at them burdened her conscience, and the injunctions to be rid of them exceeded her abilities and will-power. She tells also of the immense relief brought to her by Father Bañez who pointed out that, "when we see a very fine picture, we always value it even if we know it has been painted by a very wicked man, and we should never allow the identity of the painter to hinder our devotion." She reaches the conclusion that:

> Just so the good or the evil is not in the vision, but in the person who sees it, and depends upon his profiting by it and upon his humility. Where there is humility, no harm can possibly

ensue, even though the vision come from the devil; and where
there is no humility, there can be no profit, even if the vision
come from God.[17]

St. John of the Cross likewise has many pages on the misunderstandings and harm that can come even from those images and
experiences which, *ex hypothesi*, come from God.[18] They should
win the approval of psychologists who are acutely aware of the
dangers of identification or "inflation" which can accompany such
experiences.

Certainly this discernment of spirits implies a criterion of
appraisal provided by doctrine and moral results, and which is
not and cannot be given in the perceptual experience itself. Yet
depth-psychologists themselves have been compelled to seek such
standards, as Jung himself shows, whether in a would-be comprehensive theory, in the manner of Freud, or in generalizations,
such as his own, gathered from a comparative study of archetypal motifs, and "purified from all the oddities, shortcomings and
flaws of individual experience." Yet it could hardly occur to them
to regard them as substitutes for the experiences themselves. And
nor, as we shall see more clearly in the next chapter, do creeds and
dogmas function as such in the Catholic framework. It may readily
be seen that no more or less conceptualized statement *about* immediate concrete experience possesses the psychological efficacy
of the immediate concrete experience of the symbol itself, whether
it be presented from outside or from within. The latter can engage
all the functions of the psyche: it can be seen, heard and perhaps
touched, smelt and tasted, as well as imagined, intuited, felt, re-
acted to emotionally, played, painted, danced. It "does something
to us," "sends us," as the abstract intellectual concept cannot.
More important still, it can and does make us aware of the presence of what is unconscious as well as of what is conscious, of the

unknown and the mysterious as well as of the known and the comprehensible. This gives it a power of transforming and integrating psychic energy which can be possessed by no conceptualized scientific theory or credal statement alone. It must be conceded that any *substitution* of creeds and dogmas for concrete symbols would involve a grave psychological impoverishment, and "alienate consciousness from its natural roots in the unconscious."[19] Indeed, insofar as dogmas are precisely statements *about* events and experiences, they would be rendered meaningless without them.

Although Jung finds creeds and dogmas so informative about psychic processes, it is, in his view, inherent in them that they determine or restrict them, inasmuch as they (for instance) identify "God" or "perfect humanity" (the "Self") with one particular figure, whether it be Christ or the Buddha or Apollo. However estimable and psychologically potent such figures may be, they do not "comply with the indeterminate nature of the archetype," and "it is altogether inconceivable that there could be any definite figure capable of expressing archetypal indefiniteness."[20] From the standpoint of practical psychology this allegedly restrictive character of dogmatic statements about definite figures can be a very serious matter, for it will mean that psychic contents which cannot be contained within, or related to those figures will lack any means of symbolic transformation through them, and so must either remain unconscious with disastrous results, or find other symbols outside—and indeed opposed to—the given figures and the accepted dogmatic framework.[21] It was the very definiteness and exclusiveness of the Christian dogmas of the Trinity and the Incarnation which, in Jung's view, gave rise to alchemy, and gives rise to grave psychic disorders in so-called Christendom today.

These latter estimates must receive more detailed examination in later chapters. But first it is necessary to re-examine the function and inter-relation of concrete symbol and dogma within the traditional framework. Before turning to the particular dogmas of the Trinity and the Incarnation, and seeing how the intellectual formulas enable us to transcend the inherent limitations of the concrete figures, and so precisely to safeguard the integrity and "indefiniteness" of the archetype, we must attend to the nature and function of creeds and dogmas in general.

V.

SYMBOL AND DOGMA IN CHRISTIANITY

It may be readily conceded that dogma, understood as the more or less highly conceptualized credal formula, is no substitute for direct experience.[1] A dogma, though itself a kind of *symbolum*, is a statement *about* experience, an intellectualized form imparted to the raw material of certain experiences. The formula, divorced from the experience which it sets out to describe, is indeed form without matter; and it may easily be misused in the way Jung alleges, as a substitute for, even a protection against, experience. Worse, it may become wholly unrelated to actual experience, degenerate into formalism, and so become a source of psychic conflict and disturbance. It is not to be denied that this sometimes happens; and that Jung's observations, though inaccurate as a description of the fashion in which dogma should function, and normally does function, is sometimes clinically correct. Moreover, it is understandable that to the outside observer, who can see the Christian dogmas but does not share the communal Christian faith and experience, the dogmas should appear to be even opposed to, instead of statements about, experience.

But the correct functioning of a physical organ can be understood only by studying healthy specimens, and not only diseased—still less amputated—ones. And indeed the pathological specimens can hardly be treated successfully except in the light of knowledge gained from those which function correctly. It thus becomes necessary to say something of the regular function of dogma as seen from within the whole Christian organism, and its relation to the believer's experience.

We cannot here undertake a phenomenological description of the distinctive Christian experience.[2] It must however be recalled that dogmatic formulas are clearly formulas *about* direct experiences: they neither drop ready-made from the skies nor emerge ready-made from the unconscious, unrelated to such experiences. These experiences, sensory or imaginative or both, are recorded in the Scriptures, and as such are the raw material of what we call revelation. Rightly appraised *sub specie aeternitatis*, they precisely *are* the Judaeo-Christian revelation.[3] The dogmas about the Trinity and the Incarnation have been called forth by the empirical facts, the direct experiences, both interior and exterior, recorded in the Bible. They are answers given by the Church to the questions raised by the experiences of the activities in the world and in man of the Creator, the Lord God of Israel, in the Old Testament, and by direct acquaintance with Jesus Christ and the power of the Spirit, in the New.

It is true that these original revelational experiences were directly given only to the "prophets and apostles," who were the original witnesses of these events. But they are shared with the whole Church, in every time and place, whose very foundations rest upon these experiences of the prophets and apostles. The communication and re-living of these original experiences belong to the Church's very *raison d'être*. And they are shared, first and foremost, not by the imparting of conceptual information from outside, but by the direct sensory and imaginative processes of the recipients. These experiences are communicated in the hearing of the Word, the reception of the Sacraments, and the whole life of prayer, meditation, ritual and devotion. Thus, for instance, to a practising Catholic, the doctrine of transubstantiation is not an intellectual theory with no relation to his experience: it is a statement about the facts of his familiar experience in attending Mass and receiving Communion. The crucifix is a familiar fact to him before he learns any conceptualized doctrine of the atonement, and when he does learn such a doctrine it is meaningful only in relation to that experienced fact.

But, on the other hand, the experienced fact of the crucifix may mean anything or nothing without the doctrine.[4] The dogmas of Mary's divine maternity or bodily assumption are statements about someone whom he knows in the direct acquaintanceship of an I-Thou relationship which began with his first "Hail Mary." It will never occur to him that the dogmatic statements of Nicea or Chalcedon, or their formulations in his catechism, are any substitute for his direct encounter with Jesus Christ or the workings of the Spirit, any more than it will occur to a scientist that his theories and hypotheses are a substitute for direct experiment. Still less will they protect him from other direct experiences, whether in his waking life or his dream life, although they may give him a valuable framework of reference for such experiences. The dogmas will be of interest to him only insofar as they are divinely guaranteed descriptions of that with which his direct experience has to do. Whether or not they are also descriptions of the basic archetypal structure of the psyche he will seldom know or ask; though he may be prepared to allow the possibility if indeed it be true that the Holy Trinity, Jesus Christ, the Blessed Virgin, Transubstantiation, are also supreme realizations of archetypes. This is a matter into which we must presently inquire, and into the function of the dogma with respect to these archetypes.

But we first have to ask, in general terms, what is the function of such dogmatic statements in the Christian soul or psyche? To Catholics—and indeed to Christians generally—creeds and dogmas are an expression of faith. And only in this context of faith can we hope to understand their function.

Faith is the very beginning and foundation of the Christian life, without which the rest collapses and becomes at best meaningless, at worst a sham. This is vividly expressed in the ancient ritual which precedes baptism. When the seeker for admission into membership of the Church first arrives in pursuit of his quest, the priest awaits him outside the church door, and asks him what he wants. His appointed answer is the single word, "Faith." "What does faith hold out to you?"[5] asks the priest. "Eternal life," comes the reply.

These simple questions and answers are pregnant with meaning. The quest for faith stands quite literally at the beginning, at the threshold to the *temenos*—the sacred enclosure of the Christian community. Faith is *all* that is asked, though the priest presently adds the warning that faith implies deeds—inner and outer:

> If then thou desirest to enter into life, keep the commandments. Thou shalt love the Lord thy God, with thy whole heart, with thy whole soul, and with thy whole mind; and thy neighbour as thyself.

"Now, there abide these three: faith, hope and charity," writes St. Paul, "but the greatest of these is charity."[6] But faith remains the first, in the order of appearance though not in the order of importance, and it is the foundation of the others. "By faith the mind first apprehends what it then hopes and loves."[7]

The conviction that faith brings with it eternal life, that is to say, the divine life of God himself, sums up the accumulated experience of centuries. It carries the mind out of the dimensions of space and time. It is what is meant when, together with hope and charity, it is technically though sometimes obscurely called a "theological virtue." Unlike the purely human, moral virtues, it describes, not just an habitual mental attitude to oneself, to others, or to things, but to God himself. "These virtues are called theological, because they have God for their object inasmuch as by them we are orientated towards God himself, because they are imparted to us only by God, and because such virtues are made known to us only by divine revelation in holy Scripture...the object of the theological virtues is God himself insofar as he transcends the apprehension of our reason."[8] Faith, in particular, is "the conviction of things not seen."[9] Its concern is with ultimate reality (*prima veritas*) and implies acceptance by the mind of the unseen (*non visum*) and the unknown (*non scitum*) beyond phenomena and rational comprehension.[10]

Psychologically regarded, such a faith clearly means a surrender of the claims of ego-consciousness to omnicompetence. At the same time it discourages the swamping of the ego by the unconscious, for it inculcates a definite attitude—an attitude of voluntary and reverent acceptance, and therefore of clear differentiation of the ego from the unknown. A mature faith is thus the very opposite of involuntary, unconscious projection. Although it involves a certain courageous surrender of the ego to a mystery which transcends it, the surrender is willed and intended, and by that very fact establishes a relationship to the mystery which excludes unconscious identification with it. Involving lowly obedience, it is a preservative against psychological inflation (i.e., identification of the ego with the "numinous" contents of the unconscious). To a very limited extent such a surrender is made by the individual also in purely *human* "faith," that is to say, in accepting trustfully from fellow human beings information which the individual has not experienced or known for himself. Such purely human "faith" requires no specific virtue or courage, still less any super-human gift of God. Its presence is a basic demand of social existence, human development and education: for the individual himself it is a quasi-instinctive preservative from schizophrenic solipsism, and from the obsessional's demand for individual certainty.

We may also speak of a certain "faith," not only in information provided by fellow human-beings, but also in nature itself insofar as it provides information to consciousness. Some such "faith" is presupposed to all science. It is not limited to physical and external, but may be extended to psychic and interior, phenomena. This is presupposed by all psychology, and especially by depth-psychology which presupposes that the manifestations of the "unconscious" can, at the very least, supply some information to the individual consciousness which it does not already possess. In psychotherapeutic practice, this is no merely theoretic presupposition. A certain faith-like confidence in the products of the unconscious on the part of the analysant—often notwithstanding powerful resistances from the side of consciousness—is indispensable to successful analysis. Experience shows that it often issues in something more than a mere extension of the ego's field of awareness. For the ego must often abandon its own self-centeredness, its own familiar world and attitudes, in order to enter into this strange and often frightening world of experience, and so itself undergo a transformation in the process. As Jung has often pointed out, it results not merely in additional knowledge, but often in a "reversal of one's being,"[11] a new centre of awareness in which identification with the former sick ego (the "old man") is broken down, and in a certain "rebirth" which issues in a new kind of life.[12]

Such experiences and such "faith" are not of course confined to the consulting room, nor are they anything new in human history. Depth-psychology has merely rediscovered their existence, their function, and techniques to activate them in modern human beings who have become estranged from them in our ego-centred and mainly extroverted civilization. To the extent that some god has been thought to produce and sanction such experiences, and to give or encourage such confidence, we may already speak of a religious faith of some sort. Indeed the findings of comparative religion, of anthropology, and of the extensive researches of the Jungians themselves, point decisively to the opinion that religious beliefs and practices universally have this psychological and social function; and also that they have to do with archetypal figures and processes found in all times and places throughout the world, as well as within the psyche of modern man. This view seems no longer disputable; and it will not in these pages be disputed.

We shall presently see that the sort of "faith" which we find in the Hebrew and Christian Scriptures, the faith which "justifies" us before God, and which is sought and given in baptism, is something more than this confidence in the spontaneous products of the unconscious and in the effectiveness of our response to them. But it is something more, not something less. It will fulfil rather than destroy them; it will presuppose and give a new amplitude to the archetypal experience, even though in so doing it will dethrone it from any claim that may be made for it to primacy.

In this connection we may fittingly recall the very concrete preliminary experiences to which the candidate for baptism is subjected, and note their evidently archetypal character.[13] Directly after the questions and answers at the church door, which we have already noted, the priest "breathes lightly on the face" of the candidate. This action evidently recalls Genesis 2:7: "The Lord God formed man (in Hebrew, the *Adam*) of the slime of the earth (the *Adamali*), and breathed into his face the breath of life; and man became a living soul." It thus indicates the imparting of breath, and therefore of life, *nephesh, psyche*, to dead matter: the same term, diving soul" (*nephesh khayah*), has already been used for the creation of the reptiles, fishes and birds (Genesis 1:20) and of the other animals (1:24). St. Paul will quote this same passage to indicate a new creation, the imparting of a new life by Christ, to that which, though "physically" living is as yet "spiritually" dead.[14] A corresponding idea is evidently operative here. For the priest bids an "unclean" spirit (or life) to leave the candidate and make room for the Spirit of God. We may notice in this breathing a concrete experience and symbol which is not *only* Scriptural, for it is also quite certainly a universal, archetypal symbol.[15] We may also note in passing that the accompanying verbal formula,[16] precisely by defining the meaning of the symbol, gives it in fact an infinite meaning—that of the infinite Spirit of God which the concrete symbol alone cannot indicate. We shall find a similar feature in the Church's verbal formulas, dogmatic and sacramental, generally.

After the breathing, the priest marks the forehead and breast of the candidate with his thumb in the form of an equal-armed cross. This, as Jung has frequently noted, is a widespread symbol of psychic differentiation; of human and conscious as distinct from the undifferentiated psychic life which man shares with the animals and reptiles.[17] Here it is imposed separately, and with the dry thumb on head and heart, the seats respectively of thought and feeling. Later in the ceremony, and after the entry into the church, this marking with the cross will be repeated; but this time with the "oil of catechumens" and on the front and the back of the candidate's body. After the baptism itself, the top of the head only is marked with the cross: this time with the oil set apart for consecration.

The first marking with the cross is followed by a laying-on of hands: a widespread expression for imposing power, whether beneficently (as in "when Paul laid his hands on them, the Holy Ghost came upon them"—Acts 19:6) or malevolently (as in "they laid hands on them and put them in prison"—Acts 4:3).[18] Next, a morsel of salt is placed in the candidate's mouth—the sense of taste is brought into play as well as sight, hearing, touch and (later, with the "odor suavitatis" of the oil) of smell. The priest here calls it the "sal sapientiae"—salt of wisdom.[19] This is followed by the first of several exorcisms, a bidding of the evil one to depart, which in psychological terms means a differentiation of the ego from the shadow, and a dissolving of identification with it,[20] and thus an activation of moral consciousness regarding good and evil. On this follows another marking with the cross (this time on the forehead only), and another laying on of hands.

Only now is the candidate admitted into the church, with the invitation: "Come into the temple of God, that you may share with Christ in eternal life."

These preliminary rites, devised before infant baptism became general, were not originally squeezed into the single baptismal service as now. They were spread over the months and years of initiation and instruction (the "catechumenate") before the rebirth of baptism into the new life of Christianity and Church-membership was normally permitted.[21] It seems that they marked "graduations" within that process, and indeed were an integral part of it. For such initiation means, not merely intellectual indoctrination in dogma, but a transformation of the whole personality such as only the concrete symbol can effect. Analytical psychologists will have no difficulty in recognizing in these preliminary rites familiar symbols of progressive psychic growth: from the undifferentiated, "uroboric" psyche[22] (the breathing), through the differentiation of thought and feeling (the double "crossing"), the strengthening of the ego (the laying-on of hands), the activation of wisdom (the salting), the separation from the shadow (the exorcism), the further differentiation of thinking and the renewal of power required for the combat which this separation of good from evil imposes.

It is only when he at last enters the church that the candidate hears *dogma*. But it is the very first thing he hears. For within, as he enters, the creed is being said or sung. He had said that he had come to the church to seek for faith, and as he enters it the Church's confession of faith is the first thing that falls on his ears.

The fact should induce us to look more closely at the relation between faith and creed or dogma.

We have quoted St. Thomas Aquinas as saying that there is a kind of faith which is made known to us only in the holy Scriptures. We might be tempted to dismiss this as a characteristic piece of theological bigotry. But students of empirical comparative religion have remarked that the "faith" of the Bible and of the Jewish and Christian communities is notably different from anything found elsewhere. Attention has been drawn to this in emphatic terms by Professor Mircea Eliade:

> The classic example of Abraham's sacrifice admirably illustrates the difference between the traditional conception of the repetition of an archetypal gesture and the new dimension, *faith*, acquired through religious experience.... What is called "faith" in the Judaeo-Christian sense differs, regarded structurally, from the archaic religious experiences. The authenticity and religious validity of these latter must not be doubted, because they are based upon a universally verified dialectic of the sacred. But the experience of faith is due to a new theophany, a new revelation, which, for the respective elites, annuls the validity of other hierophanies.... Whereas, for the entire Paleo-Semitic world [the sacrifice of the first-born], despite its religious function, was only a custom, a rite whose meaning was perfectly intelligible, in Abraham's case it is an act of faith. He does not understand why the sacrifice is demanded of him: nevertheless he performs it because it was the Lord who demanded it. By this act, which is apparently absurd, Abraham initiates a new religious experience, faith.... Between God and Abraham yawned an abyss; there was a fundamental break in continuity. Abraham's religious act inaugurates a new religious dimension: God reveals himself as personal, as a "totally

distinct" existence that ordains, bestows, demands, without
any rational (i.e., general and foreseeable) justification, and for
which all is possible.... We have cited this example to illustrate
the novelty of the Jewish religion in comparison with the traditional structures.[23]

But just what is this new dimension which the Bible calls
"faith"? Biblical students will generally agree that:

> To understand the Biblical use of the words [the noun "faith"
> and the verb "to believe"] it is essential to realize that they
> contain no suggestion of an apprehension inferior to reasoned
> knowledge, "believing what we cannot prove." The New Tes-
> tament usage owes little or nothing to Plato. In some instanc-
> es the noun means little more than the Christian religion, and
> the verb loyal adherence to it, but in the vast majority of cas-
> es the meaning goes back to a Hebrew concept which was
> brought to full actuality in the relation with God established
> for Christians in Christ. The core of this Hebrew concept is
> firmness, reliability or steadfastness. To believe is to hold on to
> something firmly, with conviction and confidence. It is implied
> that steadfastness is sought in the object believed, and that,
> in laying hold of that object, the believer himself will become
> steadfast.[24]

This means, in psychological terms, a certain stabilization
through the surrender or "obedience" of the ego to a centre beyond itself, and in that sense unconscious: whether or not we may
identify that centre with what Jung calls the Self.[25] It implies a
courageous sacrifice of egocentricity. Although the ego voluntarily
participates in this, the initiative, the demand for it and the ability
to effect it lie beyond the ego's conscious and available resources.

In the language of the Bible and of theology, faith is a gift of God, a supernatural grace:

> The loyalty to God which is found in a man of faith, and all derivative loyalties, are themselves created by *God's* act. On the basis of man's helplessness and instability, God makes the believer firm and trustworthy.[26]

The certitude and reliability of faith is not found, where some Christian apologists have sought it, in the act of faith itself as a psychological event, the voluntary assent of the ego, but solely in its object—in the God in which the ego is enabled to put its faith.[27] According to the Bible:

> The efficacy of faith for salvation and for right relationship with God is not to be sought in the act itself, but rather in that to which a man holds firm by believing.... It is not true to say that this act of utter reliance on God is a relapse into quietistic fatalism. The true nature of existence "in faith" depends entirely on that which is believed. And in the Old Testament as in the New Testament, that upon which the believer lays hold is the promised acts of God by which he is sustained and indeed recreated.[28]

We should note in passing that for Catholic theology—and, we believe, for the Bible also—faith is not only an act, or a number of disconnected acts—"telegraph posts without the wires."[29] Still less is it a passive "being acted upon" spasmodically from without. Even as an act, although the initiative, the demand for it, and the power to achieve it, come from God, it is a human act requiring human co-operation, and the utmost of human capacities. Catholic theology will not allow that God is glorified by minimizing his human creation, or that the principle of "grace alone" is the better vindicated by annihilating human nature and the human partnership with God which his grace affects. Rather does this disparage the power of grace and dim the glory of God as it shines through his creation.[30] But faith is not only acts, it is also a continuous life, an habitual state of mind. It is truly a gift, a something which is put at man's disposal to possess and to use, but which he can neglect. As such, it admits of degrees; of more and less, of growth and development. While faith demands God-centredness, it seldom at once conquers ego-centredness. We cannot, with Professor Paul Tillich,[31] equate faith with actual "total commitment"; not only because there are "total commitments" which are the very antithesis of faith, but also because there is faith which falls short of "total commitment." There is smoking flax which the Gospel forbids us to quench, for this also is the gift of his Spirit; and there is a genuine prayer, "Lord, I believe, help thou mine unbelief," which no perfectionism should make us despise.

So faith is both act and *habitus*—in the sense of something which we *have*, a gift which is put at our disposal as our possession, and which permits a greater or less though permanent "living by faith"—even when explicit acts of faith are not being made.

But what is it "to which a man holds fast by believing"? The days are happily past when the exegetes or controversialists of the Reformation felt it incumbent to understand faith only and always as simple and immediate trust in God (*fiducia*), and those of the Counter-Reformation only and always as assent to "revealed truths" (credence).[32] It is now generally understood that each implies the other: that *fiducia* in God is empty if God is not revealed in truths which demand our trustful assent, and that the only ground for assenting to the truths is trustful confidence in the God, the First Truth, from whom they come. "There is no faith without a content toward which it is directed. There is always something meant in the act of faith. And there is no way of having the content of faith except in the act of faith."[33] Recent Biblical and Patristic studies of the apostolic *kerygma* ("preaching") have emphasized the inseparability of the New Testament conception of "faith" from "truths" requiring assent: "it is impossible to overlook the emphasis on the transmission of authoritative doctrine which is everywhere found in the New Testament."[34]

This has always been understood in the traditional, integral analysis of faith. Faith means not only that (the act or *habitus*) *whereby* we believe (*fides qua creditor*), but also that which we believe ("*the* faith"—*fides quae creditur*): and each is meaningless without the other. Faith itself, as act or *habitus*, just because it means believing God (*credo Deo*), and a willing "motion towards" God (*credo in Deum*), also means believing truths or affirmations *about* God (*credo Deum...*)—believing *that* God is this or that: eternal, almighty, love, one, three, incarnate, etc.[35] Just *because* faith is a theological virtue, whose concern or "object" is God, the ultimate reality, unknown and unseen, and because God can only be mediated in what can in some measure be known and seen—in what Eliade calls hierophanies or theophanies[36]—the content of faith can only be mediated and expressed in *enuntiabilia*.[37] They are not necessarily explicitly formulated propositions, but are at least capable of propositional statement—they are *enuntiabilia* whether or not they are also actually *enuntiata*. For, humanly speaking (and faith is a human act, however it may be divinely initiated and enabled), truths and untruths can be apprehended and expressed only in affirmations and negations—in propositions.

Dogmas are precisely these affirmations and negations, these propositional statements, explicitly made by the Church as the believing community (the *communio fidelium*), whereby the content of her faith is mediated and expressed. They should never be divorced from the original revelational experience, for they are called forth precisely by that experience and the need to describe, communicate and understand it, truthfully and not erroneously. They state what is revealed, though they are not themselves revelations.[38] A Catholic will believe that, being utterances of and for the whole believing community through its accredited mouthpieces, they are infallible or inerrant descriptions of what is revealed; but they are essentially "articles of faith" and not articles of revelation; not direct "acts of God" in nature, in history, and in the prophet's or apostle's soul, as is revelation itself.[39]

It is true that the original revelational experience itself sometimes consists in explicit propositions.[40] These may be either heard (as in "this is my beloved son") or uttered (as in "thus saith the Lord"). And these particular propositions are peculiar to the Biblical revelation; and they are themselves experienced facts about experienced facts—for what is heard or uttered is *about* the sight of the baptized and transfigured Jesus, or of the woes of captive or defeated Israel. They give a certain meaning to what otherwise is a mere perception, no matter how impressive and even "numinous." Not only do they transmute neutral fact into symbol (that is already achieved by the intuitive perception of the fact as a theophany: as being not only fact for sense-experience but as somehow manifesting the sacred through "perception by way of the unconscious"[41]), they are either true or false, for they declare that the original experience *is* this or is *not* that. No perceptual fact, be it sensory or imaginative, is of itself true or false. The question of truth or error only arises in the judgment, in some affirmation or negation about it. The onlooker by the Jordan, or on the mount of Transfiguration, sees only what he sees. The "voice from heaven" says something about it; and what it says is no less than "this is my beloved Son."[42] Here is a statement which must be either true or false, not *only* a psychological fact, though it is that also. It is understandable that, without faith, it is judged false or even meaningless. But accepted in faith, the revelational fact is already declaring what Nicea and Chalcedon[43] will formulate as dogma: that this son of man, Jesus of Nazareth, is also son of God, of one kind (*homoousia*) with the Eternal Father.

All this becomes obscured in the Jungian's confusion between fact and truth.[44] In a bare factual experience, just as there is no question of truth or falsehood, so there is no question of orthodoxy or heterodoxy. Yet Jung writes of "heretical" dreams,[45] of the "unorthodox" visions of St. Nicholas von der Flue,[46] of the "heretical" or "pagan" images conjured up by the alchemists.[47] One of his most distinguished disciples has interpreted the visions of St. Perpetua on the strange supposition that images are of themselves "pagan" or "Christian."[48] Yet it is difficult to see how a dream, a vision or any other psychic experience, can be "orthodox" or "heterodox," or even "pagan" or "Christian"; though doubtless there may be orthodox, heterodox, pagan or Christian ideas affirmed or denied *about* them. It must even be doubted (and Jung's own works go far to confirm the doubt) whether there is such a thing as a distinctively Christian image. Christianity did not create new images; it was a "rebirth of images" insofar as it brought perennial images into new relationships with one another,[49] and made statements about them which were never made before, which can never be confidently affirmed as "truths" save on the basis of faith.

But, we have to ask, just what sort of "truth" is claimed for the dogmas? Clearly, they are not mathematical, physical, chemical, historical nor, in any ordinary sense of the word, psychological truths. They may, some of them do, make statements about the physical world, about what has happened in time, or about the human soul or psyche. But these statements are not verifiable as true by the physical or historical, or even the psychological sciences: they can be asserted with confidence by faith alone. It is however claimed for them that they are objectively true, and not merely subjectively useful.[50] They make statements, claimed to be true, about God himself and his dealings with mankind. They are, however, in no way substitutes for God, nor do they pierce the mystery and inherent unknowability of God to the human mind:

> For the divine mysteries by their very nature so transcend the created mind, that even when they are delivered by revelation and received by faith, they remain covered by the veil of faith itself and, as it were, wrapped in cloud; for, so long as we are in this mortal life, "we are exiles from the Lord, and walk by faith and not by sight."[51]

The dogmas are pointers to the mysteries, never substitutes, still less the mysteries themselves. God still remains the unknown, unseen God; all that is immediately experienced is facts, but facts perceived to be his effects and manifestations. As Aquinas put it:

> Neither a Catholic nor a pagan knows the nature of God as it is in itself.... By revelation we do not know in this life what God is...but it enables us to know him more fully insofar as it displays to us both more and better effects, and to attribute to God certain things which are beyond the scope of our natural reason, such as that he is three and one.[52]

While the dogmas add new dimensions of meaning to the experienced facts which evoked them, they never comprehend those dimensions.

Since these formulas can never circumscribe what they present, why such care over precision of formulation, such anathemas against other, "heretical," formulations? Since all formulas are infinitely inadequate to express the incomprehensive mystery which is God, and are at best certain analogies, how can one formula be more true or more false than another? What should it matter, and to whom should it matter, whether we say God is Three in One and not Four or Five in One; or that the Son is *homoousios* with the Father and not only *homoousios* or that the presence of Christ's body and blood in the Eucharist is wrought by transubstantiation and not consubstantiation or the faith of the communicant? Why should salvation be attached to one statement and damnation to the other, since all alike are but fumbling attempts to express the inexpressible?

The seeming extravagance and intransigence of these claims made for dogma have, perhaps more than anything else, led to the modern revolt from dogma, to the point that, even on the lips of many earnest and devout Christians, the very word "dogma" has become a bad word. The revolt has long ago reached the point where "orthodoxy," which etymologically means "right-thinking," has come to mean wrong thinking[53] and is a term of opprobrium; and "heresy," which etymologically means choosing only what we can grasp,[54] is a matter for congratulation. Yet, the care which the Church has always exercised in the formulation of dogma, her fulminations against defective or contrary formulations, have rested on the conviction that the integrity of the images or symbols which dominate a man's soul are of the utmost importance to his own well-being, and that it is a matter of the highest importance to him what he thinks and says about them. The dogmas are indeed "objectively true," but the truth of them is, above all else, *veritas salutifera*—healing or saving truth. Though objectively true, they are also in the highest degree subjectively relevant to his health and wholeness; and if they were to distort the full significance of the symbol they will be hurtful and harmful to him. It is not an academic fondness for precision, let alone an idolatry for mere words, that has prompted the Church's dogmatic definitions or her passionate condemnation of heresies, but her concern for the *salus humana*—human health and wholeness.[55] It is in this light that we should understand such pronouncements as those opening words of the Athanasian Creed, which may otherwise seem so monstrous:

> Whosoever wills to be *salvus* (i.e., healed, whole, salved), before all things it is needful that he hold that Catholic faith [i.e., the faith which is for all]; unless he keep it whole and undefiled, without doubt he will perish in eternity.[56]

The meaning is not that the "correct" formula, *homoousia* or transubstantiation, is a sure password through the heavenly gates, and *homooisia* or consubstantiation, an equally arbitrary ticket to eternal damnation. The Catholic or universal faith, so called because it is for all men and the whole man,[57] is healing or whole-making in *this* life. (Only in this life do we live by faith and not by sight: there are no dogmas, because no faith, in heaven!) And what a man believes, and thinks about what he believes, is the first thing needful for his *salus*, for on this all else—his whole pattern of behaviour—will depend.[58] And any inadequacy in his dominant symbols, or any thoughts or statements about them which will narrow their amplitude, will be a source of disintegration and destruction—hence the traditional description of heresies as "poisonous." And this will be "in aeternum"; not on the temporal plane of his commonplace cogitations, but on the timeless and spaceless plane of his relation to God. Or, in psychological terms, in the realm of the timeless archetypes, and the objective, collective and supra-individual unconscious.

It should not, then, be a matter of surprise to the theologian, still less of pained resentment, that dogmas are found to be highly relevant to psychological health and sickness, and their manner of functioning in the psyche a matter of profound concern to the practical psychotherapist.[59] It is rather the psychologists themselves, and notably Jung, who have been astonished to find themselves concerned with such things. We find him, in fact, on purely practical grounds of the unity and integrity of dominant symbols, profoundly concerned with the formulations of the Trinity,[60] vindicating the *homoousia* against the *homooisia*,[61] suggesting that transubstantiation—the conversion of the whole into the whole—alone ensures an adequate symbol of psychic transformation, where other Eucharistic doctrines fail.[62] The fact that we have had to criticize some aspects of his understanding of dogma generally, and will have to criticize his handling of some dogmas in particular, must not allow us to be any less grateful for his having raised and expounded the question of the psychological function and relevance of dogma at all, and penetrated it so boldly and deeply. Although the Church has rightly insisted that dogmas were all a *verbum salutis*—a message of health and wholeness—and heresies a destructive source of disintegration, it has not been her business to explain how and why it should be so. Nor, perhaps, in past ages, has any such explanation been required; neither, in fact, was methodical empirical psychology sufficiently developed to be able to provide such an explanation in its own terms. But now that it is, above all, the *relevance* of revelation and dogma to human needs that is most in question, we may find that analytical psychology supplies a valuable aid to our understanding.

Yet it is clear that this whole claim for faith and dogma as promoters of stability, health and wholeness is open to very serious objection. Although statistics suggest some indication that the incidence of mental and emotional instability and disorder is lower in the Western world among adherents to dogmatic religion than among others,[63] it is certainly by no means uncommon or less serious among them. To this, three things must at once be said. Firstly, that it is not of course claimed that mental health and wholeness depend on archetypal factors or their elaboration in dogma alone. Personal, hereditary and environmental factors are not thereby excluded. Secondly, the objection can hardly be satisfactorily met until we have decided just what it is that we are to understand by psychological stability, health and wholeness. Of this we shall have something to say in a later chapter. Thirdly, just because dogmas point to living in accord with the archetypes, preserve their integrity, and are (as Jung puts it) their "hitherto most perfect" presentation,[64] they so render them all the more demanding. Failure to meet their demands will be a source of disturbance, conflict and of the sense of guilt to a degree usually unknown to those who are ignorant of them. Moreover, possession of faith and dogma, and adherence to the moral principles and standards which they imply, will give rise to problems and conflicts in adaptation in a society conditioned by quite different, and often opposing, values—the values of what the Scriptures call "the world." The *beati possidentes*—the happy possessors of faith of whom Jung writes rather enviously (possibly rather condescendingly)[65]—are in fact subjected to stresses and strains of a kind which others are spared; and, humanly speaking, breakdowns should not be surprising, especially if these are judged by the criteria of that same "world."

But dogma-in-general does not exist. What exist are particular dogmas. And to the most important of these, and their psychological function, we must now turn.

VI.

TRINITY AND QUATERNITY

A wit has said that what Freud did for Sex, Jung has done for the Number Four. Even the most casual acquaintance with his later books shows that nothing has impressed him so much, in his observations of the spontaneous products of the unconscious, as the frequent emergence of quaternary images, and no other psychological phenomenon has been for him a subject of more intensive and extensive investigation and reflection. These images, usually but not always visual, may take quite simple, rudimentary forms, such as a square or a cross, often enclosing, or enclosed by, a circle. They may be little more than geometrical designs, of greater or less structural complexity, or even abstract numbers, and with little or no qualitative content. Sometimes they take the familiar forms of a four-legged table, a public square, a cruciform building: hardly remarkable in themselves, but found to be significant in their relationships to the beholder or to other objects—the beholder's position at the table, the angle from which he views the square and what is taking place within it or outside of it, the conjunction and dissociation of the building in respect of other objects. Sometimes these images are quite static, but sometimes in motion, perhaps expanding and contracting. Sometimes they are flat, two-dimensional surfaces, but sometimes cubes or other solids with quaternary characteristics. Often they are not such simple quaternities, but more complex patterns of multiples of four: an octagon, a wheel with twelve spokes, the foursquare Heavenly Jerusalem in the vision of the Apocalypse, with equal height, length and breadth, but with twelve foundations and twelve gates—and which, we may be baffled to be told, is the "measure of a man which is of an angel."[1] Sometimes in addition to formal quaternary structure, there is qualitative content: there are four different colours variously distributed, or the four constituents which make the quaternity are themselves of different shapes. The fourfold pattern is sometimes made up of representational figures, conspicuously distinct from one another, like the four living creatures with the distinct faces of lion, ox, man and eagle, in another vision recorded in the Apocalypse.[2] In the parallel but more complex vision of Ezechiel, the four living creatures are like one another, but each has the four faces of the same four animals.[3] Sometimes, in contemporary dreams, there is fourfold content without noticeable form or shape: four floors to a building or four *dramatis persona*. It is not uncommon for there to be some peculiar difficulty in reaching the fourth floor from the third—the lift gets stuck or oscillates crazily between them—or there is some confusion about which floor is which. In dreams, especially at a certain stage of analysis, there is sometimes something enigmatic about a fourth person by comparison with a trio; he or she sometimes manages to be remarkably conspicuous by his or her absence. But these quaternities, while they more often consist of familiar or at least possible objects, occasionally assume forms which neither do nor could exist in the realm of outer sense-perception subject to the laws of macrophysics, any more than they could have been formed, as was claimed, by the chemical prescriptions of the old alchemists. It is not unknown for them to combine, not only the three dimensions of space, but also the fourth dimension of time, and even a rhythm of different times.[4]

Quaternary images have been found to be of frequent occurrence in the dreams of modern people, and in their spontaneous paintings, doodles and phantasies. Examples abound in Jung's works and elsewhere. Sometimes, though by no means always, they appear to carry a powerful emotional charge, and to make a great impression on the dreamer, even to the extent of radically changing his whole outlook on life. They appear to be loaded with some deep and scarcely comprehensible significance, to make some sort of revelation. They are "numinous" in the sense of a manifestation from far beyond the range of ordinary human awareness and its expectations, and of being both awesome and fascinating. This atmosphere of mystery sometimes enshrouds the whole, but sometimes more particularly the fourth of a series.

Jung has also drawn attention to the extreme antiquity and universality of these quaternary images, to which countless artefacts and documents from almost every place and time bear witness. Most have no possible utilitarian function, nor do they usually appear to be purely representational. (It is clear that neither a city, a man nor an angel can possibly *look like* a cube of twelve thousand *stadia*.) They are certainly to be found among relics from the Bronze Age, and apparently in the so-called wheels depicted in the Rhodesian rock-drawings which may antedate the invention of the wheel itself.[5] Mandalas, designs which combine circles, squares and crosses and which are sacred objects for meditation in the Far East, have received Jung's special attention on account of their striking resemblances to the paintings and drawings of modern analysants.[6] In the West, quaternary symbols abound in ecclesiastical art and literature, as well as in the designs and prescriptions of the alchemists.[7] It is now hardly questionable that such symbols are to be found, at every level of culture, quite literally from China to Peru and dating back into the mists of prehistory.

Abundant additional evidence has been collected by scholars with no Jungian axe to grind. Dr. Arnold Ehrhardt has presented instructive information about their prevalence in classic antiquity.

The figure of "the foursquare man without blemish" first meets us in Simonides of Cos, but again in Plato, Aristotle, Methodius of Philippi, Julian the Apostate and Damascius.[8] Quite independently of these, the same image appears again in the early Middle Ages with the English disciples of St. Anselm, in pseudo-Anselm's *Similitudines*, and in Eadmer's sermon on Gregory the Great, in which again *vir bonus quadrato lapidi comparatur*—the good man is likened to a squared stone or cube.[9] We find it again in the "Human Fourfold," the "Four Zoas" of our William Blake.[10] In antiquity, not only was the good and mature man, the microcosm, likened to a quaternity, but also his environment, the macrocosm. The quaternity was not only the measure of a man, but also of his dwelling-place, the city, mother earth herself. And it was not just *either* microcosm *or* macrocosm, but both: and also "it is the connecting link between the microcosm, man, and the macrocosm, the world."[11]

It was among the Pythagoreans that the veneration of the *Tekraktys*, the fourfold, was most explicit and prominent. Cornutus, a first-century Pythagorean, said that it symbolizes firmness and reliability.[12] But it is risky to define too definitely what a symbol symbolizes. A symbol is much more than a sign for an already conscious preconception. A living symbol *presents*; it does not just *represent* what we already know. From it, our mind may derive some more or less abstract concepts, but it is prior to them and never exhausted by them. Firmness and reliability are among the notions which we may derive *from* four-legged tables and chairs, and from foursquare things generally, but they leave much more about them unsaid. Similarly, the equal-armed cross embodies and presents much that we may translate into the comparatively abstract terms of a balance of opposites, a polarity of contraries, an equilibrium of opposing weights poised on a central point. The solid cube adds what we can still only call solidity. Both square and cross present to our perceptions a certain completeness and finality. So, of course, does the circle or sphere, to which God, man and cosmos have also been likened.[13] Indeed, there is considerable evidence that the Greek *telos*, which came to have the very abstract meaning of end, completeness or termination among the philosophers, originally meant a circle or some circular object.[14] But the circle, the square and the equal-armed cross (especially when this is, as is usual, enclosed) present it very differently. Although a circumference sets a fixed boundary or bond (and that was another meaning of *telos*[15]) it has itself no beginning or end, and presents no distinction or differentiation whatsoever. It is "natural" in a sense in which the square and the cross are not. It corresponds to man's original state, as a baby, when he is indeed a complete whole, but has not yet begun to think and so to distinguish.[16] It corresponds also to the formless horizon of which man experiences himself as the centre. The square, on the contrary, is the habitation which man makes for himself in the formless: the equal-armed cross, as the four points of the compass, are what man's mind does to the horizon when he has to find his own bearings, his own place, in his natural environment. It is also what he does to his own unthinking completeness so soon as he begins to distinguish this from that. "The cross signifies order as opposed to the disorderly chaos of the formless multitude." And hence "in the domain of psychological processes, it functions as an organizing centre."[17] It presents manmade and artificial division as opposed to the unconscious and purely natural unity of the circle; it is the *complexio oppositorum* on which man must be stretched, and the "old man" must die if he is to be whole and to live.[18] The square is that which man clears out, by his own art and labour, from the boundless forest: "Roman geodesy was the art of dividing the land into squares."[19] The cube or the block is what man hews from the shapeless rock. Emerging from his earlier dwelling within the caves of the rock, man shapes the rock into blocks for his housing of his own making; the forest clearing he makes eventually into cities, which are ideally built as, or around, a square, where the roads meet at right-angles at a cross-road.[20] The derogatory sense which the word "square" has recently acquired for a "beat generation" confirms, rather than contradicts, its archetypal symbolism.

For the ancients, man the microcosm, no less than the macrocosm, is composed of the four elements; and no discoveries of chemistry or physics have radically changed our fourfold common-sense experience of "matter" as solid (earth), liquid (water), gas (air) or flame. So also was the "foursquare" man to be composed by acquiring the "second nature" of four cardinal virtues. Jung, as is well known, has gone further and detects in the psyche a basic structure of four irreducible functions.[21] Of these, the perceptual function of sensation is diametrically opposed to, but also counterbalanced by, the perceptual function which he calls intuition; the judgment by way of thought opposed to, but counterbalanced by, the value-judgments which he calls "feeling." Sensation is prosaic, matter-of-fact perception of objects as they appear to our senses; intuition, on the contrary, is a "hunch" of uncertain origin which "divines" possibilities and analogies which seem ruinous to precise and objective sense-observation. The calculations of exact thought, with their concern for objective analysis, organisation and efficiency, are a way of appraising reality which appears murderous to the value-judgments of "feeling" in terms of the agreeable and the disagreeable, and vice-versa. The mentality which is characteristic of the opposite to our own—the fourth or "inferior" function—appears to us disturbing and terrifying, because destructive of the whole world in which we have been accustomed to live. Yet it may also appear fascinating and irresistible, because it appears to promise fulfilment of our own incompleteness and of our innate longing for wholeness. Hence many conflicts in the individual;

and the seemingly unbreakable bondage of love and hate which both unites and divides many couples of opposite "types." Bodies politic and ecclesiastical can be similarly afflicted.

So it would be wrong to suppose that Jung's concern with quaternities is prompted by some pseudo-mystical eccentricity or by a fondness for collecting curios. If the quaternity is the basic pattern of man's whole being, it is also the ineluctable goal of his becoming: the squaring of the circle, the crucial balancing of opposites, are both his fate and his task as he grows in consciousness. This is why the ancients saw that it imposed "moral demands,"[22] and why modern psychologists find that this symbol of the "self," of conscious and differentiated human wholeness, functions for weal or woe as a sort of categorical imperative, a "goal for realization" which "challenges and leads one to ethical decisions."[23]

It is therefore a matter of the utmost importance in practical psychology and psychotherapy. If the inborn pattern of our balance and wholeness is a quaternity, yet we are wittingly or unwittingly trying to live in accordance with some other model (for instance, a straight line or a triangle), we shall not be whole, and we may well become unbalanced and ill. If one, two or three constituents of our wholeness are exaggerated to the neglect of a fourth, we shall be lop-sided. An individual, a society or a civilization may be able to live in this way for a time; but the fourth is not eliminated because we take no notice of it, or because it is unconscious. There may be periods in the life of the individual, especially in his youth, when it is imperative that he develops one side of his personality, for example his intellect, to the neglect of another. The growth of a civilization makes similar demands; modern technical achievements would, for instance, have been impossible without such one-sided development of human capacities. Such a one-sided, two-sided or three-sided specialization may even, in Jung's view, make for a certain "perfection" (*Vollkommenheit*), and it is

in this sense that he seems to understand the ideal of "Christian
perfection." But it does not make for, and is often destructive of,
the wholeness of the "foursquare man without blemish" (*Voll-
ständigkeit*).[24] Nature must eventually protest against the violence
done to her integrity. The neglected function or functions, just
because they are unconscious, will constantly disturb our accepted outlook and way of life in unpleasant and disturbing ways; and
the more they are ignored, feared and repressed, the more primitive and destructive they will become. But this unconscious and
neurotic complex, however objectionable and disturbing to the
conscious ego, is itself an effort of nature to restore the lost balance.[25] It threatens the peace, security and efficiency both of the
individual and of society until it becomes conscious and integrated.[26] It is when this begins to happen that the archetypal pattern
of the fourfold commonly begins to emerge, and the neglected,
despised or totally unknown "fourth" demands admission. But
this can only happen when the former conscious attitudes, and
their claim to all-sufficiency, are abandoned; and a new centre—
the centre of the quaternity—is discovered and accepted. If the
symbols whereby a man lives are inadequate to express even his
potential wholeness, and even positively exclude the unconscious
fourth, the latter has no means of entering consciousness; it will
be repressed and may prove highly destructive. If man is, by nature, a quadrangle but tries to live indefinitely as a triangle, he will
do violence to himself, as he will to a square rubber sponge which
he tries to force into a triangular box.

Now the central and most venerated Christian symbol is not
a quaternity, but the holy and undivided Trinity. Jung seems to
have sensed at an early age that the doctrine of the Trinity was
somehow of vital interest and importance. He relates how, as
a boy, he received religious instruction from his father, a Swiss
Protestant pastor. It bored him to death. But one day he looked

ahead in the pages of his catechism and came across those which dealt with the Trinity. He waited impatiently till the day when his father would explain them. "But when the longed-for time arrived, my father said, 'We will skip this section. I cannot make anything out of it myself.' With that my last hope was laid in the grave."[27] In his later writings he has given much attention to the psychological function of the symbol and the dogma. In his *Psychology and Alchemy* (1944), he explained the strange doings of the Christian alchemists, with their rich quaternary symbolism, as being, in large measure, an unconscious attempt to compensate for the inadequacies of orthodox Trinitarian symbols and dogmas, and to integrate the fourth which they are alleged to have excluded. In his Terry Lectures at Yale in 1937,[28] he had already related the psychological adventures of a brilliant young agnostic scientist. He had been brought up a Catholic, had abandoned his religion for a hard-headed positivism, and a serious breakdown had ensued. The turning point in his healing came with the progressive emergence, after many struggles and some regressions, of quaternary images. This, with similar experiences, stimulated Jung to further research and reflection on the subject. They bore their fruit in his *Versuch zu einer psychologischen Deutung des Trinitätsdogmas* in 1948.[29]

We can record only a few salient points of this closely packed and penetrating essay. The preface gives a reasonable apology for dealing with so sacred a subject at all:

> The timid defensiveness which some moderns display when it comes to thinking about symbols was certainly not shared by St. Paul or by many of the venerable Church Fathers. This timidity and anxiety about Christian symbols is not a good sign.... If the ancients had not done a bit of thinking we would not possess any dogma about the Trinity at all. The fact that

a dogma is on the one hand believed and on the other hand is an object of thought is proof of its vitality.... To many people it may seem strange that a doctor with a scientific training should interest himself in the Trinity at all. But anyone who has experienced how closely and meaningfully these *représentations collectives* are bound up with the weal and woe of the human soul will readily understand that the central symbol of Christianity must have, above all else, a psychological meaning, for without this it could not have acquired any universal meaning whatever, but would have been relegated long ago to the dusty cabinet of spiritual monstrosities....[30]

In the essay itself we are first reminded that "Triads of gods appear very early, at a primitive level," and subsequently almost universally. In psychological terms this means that "arrangement in triads is an archetype in the history of religion."[31] Jung gives us some examples from Babylonia. Even more interesting is the prefiguration of the Trinity-doctrine which he finds in ancient Egypt. Here God, as Father and Son, are united in Ka-Mutef. "To the extent that Ka-Mutef is a special manifestation of the divine *Ka* [double or spirit], we can actually speak of a triunity of God, king and *ka*, in the sense that God is the father, the king is the son, and *ka* the connecting-link between them."[32] Jung makes much of this, as being already a doctrine of *homoousia*, and he quotes Karl Barth's formulation, "There is indeed a unity of God and man: God himself creates it.... It is no other unity than his own eternal unity as Father and Son. This unity is the Holy Ghost."[33]

In Greece we find, among other things, the mathematical speculations of the philosophers. The Pythagoreans venerated not only the *Tetraktys*, but also paid much attention to the properties of the number three. Zeller thus summarizes their views:

One is the first from which all numbers arise...two is the first even number; three the first that is uneven and perfect, because in it we first find beginning, middle and end.[34]

The "third" also plays a considerable part in Jung's own psychology as the "reconciling function" which is found to emerge from the tension of opposites, the "one" and the "other" expressed in psychological conflict. Thus understood, "Three appears as a suitable synonym for a process of development...and thus forms a parallel to the self-revelation of the Deity as the absolute One unfolded into three."[35] The Pythagorean notions are expanded in Plato's *Timaeus*. This difficult Dialogue opens ominously with the question, "One, two, three—but where is the fourth?"—and we are told that this fourth expected participant is absent because he is unwell! Plato agreed with the Pythagoreans that "two things alone cannot be satisfactorily united without a third" to function as mean (*meson*); but he also saw that:

If it had been required that the body of the universe should be a plane surface with no depth, a single mean would have been enough...but in fact the world was to be solid in form, and solids are always conjoined, not by one mean, but by two.... For these reasons, and from constituents four in number, the body of the universe was brought into being.[36]

In other words, "the union of one pair of opposites only produces a two-dimensional triad.... This, being a plane figure, is not a reality but a thought. Hence two pairs of opposites, making a quaternion, are needed to represent physical reality." In Jung's view, Plato stumbled on the problem of the four, and the inadequacy of the three, but thereupon evaded it, and retired into the triadic world of pure thought—the Ideas—away from concrete reality. It ensured that "Plato would remain a bachelor to the end of his life, as if affirming the masculinity of his triadic God-image"![37]

But whatever Greek philosophical thought may have contributed to later elaborations of the doctrine of the Trinity, Jung is well aware that the doctrine itself could not consist of conscious borrowings either from the philosophers or from other religions. "The sole reason for the doctrine lies in the 'Christian message.' "[38] The impact which Christianity made would be unintelligible were it an artificial syncretism of already existing ideas; rather was it experienced as a totally new, unique and saving revelation.[39] Jung recognizes that, even if we set aside the Johannine comma[40] and the baptismal formula[41] as later additions, the New Testament is already saturated with the doctrine.[42] The doctrine is prompted by the question, "What think you of the Christ, whose son is he?" and the suggestion of a duality in the one God implicit in the acknowledgment that he is the Son of the Living God: this duality is both extended and resolved in a Trinity through the experience of the Spirit in the apostolic Church. Nevertheless the doctrine corresponds to an archetype—even though it "represents the most perfect form of the archetype"[43]—as we know from the universality and antiquity of triads and other ternary symbols. Moreover, "All the controversies, sophistries, quibbles, intrigues and outrages that are such an odious blot on the history of this dogma, owe their existence to the compelling numinosity of the archetype."[44]

Jung's insight into the meaning of the dogma, based on psychological observation rather than theological knowledge, is astonishing. A theologian is amazed to find that he stumbles on many of the most recondite problems of the theology of the dogma without having obtained it from theologians, but from his direct experience of psychic happenings; we may instance his comments on the "a-logical" character of the second procession,[45] and on the impossibility of giving a distinctive name to the Third

Person.[46] Although, of course, he has no theological or denominational axe to grind, he has shrewd observations to make about the various efforts—gnostic, modalist, Arian, liberal—to make the doctrine more acceptable to the prosaic mind.[47]

Here, however, we must confine ourselves to what Jung has to say about the problem of the recalcitrant or missing fourth. This should be read in his own carefully chosen words which are more *nuancés* than a brief summary might suggest. But we can all see for ourselves that a fourth is conspicuously absent from the Three in One. It supplies a symbol for threefold "perfection," but not for the integration of the fourth, the "inferior" function, and therefore not for the total completeness or wholeness of the "self." Moreover, it seems, certain qualitative contents are excluded from the Christian Trinity. Father, Son and Holy Ghost are all masculine—femininity, which we know to be a constitutive of wholeness, is absent. Furthermore, the Three Persons of the Trinity are good—evil is likewise absent. This means that, psychologically speaking, the central Christian symbol lacks any presentation of the "inferior function," of the "anima," or of the "shadow," and can only do so if it be "expanded" into a quaternity. It appears that a ternary symbol, employed as a symbol of the "self" or of human wholeness, can become inadequate, outgrown and even positively harmful. We must presently inquire if the symbols and doctrines of the Trinity do in fact function in this way in the Christian life and in their Christian context.

But we may well ask whether this is a genuine problem at all. Even apart from the doctrine of the Trinity, are we *always* compelled to ask, when confronted with the number three, "Where is the fourth?" Are we to suppose that always and everywhere the number three is to be understood only as four minus one?—that every triangle is only a failed square?—the capital "T" nothing but a decapitated cross? Or could it possibly be that ternary symbols are, so to speak, archetypal images in their own right, which present a content distinct from that of the quaternity? The Pythagoreans, as we have seen, certainly seem to have thought so, and on that account attributed a certain perfection to the number seven, precisely as the sum of four and three.[48] The alchemists too—Jung's prize witnesses to the collective unconscious—appear to have experienced ternary and quaternary images as quite distinct. There is plenty of evidence for this in the records and pictorial illustrations of their *opus* collected by Jung himself in his *Psychology and Alchemy*.[49] The differentiation of the three from the four seems to have been to them of no less importance than the squaring of the circle itself. There was no question for them, as there is for Jung, of expanding the three into the four. One of their prescriptions runs: "Make a round circle, and extract the quadrangle from this, and from the quadrangle the triangle."[50] The famous alchemical axiom of Maria Prophetissa runs: "One becomes two; two becomes three; out of three comes the One as the fourth." Of this eminently trinitarian formula Jung writes that "the quaternity is muffled and alembricated."[51] Could it be that this is not so, and what is described is precisely a *procession* of the other from the one and of the third from them both, as distinct from a completed quaternity and something quite different from it? There is a passage in which Jung himself, commenting on a dream, contrasts its expression of "the Deity through its threefold rhythm, and the soul through its static quaternity."[52] What is presented by a dynamic ternary image, in which the second and the third issue from the first, and are dependent upon it, is quite different from what is presented by a static quaternity of four mutually independent and irreducible constituents. It is therefore difficult to understand why we should ask of such ternary images, as Jung asks of the Trinity, "Where is the fourth *function*?" For, Jung tells us, he differentiates his "functions from one another because they are neither mutually relatable nor mutually reducible."[53] In the dynamic process of the three, on the contrary, and notably in the holy Trinity, the Second and the Third proceed from the First, and, according to traditional Western theology, the distinctiveness of the three consists precisely in their mutual relations, and in nothing else whatever.[54]

Before leaving the purely empirical evidence, there is another well-known fact which needs to be recalled. However widespread and deeply rooted is the quaternity, in association with the completeness of man or the cosmos or the "world-soul," *divine* beings are far more often found in triads or with threefold attributes. Groups of four gods are very rare indeed and, although not wholly unknown, gods are comparatively seldom identified with quaternary images.[55] Thus we have the Hindu Trimurti, and the Vedantic Brahman with its three attributes of *Satchitananda* (Being-Knowledge-Bliss).[56] In Egypt we have Osiris, Isis and Horus, like many other examples elsewhere of the divine Father, Mother and Child. In view of this, it is somewhat surprising that Jung says repeatedly that there is no empirical evidence to distinguish the symbol of the "Self"—the human-cosmic totality—from the symbol of the Deity. This seems to be so only if we disregard the fact that the latter is usually ternary and dynamic, while the former is usually quaternary and static, and if we regard the common factor of occasional "numinosity" as the sole criterion for divinity. We have already suggested that this criterion is inadequate and misleading.[57]

It may be confidently asserted that for most Christians the problem of the missing fourth simply does not arise in connection with the holy Trinity. And we may note that it is precisely the dogma which almost automatically safeguards them from that confusion of the three and the four which Jung finds psychologically deleterious. For them, "The Catholic faith is this, that we *worship* one God in Trinity, and Trinity in Unity."[58] The Three

in One is to be kept at a respectful, adorable distance: it is a transcendental mystery in no wise to be confused with the intrinsic
completeness of the creature. The Three in One, according to the
same Athanasian creed, is uncreated, infinite, eternal, almighty, and
cannot possibly be confused with any human or cosmic completeness, which must at best be created, finite, temporal and of limited
power. If it be urged upon the instructed Christian that, according
to his own belief, his own soul is nevertheless made in the image
of the Trinity, he will readily agree. He will recall that, at least since
St. Augustine's *De Trinitate*, it has been customary by introspec-
tion into our own mental processes to find analogies—and indeed
manifestations—of the uncreated Trinity. But he understands that
"Imago Trinitatis est in homine solum secundum mentem"[59]—the
image of the Trinity is in man only in respect of his *mens*, the purely immaterial processes of the soul. This is so inasmuch as "memoria, intelligentia et voluntas sunt una mens, una essentia, una
vita"—memory, understanding and will are one *mens*, one being,
one life."[60] He has learnt that what makes him to be in the image of
God and *capax Dei* is precisely that which differentiates him from
the rest of creation; not the corporeity, solidity and animality which
he shares with it. It could never occur to him that this imagery of
the Trinity, to the extent that his understanding (*intelligentia*) and
will (*voluntas*) proceed from *memoria*, is the type and model of
his whole personality, or a symbol of the "self"; even though they
are that which should fashion and govern it, a prototype of consciousness. And it leaves no room whatever for a fourth: in *voluntas*
or *amor* the *process* is completed and returns to its source.[61] And
this, we notice, conforms very well with what Jung, following the
Timaeus, says about the threefold as the archetype of thought or
reflective consciousness, though not of psychophysical wholeness.

   Christian doctrine thus ensures that the symbol of the triune
God in no way functions as a substitute for, or an evasion of, the

demands of the quaternity, and that no confusion need arise between them. On the contrary, it ensures that they be kept utterly distinct, although, as we shall presently see, the doctrine of the Incarnation ensures that they be not kept utterly apart. The one is Creator, the other its creature. The emanation of the fourfold by way of creation is wholly distinct from the timeless begetting of the Second and the breathing forth of the Third in identity (*homoousia*) of being with a distinction solely of mutual relation and with no intrinsic qualitative differences.[62]

But the fact that, according to Christian belief, the holy Trinity is transcendent, infinite and adorable, and that its created image is to be found only in the higher mental processes of the psyche, does not mean that it is psychologically irrelevant. Jung sees that the doctrine has, in fact, had an enormous influence in shaping the mentality of Western man, even when he has repudiated it. A Christian will maintain that it is "objectively true," but this does not mean that it should be subjectively ineffectual; for it is part and parcel, indeed the central core, of the revealed word of God for man's *salus*. Psychological health or sickness is determined, not only by the shape or pattern—quaternary or other—in accord with which a man lives, but also by what he believes to be his supreme values, his first beginning and last end—in short, his Lord and God. The Three in One and One in Three differs from all other gods, even triadic gods, in several important particulars. He transcends and includes all created categories and contrarieties, and cannot, as can other divinities, be fitted into any one of them to the exclusion of another. He is the One, yet also the Many inasmuch as he is also the Other and the Third; the Absolute, yet also the Relative inasmuch as the Persons *are* relations identified with the absolute Essence,[63] static Being yet also dynamic Becoming inasmuch as there is eternal begetting and procession; boundless Godhead, yet also distinctive personal God[64]; the All, and yet This and not That (for the Father is *not* the Son, the Son *not* the Father, etc.). Where such a revelation of God prevails, the absolute and the relative, the static and the dynamic, being and becoming, the unlimited and the limited, the particular and the universal, the individual and the social, are all alike holy, and all have their divine prototype. The Unity preserves the psyche from that dissociation which goes with polytheism—however appropriate this may be to certain stages of its development; the Trinity of the Unity preserves it from that otherworldly contempt for the relative, the dynamic, the distinctive and the individuated which is the logical, and often seemingly the psychological, consequence of transcendental monism and a monotheism which admits of no divine differentiation—however appropriate this also may be in certain phases in the growth both of individuals and of societies. Moreover, the insistence of the dogma and of the liturgy that the Three are co-equal and inseparable, and to be "worshipped and con-glorified together,"[65] and not in isolation, should preserve the psyche from many one-sided religious aberrations. Mr. Aldous Huxley writes that union with God, for a Christian,

> is simultaneously union with the Father, the Son and the Holy Ghost—union with the source and Ground of all being, union with the manifestation of the Ground in a human consciousness and union with the spirit which links the Unknowable to the known. Union with any single person of the Trinity, to the exclusion of the other two, is not realization. Thus, union exclusively with the Father is a knowledge, by ecstatic participation, of the Ground in its eternal essence and not, at the same time, in its manifestation in the finite—Union with the Son is the assimilation of the personality to a model of loving selflessness. Union with the Holy Spirit is at once the means to, and the fruit of, the individual's self-transcendence

into loving selflessness. Together they make possible the awareness of what, unconsciously, we enjoy [*sic*: a Catholic theologian would prefer to say *is there*—in virtue of the divine omnipresence] at every moment—union with the Father. In cases where union with the Son is pursued too exclusively— where attention is centred upon the humanity of the historical mediator—religion tends to become an affair, outwardly of "works," and inwardly of imaginings, visions and self-induced emotions.... A too exclusive union with the Spirit is no less unsatisfactory than a too exclusive union with the Father in world-obliterating ecstasy, or with the Son in outward works and inward imaginings and emotions. Where union with the Spirit is sought to the exclusion of other unions, we find the thought-patterns of occultism, the behaviour-patterns of psychics and sensitives.... Foredoomed to failure are all those who aim exclusively at union with the Spirit. If they ignore the call to union with the Son through works, if they forget that the final end of human life is the liberating and transfiguring knowledge of the Father, in whom we have our being, they will never reach their goal. For them there will be no union with the Spirit; there will be a mere merging with spirit, with every Tom, Dick and Harry of a psychic world, most of whose inhabitants are no nearer to enlightenment than we are.[66]

It might be added that union with the Begetter and the Logos, to the exclusion of the Holy Spirit, tends to that "objectification" which, according to Berdyaev, is the disease at the root of our modern mentality, even, and perhaps especially, of our modern religious mentality when the letter so often kills the spirit.[67] The unbridged duality of subject and object, of the observing "I" and the observed "not-I," of the Thinker and the Thought, unresolved by any uniting "third," is at the source of much modern scientific achievement, but also of much of the distress of Western man.

Although the Trinity is not, and in Christian doctrine and worship is never presented as being, an archetypal pattern of human or cosmic wholeness, it *is* presented as the prototype of that distinctly human mental *process* which we call consciousness, and which St. Augustine and St. Thomas called the image of the Trinity which is "solum in mente"—in the reflecting mind alone. And the image, they insist, is not realized in mere "objectification," the production by *memoria* of an intellectual thought or *verbum mentis*, but in a "third" relationship of *amor* or *voluntas* which relates the knower and the known and resolves the subject-object duality.[68] Jung likewise makes a sharp distinction between mere "knowing" or "having ideas" and consciousness.[69] Consciousness, in the full and proper sense, is to be described as "the *relatedness* of psychic contents to the ego...insofar as they are sensed as such by the ego."[70] Consciousness, therefore, in Jung's terminology, is equivalent to "reflective consciousness"[71]; in older language, to the *imago Trinitatis* which is "solum in mente."

But neither does the Trinity exhaust a Christian's beliefs and symbols. The same Athanasian creed continues that it is needful for our eternal *salus* that we "also believe rightly the Incarnation of our Lord Jesus Christ." While it is true that the incorporeal God of Christianity cannot and should not be expressed in a quaternity, which, as Plato saw, is required to express concrete, psychophysical reality, a Christian is also constantly confronted by quaternary symbols, as indeed Jung frequently recognizes. "The great symbol of the Christian faith, the Cross, upon which hangs the suffering figure of the Redeemer, has been emphatically held up before the eyes of Christians for nearly two thousand years."[72] Moreover "the cross and the crucified are practically synonymous in the language of the New Testament"[73]; and "the cross symbolizes God's suffering in the immediate encounter with the world."[74] But the cross is not the only form in which the quaternity presents the incarnate God. Dr. Ehrhardt says:

> The Fathers of the Church adopted the cosmological significance of the cube and of the number four. Hermas in his *Shepherd* compares Christ with a big square stone, lying in a wide plane and large enough to embrace the whole universe.... The Godman Christ is a square stone which is able to reconcile the whole world to himself.[75]

For Christian doctrine this fourfold incarnate Christ is the work of the Three. The act of the Three in One which we call the Incarnation also unites the Four to the Three in One in virtue of the hypostatic union to the second Person.[76] But the two natures in the one Person ensure that the Three and the Four are not confused. The One, the Other and the Third take concrete psychophysical reality into identity of Person with the only Begotten of the One, and thus make his creature to be also his Son, and his Son to be also his creature.[77] The Four is thus indeed brought into the life of the Three, without the Three in any way becoming four, or the four being obliterated by the Three, the creature by the Creator.[78] Jung himself has much to say of Christ as being, from his psychological standpoint, a symbol of the "self"—the psychic totality. In this, in virtue of the union of Divine and human nature, are united the four opposites of the universal and the particular, the eternal and the temporal once-for-all (*Einmaligkeit*).[79]

These considerations of the function of the doctrine of the Trinity in its Christian context do not however solve all the problems concerning it presented by analytical psychology. In the Trinity we are confronted not merely by a formal, abstract ternary symbol of the One, the Other and the Third, but also—and indeed far more obviously—with the personal figures of Father, Son and Holy Ghost. Despite some gnostic attempts to present the Holy Ghost as feminine, and some products of later ecclesiastical art which depict Christ as almost epicene, Father and Son are definitely and exclusively masculine, while the sex of the Third Person is at best indeterminate: certainly a "He" and not a "She." Where, it is asked, is the fourth, in the sense of the Woman?[80] Moreover, Father, Son and Holy Ghost are presented as wholly and exclusively *good*. Where, then, is the fourth, in the sense of Evil?[81] The figure of the Incarnate Lord, masculine and sinless, also lacks these constituents of reality as we know it.[82] Yet psychological experience indicates very strongly indeed that the integration of evil (the "shadow') and of the "feminine principle" (the "anima") are indispensable for human health and wholeness, and that disregard for them, or unconsciousness of them, is at the root of much of the neurosis of our time as well as of the ills of our civilization which threaten the very existence of our race on this planet. The Christian symbols, it is alleged, appear positively to exclude them, and so to provide no means for their integration, but rather to ensure their devastating repression.

To this "conspicuous absence," both of the female and of evil, from the central Christian symbols of God and of Christ, we must next give our attention.

VII.

THE MISSING FEMININE

The figure of Yahweh in the Old Testament is unmistakably masculine. He is the Lord of hosts, the God of battles, the mighty One, the King, the Lawgiver, the Thunderer. He is also a jealous God, who will have none other gods—let alone goddesses—beside him.[1] Unlike most of the gods we meet in the history of religions, he has no divine consort, no lover, no mother, no sister, no *shakti*,[2] no family. The fact is all the more astonishing when we remember that the cult of Yahweh takes place in the heartlands of the cult of the Great Mother. But his whole function in regard to his people is markedly different from that of the deities of the fertility rites of the ancient Near East. His primary, if not his only, concern is at first, not with the perennial renewal of the processes of nature on which the life of the people depends, but with irreversible and unrepeatable events of human history. His business is not repeatedly to recall his people from the temporal, the historical and the profane to the "mythical time" of the sacred and the archetypal, but contrariwise he calls Abraham out of the land of the Chaldees, and Israel out of Egypt, to make irreversible and unrepeatable history itself.[3] This is indicated in the strongest way possible by the transmutations which were effected in the old myths and rituals themselves. Thus, the old New Year rites of Spring, repeated annually for the renewal of nature and of the food-supply, became a commemoration of a deed done once for all, and with incalculable results for posterity down to our own time, when the Lord passed over the tents of the Israelites and smote the Egyptians, and led his people out of captivity to a promised land."[4] "His department," it has been said, "was the larger one of the state and not the affairs of ordinary everyday agricultural and commercial life."[5]

But this could hardly be so satisfactory when the chosen people had settled down in the promised land.

> It was not denied that Yahweh by his mighty hand and stretched out arm had brought the captive tribes out of Egypt...but in Palestine the controlling forces were the gods of the land and their prescribed rites, to be neglected at great peril. It was they who dealt with fertility rather than Yahweh, the desert divine deliverer, the Lord of hosts, mighty in battle, and jealous of his rights and privileges.[6]

Increasingly it became "essential that he should be presented and worshipped in the appropriate manner of a fertility god, rather than that of a desert god"; as Lord of nature as well as of social, political and military affairs—until eventually Hosea "did not hesitate to interpret the doctrine of the covenant in terms of the sacred marriage, in spite of its early associations."[7]

But masculine and celibate he was, and so remained; and quite alone, unaccompanied by any Ishtar, Isis or Astarte. The phenomenon is still more remarkable when we remember the extreme antiquity and universality of the goddess under a thousand different names and guises.

> Whether or not the Mother-goddess was the first deity the will of man devised, her symbolism unquestionably is a predominant feature in the archaeological record of the ancient world, from the Gravettian Venuses and the stylized images of the decorated eaves in the Palaeolithic to the emblems and

inscriptions of the Fertile Crescent, Western Asia, the Indus valley and the Aegean.[8]

The Old Testament itself bears abundant witness to the extent to which the human nature of the chosen people abhorred this vacuum. Archetypes apart, it was hardly surprising. The Ras Shamra texts show that the cult of the Great Mother, under the name of Anat,[9] was firmly established in Canaan at the time of the Hebrew settlement, and amulets and figurines of the goddess have been unearthed in many parts of Palestine.[10] The devotees of Yahweh were in constant conflict with the devotees of the old nature-religion which centred in the goddess and the Baalim, her sons and lovers.

> The conflict between the mono-Yahvists and the rest of the nation who practised the indigenous vegetation religion is a constantly recurrent phenomenon.... The graphic description of the contest on Mount Carmel[11] [...] illustrates the perennial prophetic struggle between the two opposed groups which continued throughout the period of the monarchy.[12]

Even the triumph of Yahweh through his prophet Elijah on Carmel (itself probably a shrine of Baal and the goddess) was short-lived. Very soon Elijah himself complained of the triumph of his adversaries:

> The children of Israel have forsaken thy covenant. They have thrown down thy altars, they have slain thy prophets with the sword, and I only am left: and they seek my life to take it away.[13]

Just before the Exile, Jeremias complained that, in the cities of Juda and the streets of Jerusalem, still "women knead dough to make cakes for the Queen of Heaven."[14] Ezechiel, in exile in Babylon, sees in vision the women in the streets of Jerusalem weeping with Ishtar for the suffering god Tammuz[15]—as later their descendants will weep in the same streets at the passing of the suffering Jesus.[16] Ritual prostitution, the dramatization of the sacred marriage of the god and the goddess for the renewal of fertility, was evidently widely practised among the backsliding children of Yahweh, to the indignation of his prophets, and in defiance of the Deuteronomic law.[17] In some of the Jewish communities of the Dispersion, as we know from discoveries in Egypt, the Queen of Heaven was worshipped, and female consorts with the names of Canaanite goddesses were assigned to Yahweh himself.[18]

It is tempting at this point to allude to Jung's psychological portrayal of the Old Testament figure of God in his extraordinary book, *Answer to Job*.[19] Judged from the standpoints (which it expressly disclaims) of sober exegesis and of objective fair-mindedness, it is an extravagant and fanciful caricature. Nevertheless, the figure of Yahweh in many of the earlier pages of the Old Testament is undoubtedly an enigmatic and disagreeable one—almost a neurotic one if we choose to interpret it psychologically as if it were that of a fellow human being. It often displays the characteristics of an immature "anima-ridden" male; that is to say, of a male who is unconscious of, and therefore largely dominated by, a severely repressed "anima," or feminine side of the male personality. Yahweh appears, at least in many Old Testament passages, as almost uncontrollably irascible, capricious, unreliable, moody and hungry for admiration. Yahweh's unpredictable behaviour did not of course pass unnoticed among Old Testament writers themselves. Apart from Job's own struggles with the Almighty's seeming injustice and cruelty, we recall the bewildered laments of the eighty-ninth psalm[20] which, while bravely singing the mercies of the Lord forever, complains of his heartless and flagrant breaches of his own most solemn promises. We recall also the bafflement of the unfortunate Jonas, forced unwillingly to proclaim God's wrath to Ninive, and then let down because he proves to be, after all, "a gracious and merciful God, patient and of much compassion and easy to forgive evil."[21]

We may agree with Jung that this portrait changes considerably with the emergence, in the later Old Testament, of the mysterious figure of *Sophia*—an embodiment of a distinctively feminine Wisdom. According to the Book of Proverbs, she has, after all, been with the Lord eternally, "set up from eternity from the beginning."[22] "When he established the heavens" she was there, playing and rejoicing with him.[23] According to Ecclesiasticus, she is "the mother of fair love, and fear and knowledge and holy hope."[24] Many of the emblems and symbols which the Sapiential books attribute to her, are undoubtedly associated elsewhere with the pagan Great Mother.[25] Unclear and indefinite as is her relation to the Lord, she is a definitely feminine figure. In the later prophets, the Lord had already manifested himself not only as his people's Father—sometimes stern, sometimes full of loving-kindness—but also even as their Mother: "As one whom the mother caresseth, so will I comfort you."[26]

But still he is pictured as a male God only; and in the New Testament he is still a Father and not a Mother, a Father with an only-begotten Son—not a daughter. However enthusiastically, and perhaps correctly, some writers have pictured the "androgynous" character of the human soul of Christ[27]—meaning thereby the perfect harmony within of typically masculine and typically feminine characteristics—Jesus of Nazareth, circumcised on the eighth day, is undoubtedly a male. Despite some attempts among early Gnostics to picture the Holy Ghost as feminine, their view has never gained general acceptance.[28]

Where then is the fourth, in the sense of the Woman, Maiden or Mother? To most instructed Christians in the West, the question will seem hardly a serious, let alone a vital one. They have learned that God is pure spirit, without parts or passions, bodiless and neither male nor female. He is beyond all the opposites, including the opposite sexes. Although they address God as our Father, they understand the phrase as little more than a term of endearment. Indeed, leading theologians have taught them that this form of address is only an expression of their creatureliness before Almighty God, and is not to be taken literally.[29] Certainly many of the Fathers of the Church maintained more than this; a Christian was truly *filius in Filio*: the Father of Jesus Christ was truly his own Father inasmuch as he had been made Christ's brother, and indeed a member of his body.[30] But in any case, the terms Father and Son will hardly suggest to him male as excluding female; nor will the absence of a female figure from the Trinity strike him as surprising, still less as unnatural and a source of psychological or social disturbance. This fact illustrates, once again, how the conceptualized dogma or doctrine—this time of the incorporeity and transcendence of the Deity—corrects and overcomes the limitations inherent in the purely concrete image.

But although this is so for the sophisticated consciousness of an educated Western Christian, it appears that this absence of a distinctively feminine manifestation of divinity presents a very serious problem to the minds of more primitive peoples and to those of other cultures, to say nothing of the unconscious requirements of Western man himself. Some thirty years ago there was considerable stir on the Continent (it appears to have caused hardly a ripple on our own shores) about the works of Father Joseph Winthuis.[31] He had been a missionary in New Pomerania (now New Britain) in the South Pacific, and later became lecturer in ethnology in the University of Innsbruck. The main theme in his writings was what he called the *Zweigeschlechterwesen* (bisexual character) of the primitive mentality. According to him, the difference of the sexes penetrates and dominates all the thoughts and interests of primitive peoples, and is quite inseparable from all their experiences and apprehensions of the world around and within them. Not only human beings and animals, but all inanimate objects also, are either male or female. Everything, moreover, is sterile, powerless, incomplete—unwhole and unwholesome—unless it is conjoined to its counterpart of the opposite sex. Monosexuality—i.e., being of one sex to the exclusion of the other—is imperfection and impotence, the great evil to be overcome at all costs. This basic conviction that the distinction of male and female divides and penetrates the whole of reality, and that power and completeness can be attained only by their reunion, affects not only the primitive's view of his natural environment, but is the foundation of his social structure, his magic, his religion. The tribe or clan is divided into male and female sections or moieties between which alone, but never within which, marriage is permitted[32]; magic power is to be obtained only through the conjunction of male and female objects. A spouseless God may indeed be capable of sound and fury, and even embody law, order and authority, but he would be essentially incomplete and powerless. If he should also claim to be a Father who begets a Son, he will be talking palpable nonsense. All puberty rites of initiation are directed primarily to overcoming monosexuality: the young man is initiated into the experience of being a woman also, and thus a complete adult human being.[33] Winthuis drew the somewhat startling conclusion that the comparative failure of Christian missionary endeavour after two thousand years was due to nothing so much as failure to appreciate and meet this "bisexual character" of primitive thought; to it he also attributed the individual conflicts and the social disruption which Christian missionaries had too often brought about.

He also suggested that this same "bisexual character" dominated the mentality, not only of relatively primitive peoples such as he himself had worked amongst, but also of those of more advanced cultures, and especially in the Far East. It is possible that the seemingly irrational custom of classifying nouns by gender, common to many languages, has its origin in this.

Winthuis's works caused some indignation; but in spite of a certain fanaticism on his part, it brought general approval from ethnologists, as well as much appreciation from missionaries themselves. Confirmatory evidence—much of it hardly new, but given a new significance in the light of his theory—was produced from almost every part of the world: Europe,[34] Africa,[35] Siberia,[36] Mexico,[37] India.[38] Plato's famous myth in the *Symposium* is familiar to us all. According to this, the original ancestors of mankind were hermaphrodite; but were subsequently split into the two sexes by the god's jealousy and fear of their wholeness and strength:

> Man's original body having been thus cut in two, each half yearned for the half from which it had been severed. When they met they threw their arms round one another and embraced, in the longing to grow together again.... Each of us then is the mere broken tally of a man, the result of bisection which has reduced us to a condition like that of flat fish, and each of us is perpetually in search of his corresponding tally.[39]

There are many other traces of this myth of man's hermaphroditic origin, and subsequent division into two sexes in Greek and Roman antiquity, and it is found also in many parts of the world. According to Talmudic and Cabbalistic—and some modern—exegesis, it is to be found in Genesis itself.[40] It is said to be implied not only in the Priestly-Elohist account of man's creation ("in the image of God he created him, male and female

he created them"—Gen. 1:27), but also in the Yahvist account
(Gen. 2:21–23) where the taking of Eve from Adam's side is understood as a splitting of an original hermaphrodite Adam into a
male and female. This interpretation is confirmed by the Hebrew
of Genesis 5:2: "Male and female he created them, and he blessed
them and named *them Adam* when they were created." For many
peoples, this splitting of an original wholeness into two mutually
desiring, but also mutually resisting, sexes, *is* the primeval disaster
of mankind, the fall from paradise, the "beginning of tragedy."[41]
For them also, a primary object of both exterior ritual and interior
meditation is the restoration of the original male-female wholeness. This is most explicit in Tantrism and Kundalini-yoga, where
the goddess rises from the depths of the adept to unite with her
Lord.[42] But it is hardly less obvious in many other religious and
semi-religious observances, and not least in the erotic language in
which the mystics commonly attempt to relate their experiences.[43]
The view that not only men and animals, but the whole of nature
is divided into male and female is certainly to be found not only
among primitive peoples: it is most explicit in Chinese philosophy
with its division of everything under heaven into the elements of
yin (feminine, dark and passive) and *yang* (masculine, light and
active).[44]

Dr. Alfred Bertholet, in his work on *The Sex of the Deity*, accepted and amplified Winthuis's findings, questioning only whether bisexuality was truly primitive and original, and not rather a
later derivation from worship of undifferentiated, sexless Power.[45]
The data of comparative religion on the subject permit of no simple theorizing, for "deities of the sky and of the earth, of water, of
fire, of thunder, of the sun, of the moon and the rest are all sometimes male, sometimes female; even in the same culture-area the
same deity can change its sex."[46] There are many hermaphroditic
deities; and still more divine male-female pairs. But, in Bertholet's

view, it can be asserted with complete confidence that "already on the primitive level the idea of a monosexual deity is experienced as something unsatisfying, and which needs its counterpart of the opposite sex."[47]

So "the missing feminine" may be a real problem for the missionary, and there is abundant evidence that it can often present a serious psychological problem for the modern Westerner for whom the symbols of his God lack any embodiment of the feminine and therefore of a necessary complement of his wholeness.[48] Where the god is male and father only, and where (as is commonly the case) the male or father is associated with law, order, civilization, *logos* and super-ego, religion—and the pattern of life which it encourages—tends to become a matter of these only, to the neglect of nature, instinct, biological time as opposed to clock-time, feeling, *eros* and what Freud called the "id." Such a religion, so far from "binding together" and integrating, may all too easily become an instrument of repression, and so of individual and social disintegration. It is well known that some peoples have solved the problem by having, in effect, two religions—a "Father religion" and a "Mother religion." The Pueblo Indians of New Mexico have been practising Christians for decades, but still perform the old fertility rites and dances of Mother Earth; and in Haiti and elsewhere Catholicism and Voodoo strangely intermingle.[49] The continuance and survival, in more or less disguised form, of old fertility rites and myths in Europe is notorious.[50] The civilized Western Christian, who must dismiss such compensations as superstitions, has no such outlets; and it is not at all uncommon for the repression to issue in neurosis, whether or not it is consciously experienced as a "religion problem."

It may be urged that, while the feminine principle may well belong to the created quaternity, it is unreasonable to look for it in the transcendent and creative Trinity. Nevertheless, such a conspicuous absence from the supremely Perfect, from Ultimate Reality, from the All, from the psyche's highest value, may well encourage an over-valuation of the masculine and a repression or abuse of the feminine. It should be pointed out that this is by no means a problem only for the male: the fear of femininity may be quite as serious a problem for the woman, especially in her social adaptation to a civilization which is governed by masculine values of activity, organization and efficiency.[51]

But is it altogether true that the feminine is excluded from the holy Trinity? "As verily as God is our Father," proclaimed Julian of Norwich, "so verily God is our Mother; and that showed he in all, and especially in the words where he said 'I it am.'"[52] Mother Julian, though recording her own "shewings" or revelations, is in a tradition that goes back to Clement of Alexandria:

> The food is the Father's milk, on which we little ones are reared. So he, the Beloved, poured out his blood for us, saving humanity; through him we believe in God, and flee to the "care-banishing breast" [quoting *Iliad*, 22, 23] of the Father. He alone, as is fitting, provides us little ones with the milk of love, and they alone are truly happy who suck his breast.[53]

But we are as yet little beyond the realm of metaphor; it is only said, as it was by the Second Isaias, that God acts as a mother towards us. The figure is expressive of God's attitude towards his people, but no more or less so than when they call him their rock, their shield or their refuge. It is not said that there is anything like womanhood or motherhood within the Godhead as there is fatherhood and sonship[54]; and it seems that reputable theologians have not, as yet, explicitly made any such bold assertion. Yet there are mystics who have experienced something of the sort, not of course in some fourth and feminine Person or

Hypostasis, but in the very unity of the Divine Nature or Essence which the First Person gives to the Second and the Third. Ruysbroeck writes of an

> Abyss, so dark and unconditioned that it swallows up every Divine process and activity, and all the attributes of the Persons, within the rich compass of the essential Unity.... Here there is death in fruition, and a melting and a dying into the essential nudity, where all the Divine names and all conditions and all living images...lapse into the Onefold and Ineffable.... To this the Persons, and all that lives in God must give place.... [It is] the dark silence in which all lovers lose themselves... [where] neither Father nor Son nor Holy Ghost is distinct according to the Persons.[55]

This is so, he explains elsewhere, because

> The Divine Nature eternally works according to the Persons, and is eternally at rest according to the simplicity of the Essence...the inactive abyss of fathomless bliss where the Trinity of the Divine Persons possess their rest in the unity of the Essence.[56]

A like experience of the divine Essence, as it were beyond the processions and distinctions of the Persons, is recorded by St. Ignatius of his visions at Manresa. He relates that he saw

> not obscurely, but in a vivid and highly luminous brightness, the Divine Being or Substance...without distinction of Persons.... I saw the Father's Being, but in such a manner that I first saw the Being and afterwards the Father, and my devotion attained to the substance before reaching the Father.... [At

other times] I saw how the Second and Third Persons were in the Father.[57]

This may remind patristic scholars of the notion of the *Logos endiathetos* suggested by the early apologists, Justin, Tatian and Athenagoras, and developed by St. Theophilus of Antioch. This "enclosed Logos lives in the womb of God, like an embryo in the womb of a mother, and like the embryo develops and is eventually born, and so becomes expressed as the *Logos prophorikos*"[58]— the externally expressed Word. This naive picture is, of course, inadmissible to a fully developed theology to the extent that it implies a temporal begetting of the Second Person, a time when the Son was not yet begotten, and the Father was not yet actually a Father, but only, so to speak, a pregnant Mother. Students of medieval theology may be reminded of Gilbert de la Porrée, who was accused by a Council of Rheims of making the Divine Essence something different from the three Persons, and by St. Bernard of thereby making the Trinity into a quaternity.[59] But is it necessary to subscribe to such exotic heresies in order to suggest that it is legitimate to see a prototype of motherhood, even of virgin motherhood, in the undifferentiated Divine essence? Although theologians, anyhow in the West,[60] have not yet given the matter the attention it seems to deserve, there are many eminently orthodox *theologumena* which might offer premisses for such a development. There is the basic datum of Genesis, according to which man as male and female is made in the image of God; from which it seems legitimate to deduce that femininity no less than masculinity has its divine prototype.[61] There is the axiom of philosophical theology, which maintains that all created perfections are somehow precontained in the Divine Being and Wisdom,[62] and therefore, it may be inferred, those of motherhood no less than of fatherhood. There is the teaching of Aquinas according to which, although we cannot, as did Gilbert, separate the divine Essence from the Persons, we may consider and contemplate the former without the latter[63]: this is, of course, the basic assumption of his whole treatise *De Deo Uno*.[64] There is the article of the Athanasian Creed according to which the Son is begotten in eternity, not only by the Father, but *from* the substance of the Father (*ex substantia Patris*) as he is begotten in time of the substance of his Mother (*ex substantia matris*). There is the classical interpretation, in terms of the eternal generation of "my Lord" from "the Lord," of the psalm-verse, "ex utero ante luciferum genui te."[65] There is also the *theologumenon* according to which, although there are only three Persons or distinct opposite relationships of the Godhead, there are indeed four *idiomata* or "properties," that is to say, attributes which can be predicated of one Person only. Besides fatherhood, sonship and the "spiratio passiva" of the Third Person, there is the unbegottenness or unoriginatedness which can be predicated of the Father alone. It is pure negation, the not-being-from-another (*non ex alio*): the First Person is Father only in virtue of his begetting a Son.[66] But he is nevertheless the divine essence or wisdom (*sapientia ingenita*), and it is this same essence or wisdom which he begets in the Son (*sapientia genita*). It may be on this account that St. Bonaventure sees in the unbegottenness (*innascibilitas*) of the First Person, a description of the positive divine fecundity.[67] Such considerations might seem to permit us to see in the essence or wisdom of the First Person, not only the Father, but also the Mother of the Son: that original substance which is begotten and "reproduced" in the Son: the abyss or womb from which he proceeds and with which he is consubstantial, and which "through him" is expressed and concretized in creation.[68]

But here we are, very clearly, in a realm of highly recondite and temerarious theological speculation; and one which even theologians, at least in the West, have as yet hardly approached. It is certainly no part of ordinary Christian teaching or general catechetical instruction. It is of interest only insofar as it may suggest that maternity is not in fact alien and wholly outside Christian belief about the Godhead; and that Christian teaching about God need not be purely monosexual, although—to the extent that it has not been purely spiritual and supra-sexual—it must be admitted that it has in fact usually been so presented, and so generally understood. But we are as yet very far from a concrete feminine image, let alone from a real woman of flesh and blood. Our somewhat high-falutin speculations about the divine essence and wisdom hardly supply the psychological need for a concrete feminine image of divinity; at best they give some grounds for holding that bisexual images are not theologically illegitimate.

But whatever their theological justification and interpretation, archetypal and numinous feminine figures appear very early, and thereafter continuously, in the visions and devotion of Christians, and before very long in their iconography also. Besides the Sophia figure inherited from the Old Testament, we find the pregnant woman clothed with the sun in the Apocalypse (ch. 12), and the woman who plays the dominant role in the visions of Hennas. Soon there is the Gnostic cult of the Divine *Sophia*, and by the fourth century St. Epiphanius is complaining that Christian women are still offering cakes to the Queen of Heaven, now under the name of the Blessed Virgin. After remarking that "the whole female sex is slippery and prone to error, petty and limited," he nevertheless allows that "Mary is to be held in honour," though "only Father, Son and Holy Ghost are to be adored."[69]

To the cult of Mary, Jung attributes an immense psychological importance. The doctrine of her Assumption, in particular, he regards as being, in effect, an admission of the missing feminine into the Divinity, even a step towards an expansion of the Trinity into a quaternity, called forth by the progressive pressure of the Anima-Mother archetype which the monosexuality of historical Christianity had repressed and ignored. Before examining this, we must return to examine the original Biblical revelation.

VIII.

THE FEMININE IMAGE IN CHRISTIANITY

Notwithstanding the masculinity and monosexuality of Yahweh, the answer of the Bible to the question, "Where is the Woman?" is fairly clear. But it is not in the heavens, not among the Elohim, that we must first seek her, but rather here on earth: not in the Creator but in the creature. Indeed the earth itself, creation itself, is presented as being feminine to God. Although *Tehom*, the "Abyss" of the second verse of Genesis, is not so explicitly a female figure as is *Tiamat* in the corresponding Babylonian cosmogony, it is certainly a proper name, and she is subdued by the *Ruach* (spirit or winds) of God, as is *Tiamat* by Marduk, to become the primal matter of all things under heaven.[1] The idea that everything has its origin through the formative and fertilizing action of a male and heavenly god (e.g., Ouranos) on a primeval chaos or formlessness which is thereby made the earth-mother of all things (Gaia) is not, of course, only Semitic, though only in the Bible, it seems, is the Abyss itself God's creature. In Genesis, the earth and waters once separated, both are then fertilized—that is to say, made to be mother—by the Divine *fiat*, and from them spring plants, fishes, animals and men.[2] In the earlier, Yahvist, account, man is fashioned out of the earth itself and given life by Yahweh's breath.[3] And although it is not yet said that mankind itself, male as well as female, is likewise to be feminine to Yahweh, this may be said to be implied (given the ideas of the time) in the docility, obedience and fertility which he demands of them.[4]

From all mankind, God chooses one insignificant and unde-serving people, and with them he enters into a covenant. There are, indeed, many sorts of choice besides those of a bride, and many sorts of covenant besides the marriage-covenant. We can-not interpret God's election of, and covenant with, Israel solely in terms of marriage. But it is in these terms that the Prophets prefer to understand them. The people God has chosen are his wife,[5] the covenant was his marriage to them.[6] Its consummation was in sacrifice,[7] and on this account no sacrifice was required in the wil-derness in the time of their virginity.[8] Worship and sacrifice given to other gods is adultery and harlotry.[9]

But the fact that God's people are God's wife does not pre-vent their being personified as their own mother, Jerusalem from whose breasts they are consoled.[10] Both Jewish and Christian in-terpreters identify the royal bride in the wedding-psalm,[11] and the amorous shepherdess in Canticles, with the People of God. This becomes readily understandable, especially since, in both cases, the Bridegroom is understood to be the Lord's Anointed—the counterpart in Israel to the Divine King, Yahweh's representative.

This tradition, which puts the figure of the Woman firmly on this side of heaven, and identified with God's chosen yet di-vinely exalted people—his *Ecclesia*—continues and develops in Christianity. In the Johannine writings, the Bride of Christ *is* the Church.[12] St. Paul goes further: marriage is not a mere metaphor for the union of the Messiah and his Church; rather is the latter the prototype of "two in one flesh," the very meaning hidden in the *mysterion* of marriage.[13] The sun-clad woman of the Apoca-lypse is at once understood to be Mother Ecclesia. Ecclesia too is the "old woman in shining garments," but later "young and beau-tiful," who in vision reproaches Hermas for his lust for Rhoda, and thereafter becomes his spiritual guide.[14] Mother Church is, for the first thousand years of our era, the predominant feminine figure in

Christian imagery and devotion. The evidence, both textual and iconographical, has been collected by Father Hugo Rahner in his *Mater Ecclesia*.[15] From this we learn that Ecclesia was the new Eve, the "mother of all living," brought forth from the side of Christ as the first Eve was from the side of Adam.[16] Being a new creation, a new paradise, she is a "glorious Church, not having spot nor wrinkle nor any such thing"[17] and is untainted by the Fall and original sin.[18] For St. Ambrose she is "the woman, mother of all living... the city of Jerusalem which shall never be destroyed."[19] She is the ever-fertile mother, for she is continually begetting new children from her womb,[20] the baptismal font; yet she is ever-virgin, for "she is pregnant not by man but by God's Spirit."[21] It is Ecclesia, according to Epiphanius, whom the angel greets with "Hail, full of grace."[22] And it is Ecclesia who, according to Anastasius of Sinai, is "blessed among women" and is mother of Christ as well as of the faithful.[23] For Hildegard of Bingen, even the woman at the foot of the cross, and whom the beloved disciple is to take as his own mother, is also Ecclesia.[24] For the Church is also "the weeping Mother of Sorrows, incessantly in this world bereaved of her children who are lost to her through sin, their own or others."[25] For Cyril of Alexandria, she is the dying Mother, for she is, in her members, ever dying and rising with her Son and Lord.[26] She is our advocate with him, praying for us and in us.[27] Left on earth, she is in exile from her Lord, and "the Spirit and the Bride say 'Come.' "[28] Yet she is also, for Eusebius of Caesarea, the prototype of all earthly things and the purpose of creation[29]; and for John Chrysostom the mighty conqueror of earthly powers.[30] She is already called to be the immortal, universal Queen.[31] It is she, says Ambrose, who is assumed bodily into heaven when we, her members, are "taken up together...to meet Christ, into the air, and so shall we be always with the Lord."[32] This assumption, that of the bride of the Whole Christ, is more glorious, he says, than was his first ascension.[33] Chrysostom goes further, declaring that "heaven is created for Ecclesia, not Ecclesia for heaven."[34]

Just who, or what, was this Ecclesia? The texts hardly permit us to say that she was no more than an artificial, allegorical figure who represented the Church in the way that Britannia represents Britain. Ecclesia is, quite clearly, their name for a living symbol which sometimes appears unbidden in dream and vision, inspires devotion and awe, and is instinct with mystery. On the other hand, she is certainly not a mere object, wholly alien from the subjects who behold and experience her, for she *is* the Church and so are they, and in some way she is their own image and reflection. She is human and of this earth, yet equally clearly she is divinely exalted and manifests something divine. The texts force us to conclude that, even before the rise and growth of a widespread and explicit cult of the Blessed Virgin Mary, a "numinous" feminine figure was never absent from Christianity, and it was no wholly novel phenomenon, but understood to be in direct continuity with Biblical revelation in both Testaments. This fact, which has too often passed unnoticed, makes highly questionable Jung's supposition that, viewed from the psychological angle, the growth of veneration for a feminine figure was a comparatively late and gradual compensation for the alleged inadequacies of the all-masculine Trinity. It is, however, certain that, though Ecclesia was, albeit decreasingly, the dominant feminine figure in the first ten centuries, she has by degrees virtually disappeared under that name as a living symbol from Christian thought, experience and iconography. Should we say that she has been *replaced* by Mary, for it is she who has for long been, for most Christians, *the* Virgin Mother, untainted by original sin, the advocate, the universal Queen assumed into heaven, even the channel of divine grace? This would be misleading, for the early Church knew no such distinction between Ecclesia and Mary. It is hard for us to tell whether some pictures from those times represent Mother Church or Mother Mary; it is probable that the artists did not know themselves, so indissolubly were they linked, and indeed identified. As Rahner says, "Eve, Mary, Church: early theology always saw these three personages as it were through a single transparent image."[35] Not only Ecclesia, but also Mary, was the new Eve and, according to Irenaeus, she is the new earth-mother too:

> The substance of the first-formed man was from the will and the wisdom of God, and from the virgin earth. "For God had not sent rain," the Scripture says, "upon the earth" before man was made, and "there was no man to till the earth." So then the Lord, summing up afresh this Man, took the same dispensation of entry into flesh, being born from a virgin by the will and wisdom of god.... Just as through a disobedient virgin man was stricken down and fell into earth, so through a virgin who was obedient to the Word of God man was reanimated and received life.... It was necessary that Adam should be summed up in Christ that mortality might be swallowed up and overwhelmed by immortality, and Eve summed up in Mary, that a virgin should be a virgin's intercessor, and by a virgin's obedience undo and put away that disobedience of a virgin.[36]

St. Ambrose[37] and St. Paulinus of Nola[38] imply the essential identity of Ecclesia and Mary, and St. Epiphanius is quite explicit:

> The Church is she who was greeted by the angel, "Hail, full of grace." The Church is she who had been foreshadowed in Eve, the mother of all living.... From the Virgin Mary, Life was born in Person, and thus did Mary become the mother of all living. Mary and the Church are meant at one and the

same time when the Scriptures proclaim that "two shall be one flesh." The Lord fashioned his body from Mary, and the Church from his side when his breast was pierced.[39]

We cannot then speak of a progressive substitution of Mary for Ecclesia, and still less of an outburst from the unconscious of a feminine figure unknown to the early Church or the Bible. But it is certain that, after the first five or six centuries of the Church's history, it is Mary rather than Ecclesia that is the name of *the* Virgin, *the* Mother. In default of an exact historical study of the matter, we can only surmise why this came about. With the definition by the Council of Ephesus that Mary was *Theotokos*, Mother of God, came an increasing realization of her vitally important role in the *Heilsgeschichte*.[40] A real woman of flesh and blood, who had actually been so highly favoured by the Lord, and on whose *fiat* the Incarnation and all that followed from it had been made to depend, may well have been felt to be a more concrete and satisfying symbol than the somewhat abstract Ecclesia. The Mother and Beloved of the flesh-and-blood Jesus must be equally flesh and blood, and no mere metaphor. The growing disparity between the empirical Church with its sins and mediocrity on the one side, and the spotless and radiant virgin-mother Ecclesia on the other, became more and more of a problem after the conversion of the Empire, and may well have encouraged the veneration of one who was in fact what the Church was supposed to be. Never, of course, was it quite forgotten that the Church was the Bride of Christ, and the fact is still recorded in the Roman liturgy on such appropriate occasions as the dedication of a church,[41] and elsewhere in such popular and dogmatic hymns as "The Church's One Foundation."[42] But with the decline of liturgical, and the growth of individual, piety, the Bride becomes more often the individual soul, notably the soul of the mystic in her intimate communings with God[43]; and, most especially—one might sometimes suppose, almost exclusively—the dedicated nun.[44] These developments, encouraged by St. Bernard's sermons on Canticles, may have been regrettable to the extent that they distracted attention from the Biblical truth that the whole Church is Christ's Bride, and not only some select souls on to whom the rest could transfer their marital privileges and obligations. But it was still in line with the Bible, inasmuch as it identified the feminine figure with human beings, and with God's chosen.

On the other hand, the Blessed Virgin was never presented as a mere cult-object requiring only veneration but not imitation. The fact that she is the prototype of the whole Church and of her members, a reflection of what they were called to be, was never quite forgotten. Popular preaching, we may suppose, set her forth as an example, *the* example, of the graced soul; and mystical guides point to her as the model and reflection of the untainted, God-centred soul, filled with the Spirit of God, and so pregnant with the divine Word.[45] Yet there is an undeniable human propensity to turn an image into an idol and a substitute for what it should reflect. (To this matter of the ambivalence of images we must return in a later chapter.) If this happens, the figure of the Madonna may indeed become an obstacle to the realization of what she reflects, namely the immediacy of the soul to God and its fruitful openness to his grace. The motives of the Reformers in destroying the cultus were doubtless mixed, but we should probably take seriously their protestations that it had become, at least for themselves, idolatrous. Catholic writers like St. John of the Cross could be no less emphatic that there are times when images, whether interior or exterior, must be renounced in the interests of the reality they represent.[46] But for the Reformers, the cultus seemed not only incompatible with their stress on justification by faith and immediate personal responsibility before God, but their doctrines—at least as they were generally understood—of total, irremediable corruption and extrinsic imputation, and their muting of the doctrines of efficacious baptismal regeneration and of the Church, left little reality for the traditional figure of Mary to reflect either in the individual soul or in the community.

Even so, the fading of the Maiden-Mother image was not immediate, and we owe to Luther himself one of the most touching of love-lyrics to the figure of the Church:

> *She is my love, the noble Maid,*
> *Forget her can I never;*
> *Whatever honour men have paid,*
> *My heart she has forever.*[47]

The subsequent virtual elimination of any feminine figure from religion has, in Jung's view, brought a grievous impoverishment to the Protestant world, and set it serious psychological and social problems, even though the individual Protestant is presented with unique opportunities by reason of the very destruction of supposedly "protective" images and devices.[48] Indeed, the elimination of religious images and, it is implied, of feminine images especially, has helped to bring the whole world to the brink of disaster:

> The Protestant lost the sacred images that expressed important conscious factors, together with the ritual which, from time immemorial, has been a safe way of dealing with the unpredictable forces of the unconscious. A vast amount of energy was thus liberated and instantly went off into the old channels of curiosity and acquisitiveness. In this way Europe became the mother of dragons that devoured the greater part of the earth.[49]

Jung is particularly scathing, and certainly less than just, in his comments on the hostile reaction to the papal definition of the Assumption in Anglican and Protestant circles. But it cannot be said that his own reaction is altogether satisfactory from a Catholic standpoint. He understands the position well when he writes, "Mary was the instrument of God's birth, and so became involved in the trinitarian drama as a human being. The Mother of God can therefore be regarded as a symbol of man's essential participation in the Trinity."[50] He is, of course, aware that "the dogmatizing of the Assumption does not, however, according to the dogmatic view, mean that Mary has attained the status of a goddess."[51] But he seems disappointed that the dogma does not, in fact, make Mary a fourth co-equal Person of the Godhead, even though he appears to have supposed that it "paved the way for...her ultimate recognition as a goddess."[52] On the one hand, in Jung's view, her immaculate conception and the virginal birth of her Son remove her from ordinary humanity; on the other, as a mere creature, her inferiority to her divine Son confirms the old monosexuality which is "carried over from the Old Testament into the New, and despite all the recognition and glorification of the feminine principle this never prevailed against the patriarchal supremacy."[53] However great the glories of Mary, they are all the gift of the masculine Trinity, because, in her own words, "*he* that is mighty hath done great things to me,"[54] and she contributes nothing but her own humility and passive obedience. But "the more the feminine ideal is bent in the direction of the masculine, the more the woman loses her power to compensate the masculine striving for perfection," with disastrous results.[55] For, as Jung has pointed out elsewhere, "as long as a woman is content to be a *femme à homme*, she has no feminine individuality. She is empty and merely glitters—a welcome vessel for masculine projections. Woman as a personality, however, is a very different thing."[56] Such development of personality will be inhibited so long as she remains a merely passive reflection of male requirements and male dreams. Wholeness can come only from a balance of equal personalities, in which neither male nor female predominate at the expense of the other, whether it be achieved interiorly in the individual psyche or symbiotically in marriage. A heroine who is essentially inferior to the hero, and whose only glory lies in her passive acceptance of the glory conferred on her by his gracious condescension sets a premium on immaturity, and in effect ensures that her female devotees will contribute nothing of that "feminine principle" either to their menfolk or to society.

Movements for "feminism" and "sex-equality," though praiseworthy reactions to grave injustice and repression, only make matters worse to the extent that in practice they commonly mean further assimilation of the woman to the male, her equal competitiveness in man-made society, and the further repression of Eros.[57] The virtual elimination of Eros as an effective social and psychological force has, in Jung's view, done more than anything to bring mankind to the brink of final catastrophe. For "where love rules, there is no will to power; and where power predominates, there love is lacking. The one is the shadow of the other.... Life is born only of the spark of [these] opposites."[58] Where one is lacking, there is only decay.

But even though it may happen that the inequality between God and Mary may in some cases be misinterpreted to encourage such a catastrophe, it is clear that her image is not presented by the Church as an embodiment of the ideal attitude of woman towards man, but of man—both male and female—towards God. Moreover, there is no inequality in kind between mother and Son as touching his manhood. Here once again we see how the conceptualized doctrine corrects the false impressions which might be gathered from the concrete image alone. For it is no mere concession to outmoded tradition or to the "patriarchal principle" that the Church refuses to allow that Mary is by nature divine, or that the adoration of *latreia*—the total submission and surrender symbolized in sacrifice—should be paid to her. For all her glory consists in the fact that she is a fellow-creature of our own flesh and blood whose lowliness has been raised, and whose emptiness has been filled, by the grace and glory of God.[59] To make her God (were that in our power!) would be positively to destroy even her symbolic function.

Yet perhaps there is more to be said which Western theology has as yet insufficiently recognized. It is even questionable whether Western theory has quite kept pace with Western practice in this matter of sacred images. Theory in the West has been largely governed, anyhow since Aquinas, by Aristotle's distinction between a representation and what it represents, and the different mental attitude which each arouses.[60] On this showing, according to Aquinas, no honour or worship whatsoever is to be paid to an image or representation for its own sake, for honour is what is due only to excellence, and an image, insofar as it is a mere thing, is inferior to the human person who pays the honour.[61] Honour or reverence is to be paid only to what the image represents. Hence the adoration (*latreia*) due to God alone may be paid before an image of Christ—not to the image as an object, to which no reverence at all is due, but on account of the Godhead of the human figure which it images.[62] But no such honour is to be paid to the Mother of God, for she is a human person, honourable in her own right, and no mere image. Only *douleia*, the reverence due to a fellow-creature, is to be paid to her, though "more eminently than to other creatures because she is the Mother of God."[63]

The reasoning is eminently sound and hardly disputable. For even the most ignorant devotee of Mary, her excellence consists—as we have seen—in the fact that she is a fellow-creature, glorified by God, but emphatically not God. Yet the theory may seem to call for supplementation if it is to cover the psychological facts of what is actually experienced by the entranced crowds at Marian shrines at Lourdes, Fatima, Chartres, Einsiedeln. They are certainly not supposing that the Mother of God is God, and their fellow-feeling with a fellow-creature who embodies mercy but *not* omnipotence is an important feature of their devotion. But their bearing hardly permits us to suppose that they are carefully distinguishing *latreia* from *douleia*. Gan they be finding in her image less than a true theophany, a manifestation of something truly divine, and which they do not find in other images? To claim less, in the name of a theory or as a riposte to the charge of idolatry, is to tax credulity very far. Hardly less disingenuous are protestations that the frequent applications in the liturgies of Scriptural passages about the Divine *Sophia* (and, more recently, even about the Throne of Grace) to the Blessed Virgin are mere accommodations—i.e., the use of appropriate verses to mean what originally they do not mean. The principle of *lex orandi, lex credendi* calls for a more comprehensive theory to cover the psychological, and even the liturgical, facts.

It has often been pointed out that the Thomist theory, however sound in itself, is difficult to square with the definitions of the second Council of Nicea, of whose terms Aquinas was evidently unaware.[64] The Council recognized, of course, the basic principle that "reverence paid to an image passes to its prototype,"[65] but it knows no clear-cut distinction between the image and the imaged. Images of the Saviour and his Mother, of angels, saints and "worthy men," the cross, and even books of the Gospels and liturgical vestments and vessels, are all put on the same footing, and to all of them reverence (*timētiken proskunēsin*) is due; to none of them *latreia*.[66] Eastern theory on the subject of ikons has been governed less by the Aristotelian distinction of image from imaged, than by the Platonic idea of participation. According to this, all phenomena are a reflection of the transcendent realm of ideas; a realm which, from Philo onwards, Jewish and Christian thinkers (not excluding Aquinas himself) identified with the Divine Wisdom, itself identified with the Divine Essence. The images or ikons were thus so many reflections and refractions of the undivided Divine Light, mirrors reflecting the Divine Wisdom of the Creator and Saviour. No one of them could ever adequately reflect its Divine source; others were always required to reflect some other ray or facet. Each *presented* the Divine Wisdom reflected in visible creation, and the possibilities, with God's grace, of the human soul, whether it *represented* the human features of the God-Man, or St. Nicholas, St. Michael or the *Theotokos*.

The basic theory of participation and reflection was taken over by St. Augustine and Western theologians generally, and notably by Aquinas himself, who incorporated it into an Aristotelian structure, and established it on an Aristotelian foundation.[67] But its application to sacred images, exterior or interior, has been little developed in the West. Some such development seems to be required to supply a theory adequate to meet the facts and problems which we have discussed: the bisexuality of the primitive and unconscious mind with all its immense implications for evangelization both at home and abroad, the psychological facts of the presence of the feminine archetype and its deleterious effects when repressed or ignored; the hardly less harmful results when the heroine is presented as inferior to, and wholly dependent on, the male; to say nothing of the psychological and liturgical facts. It might also go some way to bridging what is perhaps emotionally and devotionally, if not intellectually, the most obstinate of all the obstacles to Christian unity. For, although the Council of Trent regarded the invocation of the Mother of God, as of other saints, as optional, though commendable, for Catholics,[68] a piety which has no vitally important place for her has become almost unthinkable for them, as well as for Eastern Christians. On the other hand, the assignment to her of any such place has become equally unthinkable for most Christians brought up in denominations which originate in the Reformation, who recoil from anything which may appear to interfere with their immediate and confident approach to the Almighty and most merciful Father. A keener realization on both sides of the psychological function of the figure of the Madonna as a created symbol both of the wisdom and hidden things of God, and of his saving activity in the community and in the soul, might do much to bridge the gap, and provide a safeguard against substitutional objectification[69] on the one side, and an important image for integration on the other.

Although we cannot follow them in every particular, the Russian Sophiologists have opened up a line of theological thinking which deserves more consideration in the West. Father Bulgakov insists, in the strongest possible terms, on Mary's everlasting creatureliness and humanity. By her Assumption she is indeed "deified" with that *theosis* which awaits all the elect, but there is "no penetration into the Holy Trinity" (he recalls the troparion in the Greek liturgy according to which, "at her falling asleep, she did not forsake the world").[70] To her, as a fellow-creature, no divine honours may be paid. Yet she is not *only* a fellow-creature, but also a unique created revelation of the uncreated Wisdom. This Wisdom is the Divine Being itself, which is unbegotten in the Father, begotten in the Son, "breathed" in the Holy Spirit; and, though changeless Being in the Godhead, is yet refracted in ever-changing forms, in the Becoming of creation.

> In the resurrection and assumption of our Lady, the creation of
> the world may be said to be completed, and its end achieved,
> and "Wisdom is justified of her children..." In her, creation is

utterly and completely divinized, conceives, bears and fosters
God.... In relation to the Father she is named Daughter; in relation to the Word, Mother and Bride; while in relation to the
Holy Ghost she is the Spirit-bearer, the glory of the world...a
manifestation, not an incarnation, of the Holy Ghost.... She
has arrived at that fulness of Godlike grace which for the rest
of creation remains to be revealed.[71]

For all her creatureliness, and indeed because of it, Mary is
thus a unique revelation of God. What the Sophiologists call the
Divine Humanity—humanity as it pre-exists in the Divine Wisdom—is not completely presented in the purely masculine figure
of her Son alone:

God-manhood is to be found "on earth as it is in heaven"—in
the double, not the single form: not only that of the God-man,
Christ, but that of his mother too. Jesus-Mary—there is the
fulness of the God-manhood.[72]

We are, of course, entitled to dismiss all this as somewhat exotic speculation. It should certainly not be accepted without examination and criticism. But it does seem to offer a theological
framework into which the psychological facts and needs to which
Jung and others have drawn attention will fit.

IX.

THE INTEGRATION OF EVIL

The question, "Where is Evil?" is not, of course, the same as the question, "Where is the Feminine?" Yet in actual psychological practice, especially with male patients, the two questions are often inseparable. The "desire and pursuit of the whole" are arduous; Thanatos guards the way to Eros. The "other half" of our wholeness is not to be attained easily; there are hostile, evil forces to be confronted before the heart's desire, the missing feminine, can be attained, and they can live together happily ever after. According to Aquinas, our loves and desires will not issue in the joy of satisfaction until we have faced and overcome *ardua*, obstacles and difficulties which will arouse our "irascible emotions" of hope and desperation, terror and daring and anger: emotions which will need to be heightened and directed by the cardinal virtue of courage (*fortitudo*), and perhaps require the Holy Spirit's gift of inspired, heroic fortitude in danger also.[1] Faint heart never won fair lady; there are dragons to be slain, fearsome witches to be outwitted and doughty deeds to be done, before the hero can marry the princess or awaken the sleeping beauty. The benign and wise Pallas Athene is shielded by the frightful Gorgon, with snakes in her hair and brutal teeth, who turns men's hearts to stone. In our own *Heilsgeschichte*, before we meet the gentle Mother of mercy, we must meet such merciless heroines as Deborah, Jael, Esther, Judith, upon whose feminine wiles for the deliverance of their people the continuation of the *Heilsgeschichte* itself was made to depend. The Saviour's own genealogy depends, not only and finally on the pure Virgin Mother, but also, according to St. Matthew,[2] on four very different specimens of womanhood: on Thamar who, disguised as a prostitute, seduced her father-in-law; on Rahab the harlot; on Ruth the Gentile widow who captivated her husband's kinsman Booz; on Bethsabee (Bath-Sheba) whose naked beauty infatuated David and occasioned his treacherous murder of her husband.

In Jungian terminology, the "shadow" bars the way to the realization of the "self," the wholeness of the personality promised by union with the "soul-image," the "other side" which, for the male, is the feminine "anima."[3] The conflict of good and evil, of light and darkness, must be undergone as an indispensable preliminary to the *mysterium coniunctionis*—wholeness and fulfilment. The "shadow" moreover "contaminates" the "anima" herself. The figure of the Mother is not always and at once all sweetness and light. Her very attractions are a perpetual menace. She has a "dual role,"[4] a double aspect; for not only does she give us life and nourish and protect it, she is also the destroyer, the terrible mother who threatens our independence, our growth, our individuality, our very consciousness. Elemental instinctive motherhood is possessive, savage and unscrupulous in keeping and protecting its young, murderous to their growth as distinct individuals, to their adjustments to society and to adult life if they fail satisfactorily to sever the emotional umbilical cord—or apron string—that binds them to her. Elemental, instinctive childishness is only too ready to be possessed, dependent, protected, crushed. The persistent mother-imago entices us back to the effortless nourishing at the breast, the dark, irresponsible unconsciousness of our embryonic state in the womb, before birth gave us solitary, independent existence, and growing consciousness made us aware of it and of our personal burdens and responsibilities. So "the battle

for deliverance from the mother" is a first stage in the attainment
of individuality:

> This struggle is variously represented as the entry into the
> cave, the descent to the underworld, as being swallowed—i.e.,
> incest with the mother. This is shown most clearly in the hero
> myths which take the form of sun myths; here the swallowing
> of the hero by the dragon—night, sea, underworld—corre-
> sponds to the sun's nocturnal journey, from which it emerges
> victoriously after having conquered the darkness.... Mother,
> womb, the pit, and hell are all identical. The womb of the
> female is the place of origin from whence one came, and so
> every female is, as a womb, the primordial womb of the Great
> Mother of all origination, the womb of the unconscious. She
> threatens the ego with the danger or self-noughting, of self-
> loss—in other words with death and castration.[5]

The phenomenon which Freud called the Oedipus complex,
and which he detected at the root of countless neuroses, marital
miseries and failures of growth and adaptation, is a powerful factor
in psychological development generally, even in "normal" individuals. But Jungians will usually understand it differently. It is not
merely a secret and repressed incestuous longing for the physical
mother, thwarted by the rival father and forbidden by the social
demands of the super-ego. The physical mother may be no more
than a bearer of an archetypal symbol which presents rest, unconsciousness, dependence, effortless security, and which, precisely by
so doing, threatens annihilation of the ego, spiritual impotence
and emasculation: a reversion from specifically human to purely instinctive, and even vegetative, forms of life. To the tenuous
ego-consciousness and will-power of the primitive it presents a
perpetual menace of "loss of soul," which many of his rituals are

designed to circumvent.[6] Puberty initiations, as we have seen, may well have as their goal the attainment of full humanity, male *and* female, but this is brought about only by tearing the boy away from home and mother and women generally, and subjecting him to physical and mental tortures which will elicit all his potentialities of courage and endurance to "make a man of him." (We probably have a survival of this in the ceremonial slap on the face which the Bishop, in the Latin rite, gives to the candidate when he administers Confirmation.) Unless the bond to the mother, which is often almost wholly unconscious, is severed, not only will growth and social adaptation be stunted, but sexual and marital relations are likely to be disastrous; the mother-imago will be projected on to the wife, or identification with it may issue in homosexuality. "A man shall *leave* father and mother, and cleave to his wife."[7] Few psychotherapists are unacquainted with the domestic tragedies which come about when the first part of this divine ordinance has, emotionally, never been successfully achieved.

The difficulty of the task, enhanced for us today by the fact that modern society provides few means for its accomplishment, lies in the fact that mere hostility or indifference to the mother-figure—to the unconscious—is as impossible as it is unsuccessful: the ego which is only severed from its roots will be as neurotic in its way as the ego which has never grown up from them. Growth demands a new, more adult and conscious, relationship to the "anima," which can only come about through the death of the old and purely instinctive one. The twelve-year-old Jesus also must separate himself from his mother if he is to accomplish his adult, messianic mission—"How is it that you sought me? Did you not know that I must be about my Father's business?"[8] It was not the final severance which came with death—"Son, behold thy mother."[9] It was a temporary separation from which a new, more responsible relationship could come, when he "came to Nazareth and was subject to them" and so "advanced in wisdom and grace with God and men."[10] But already it was a "little death," the death of the infantile mother-son identification, a death which was necessary if both were to rise to a new life of adult responsibility.

The "struggle for deliverance from the mother" is not, of course, the only struggle which confronts the psyche, nor are the terrible mother and her cohorts the only evil within it. The "shadow," the "dark" or "bad" side of the psyche contains all that the ego deems unacceptable, and the more the ego is set upon what it accounts to be "good" and "light," the worse and the darker the "shadow" will be. It will comprise not only what is disagreeable, but often what is terrifying, detestable, very probably immoral.

> Everyone carries a shadow, and the less it is embodied in the individual conscious life, the blacker and denser it is.... If it is repressed and isolated from consciousness, it never gets corrected, and is liable to burst forth suddenly in a moment of unawareness. At all events, it forms an unconscious snag, blocking the most well-meaning attempts....[11]

> The individuation process is invariably started off by the patient's becoming conscious of his shadow, a personality component usually with a negative sign. This "inferior" personality is made up of everything that will not fit in with, and adapt to, the laws and regulations of conscious life. It is compounded of "disobedience" and is therefore rejected not on moral grounds only, but also for reasons of expediency.... It lurks behind every neurotic dissociation and can only be annexed to consciousness if the corresponding unconscious contents are made conscious at the same time. But this integration cannot take place unless one can admit the tendencies bound up with

the shadow and allow them some measure of realization—
tempered, of course, with the necessary criticism.[12]

This shadow was for St. Paul "the law in my members, fight-
ing against the law of my mind"—the "sin that dwelleth in me" so
that "the good which I will, I do not; but the evil which I will not,
that I do."[13] But for others it may be the tyrannical disordered
"mind" itself whose ruthless, cold efficiency or meticulousness is
the enemy of conscious feeling values and the good life—the super-ego rather than the id.[14] The mystics, in their introverted effort to withdraw from all external distractions and find peace and
union with God, were at once confronted with it. This is their
"purgative" way, without which "illumination," let alone "union"
is unattainable. Walter Hilton instructs us:

> Thou shalt cease for a while of all bodily works, from outward
> business as well as thou mayest.... And set thine intent and
> thy purpose as thou wouldest nought seek, nor feel, nor find,
> but only Jhesu.... And if thou do thus thou shalt find some-
> what; but not Jhesu whom thou seekest. What then? Soothly
> right nought but a murk image and a painful of thy own soul,
> which hath neither light of knowing nor feeling of love nor
> liking. This image, if thou behold it wittingly, is all belapped
> with black stinking clothes of sin, as pride, envy, ire, accidie,
> covetise, gluttony and lechery. This is not the image of Jhesu,
> but is an image of sin; as St. Paul calleth it, a body of sin and a
> body of death. This image and this black shadow thou bearest
> about with thee wherever thou goest.... Nevertheless, in this
> dark conscience it behoveth thee to swink and sweat.... And
> then, when thou findest right nought but sorrow and pain and
> blindness, if thou wilt find Jhesu, the pain of this dark con-
> science it behoveth thee to suffer, and abide awhile therein....

> Thou art busy upon the might to stop the rivers without, but
> perhaps the spring within thou leavest whole.[15]

Psychology abundantly confirms that if we are unconscious of this fount of evils within us and leave it unattended, we shall either project it onto "rivers without," which we shall vainly try to stop, or it will submerge our own egos. The difference, according to Hilton, between the man who lives the life of grace and the man who does not is not that the first has no shadow, but he is aware of it and so "he beareth it." But the latter "beareth not this image of sin, but is borne by it, as a man so sick and weak that he might not bear himself."[16]

Jung's more recent writings have been much concerned with the appalling shadow-problem of modern Western man.[17] The gods and heroes of pagan antiquity were morally, and even aesthetically, ambiguous characters in whom goodness and badness, according to our standards, were fairly evenly mixed, and certainly not very clearly distinguished. Yahweh, in the Old Testament, was indeed the God of Righteousness, and to be attained only by our righteousness, but Jung considers that his own conduct was often not too unlike our own, even at our worst.[18] The concentration on sheer unmitigated goodness in Christianity has brought with it an enormous advance in man's moral consciousness, but it has at the same time immeasurably deepened man's shadow and increased his load of guilt.[19] Father, Son and Holy Ghost are all good. "God is light, and in him there is no darkness at all."[20] Where is the fourth, in the sense of darkness and evil? Mary is the pure and stainless Virgin, free from every trace of contamination by the shadow, of the terrible aspect of the mother, of the destructive wiles of the anima. Jesus Christ is all good and innocent: "he did no sin, neither was guile found in his mouth."[21] What came from his mouth were the humanly impossible, other-worldly ideals of the Sermon on the Mount, compared with which the ten commandments and the ritual precepts of the Mosaic Law were child's play. Not only does our own shadow-side, our "evil inclination" or evil imagination as Genesis had called it, find no presentation in the figure of the all-good Christ, it seems to be positively cast out and excluded—"Get thee behind me, Satan: thou art an offence unto me."[22] Repression and unconsciousness of the shadow seem to be positively encouraged. "Fornication and all uncleanness or covetousness, let it not be so much as named among you, as becometh saints."[23]

It is idle, Jung contends, to suppose that our psyche can be rid of the Christ-symbol by an intellectual disavowal of Christianity. Christ is, whether we like it or not, the *Kulturheros* of our Western civilization. "He is in us, and we in him," even in our rejection of him, his ideals and his demands.[24] Whatever may be the case for other races and peoples, for the Western white man Christ is ineluctably the embodiment of the Self, the pattern of perfect divine humanity: the one which has fashioned our Christian era, and also shaped the forms of our post-Christian and even anti-Christian revolts. Yet, as such, this Christ-figure sets Western man, and through Western man the whole world, a terrible problem, and precisely because this figure lacks that ingredient of our own personalities which we call the shadow or evil. The white man's unconsciousness of, and consequent failure to recognize and integrate, his own shadow has now brought the whole world to the brink of final destruction. Blandly convinced of his own rectitude, of the goodness and superiority of his religion, his morals, his social institutions and economic systems, of the magnificence of his conquest of nature and the achievements of his brain—and, at the same time, blissfully unaware of the evil within him and the destructiveness of his wares—he has, in his very good-doing, committed unprecedented crimes on an unprecedented scale. Western man has infected the world with his greed, his acquisitiveness and restlessness, uprooted whole cultures, proletarianized their peoples, spread physical and psychological disease and the evils of his own egotism, arrogance, nationalism, class-war and materialism. He has thereby ensured the lasting hatred of those whom he has exploited and "civilized" and whose gods and values he has destroyed; and thereby added immeasurably to his own burden of guilt. His technical achievements have now given him an almost almighty power of destruction in the possibilities of nuclear and chemical warfare, and these products of his ego are at the disposal of a shadow which his ego neither acknowledges nor seems able to master. In the "easy speeches which comfort cruel men"[25] he talks of them as mere "deterrents," seemingly unaware that the very word implies a psychological instrument for inducing terror, than which no emotion is more likely to explode into desperation and irrational, suicidal action. Already his terror progressively poisons not only the psychological, but even the physical atmosphere he must breathe, with consequences that cannot be foreseen. Having rendered this globe increasingly unendurable, even to himself, his "modern myth" is flight from it by space-travel; or, alternatively, a visitation in space-ships from other planets which will either deliver or annihilate him.[26]

All this, Jung thinks, is the inescapable fate of our Christian era: the Nemesis which awaits its *hybris*: the price to be paid for the achievements of its hypertrophied ego. The psychological law of enantidromia ensures that too overweighted a concentration on one side of the personality—in this case on real or supposed goodness and the potentialities of the ego—will produce the revolt and eventual triumph of its unconscious opposite—in this case of evil and the shadow. Moreover, the New Testament writers themselves foresaw it all. The coming of Christ paves the way for the coming of his opposite, Antichrist,[27] for the temporary triumph of Satan,[28] for the apotheosis of the shadow, "the man of sin, the son of perdition who opposeth and is lifted up above all that is called God...showing himself as if he were God."[29]

Such a brief and bald summary hardly does justice to Jung's diagnosis of the woes of our time. It deserves, I believe, very serious consideration. But he adds much more which Christians will find even more difficult to swallow. Empirical psychology, Jung points out, shows repeatedly that adequate symbols of the "self"—of total humanity—contain evil as well as good, darkness as well as light. These symbols, he maintains, are empirically indistinguishable from symbols of God. God, in fact, is evil as well as good, dark as well as light. Total reality as we experience it contains evil as well as good, and the evil is as real as the good, and at least as potent if not more so. If God is the All, in which all reality is precontained, there must be evil in God as well as good. "To believe that God is the *Summum Bonum* is impossible for a reflecting consciousness."[30] Yahweh in the Old Testament has a dark side as well as a light, as Job discovered to his cost. "I am the Lord," he says through Isaias, "I form the light and create darkness. I make peace and create evil."[31] On the principle that things are what they do—*agens agit sibi simile*—God therefore *is* darkness as well as light, evil as well as peace; and the Bible is full of the manifestations of the dark, evil, wrathful, unjust, cruel side of God. Some early Christian writers also recognized that God has a left, "sinister" side, as well as the right side on which his good Son is enthroned.[32] In God's Incarnation in the good Jesus Christ, Jung continues, God incarnated his good and light side only. This, from the standpoint of man's psychological development and his progressive psychological symbolism, was a necessary step. For, as therapeutic experience shows, the advancement of human consciousness requires the complete separation of the ego from the shadow before they can be integrated: the opposition of good and evil and the tension between them must be heightened to the utmost; evil, in other words, must be wholly excluded from the ego at this stage. The hero in all the stories must be good and pure and noble before he can cope with dragons, the blandishments and terrors of the female, or set out on his terrifying night-journey through the underworld. The Incarnation, the embodiment of God in Jesus Christ, is as yet an incomplete incarnation from which the dark and evil side of God has been excluded. But God remains dark and evil—as well as light and good—nevertheless. In the last book of the Bible this fearsome side of God breaks through into the visions of the seer with unparalleled ferociousness, in visions which foretell all the blood and tears, the vials of the wrath of God, the terror and hatred which await the Christian era. On the assumption that the visionary of the Apocalypse had indeed been the Beloved Disciple of the Fourth Gospel and the Johannine epistles, Jung writes:

> The "revelation" was experienced by an early Christian who, as a leading light of the community, presumably had to live an exemplary life and demonstrate to his flock the Christian virtues of true faith, humility, patience, devotion, selfless love, and denial of all worldly desires. In the long run this can become too much, even for the most righteous. Irritability, bad moods, and outbursts of affect are the classic symptoms of chronic virtuousness.... I have seen many compensating dreams of believing Christians...but I have seen nothing that remotely resembles the brutal impact with which the opposites collide in John's visions, except in the case of severe psychosis. However, John gives us no grounds for such a diagnosis.... It is sufficient that he is a passionately religious person with an otherwise well-ordered psyche. But he must have an intensive relationship to God which lays him open to an invasion far transcending anything personal.... The purpose of

the apocalyptic visions is not to tell John, as an ordinary human being, how much shadow he hides beneath his luminous nature, but to open the seer's eyes to the immensity of God, for he who loves God will know God.... Like Job, he saw the fierce and terrible side of Jahwe. For this reason he felt his gospel of love to be one-sided, and he supplemented it with his gospel of fear.... God has a terrible double aspect: a sea of grace is met by a seething lake of fire.... That is the "eternal," as distinct from the temporal, gospel: *one can love God, but must fear him.*[33]

The "temporal" or interim Gospel of the all-good Jesus Christ was a necessary step for the evolution of human consciousness and wholeness; and therefore, a theologian might add, in the *Heilsgeschichte*. But this Incarnation, says Jung, being one-sided, is not final; and a theologian will have to agree that the first coming was not the eschatological consummation which we still await. But Jung is evidently much impressed by a Gnostic myth according to which Jesus is not the *only* begotten Son of God. There is another Son who represents the dark side of God, and his name is Satan or Sathanel. This, his brother and his adversary, his shadow, Jesus decisively rejected in the "temptations" in the wilderness, and their fratricidal strife is the fate of our Christian era.

From most of this an instructed Christian, of any tradition, will recoil. This talk of "sides" of God will seem to him intolerably anthropomorphic—though he should remember that the talk is of images and presentations (*Vorstellungen*) of God in the human mind, and of a kind not unknown to the Bible.[34] God, he will maintain, is beyond the *opposites* of good and evil, as he is beyond the opposite sexes. And, although God is good, this does not mean that he is goody-goody, or that all he does is pleasant and agreeable to human tastes. Indeed, goodness predicated of God is never identical with goodness as predicated of any creature; like all other predicates used of God and creatures it can never be understood in the same, but only an analogous sense.[35] The fact that a cause produces something which from some points of view is bad, does not mean that the cause itself is bad. Badness can arise, and often does arise, from the very perfection of the cause.[36] To judge the infinite and almighty God by the ethical laws which are designed to govern human behaviour will seem as preposterous as to subject him to the laws of gravitation or thermodynamics. On the contrary, a Christian will say, it is we, and our ethical standards and behaviour, which should be subjected to the judgment of God. The view that Christianity encourages a smug optimism which represses evil and the dark side of life may be a welcome change from the more usual charge that it is forever harping on suffering and sin, the corruption of our fallen nature, on hell-fire and the necessity for carrying our cross. To most practising Christians, the view that Christianity disregards the wrath and severity of God will seem hardly more realistic; though it may be understandable as a memory of a late Victorian, Pelagian liberalism masquerading as Christianity.

An unprejudiced reading of the Bible, a study of the follies and woes of Christendom, a compassionate understanding of the dreads and dilemmas of our contemporaries and of what is actually taking place in the modern psyche,[37] must indeed be a shock to those brought up to identify Christianity with the myth of human moral progress under the leadership of a "gentle Jesus, meek and mild." It cannot be denied that this distortion of Christianity was a most dangerous and repressive psychological force. But it was unknown to previous ages; and St. John—to take Jung's example—had never subscribed to anything like it. Christ himself nicknamed him Boanerges—a son of thunder—on account of his eagerness to rain fire and brimstone on his opponents[38]; and perhaps nobody has been more acutely aware of the tensions between good and evil within his own soul. In one and the same epistle he asserts that "anyone born of God does not sin," and that "if we say we have no sin we deceive ourselves...we make [Jesus] a liar."³⁹ Nor was he ever unaware of the terribleness of the very love of God: the especial task of the Paraclete is "to convince the world of sin, of justice and of judgment."⁴⁰ We may well agree with Jung that Christianity has set the post-Christian world problems of unprecedented magnitude, unknown to comparatively "innocent" and relatively amoral forms of paganism. Christian theology itself asserts that while the "intolerable burdens" of the Old Testament, of which St. Peter complained,⁴¹ were humanly difficult, the life of love exemplified in Christ and portrayed in the Sermon on the Mount is utterly impossible to man without the power of the living God, the grace which he imparts in Christ and through his sacraments.⁴² The post-Christian's retention of a sentimentalized Christmas while ignoring Good Friday, his half-conscious attachment to Christian ideals and ethics while abandoning the Christian call to acknowledgment of sin and repentance, and his denial of the very reality of the devil, are indeed doomed to disaster.

But most Christians—and not only Christians—will protest that Jung has radically misunderstood the very nature of evil. Since the great Greek philosophers, it has generally been understood that evil as such does not and cannot exist.⁴³ It is not in itself a reality, an *ousia*, a substance or a thing; and badness cannot be a quantitative part of reality. Bad people, things, inclinations, actions and wills are certainly very real and very powerful, and it is at our dire peril that we pretend to ourselves that they are not. But their badness consists, we find on examination, not in some positive entity or reality which they possess, but in the absence from them of some positive entity or reality which we account as good. This is so, even when that absence is brought about by the presence of some entity or reality which excludes it, as blindness—the very real privation of sight—may be brought about by a cataract. Thus understood, evil or badness cannot possibly be something that can be added to something else and so bring about its greater completeness. Goodness and completeness are in fact synonymous, and evil or badness can never be an addition to, for it is by definition a subtraction from, that completeness. Only the crudest picture-thinking can make it a "part" or a "side" of God. Good and evil, in the abstract, are indeed opposites, but they prove on reflection to be not two positive contraries—*äquivalente Gegensätze*, as Jung calls them—but contradictories. In the concrete their opposition comes about from the presence in a subject of a positive quality (or one considered to be such) as against its absence or privation.[44] Evil or badness, in short, is a *defectus boni quod natum est et debet haberi*,[45] the absence of a good which is naturally there, and should be there. Our value-judgments of good and bad prove, on examination, to be based on the presence or absence in a subject of a quality which, on one ground or another, and, whether rightly or wrongly, we account good or desirable. An evil can never be defined except in terms of the good which it excludes; while a good can be defined, without reference to evil, in terms of the positive qualities which are attributed to it. They are opposites indeed, but not equivalent contraries.

Now just these assertions arouse Jung to unwonted indignation. This idea of evil as a *privatio boni* is, he says, a "nonsensical doctrine,"[46] a "euphemistic *petitio principii*,"[47] a "regular *tour de force* in sophistry."[48] Though unwilling, he tells us, to "get mixed up in metaphysics" he has felt it incumbent upon him to "become polemical where metaphysics encroaches upon experience and imparts to it a significance which can in no wise be verified empirically."[49] The doctrine is, he is convinced, contrary to experience, and highly deleterious psychologically. He relates:

> I should never have dreamt of coming up against such an ap-
> parently remote problem as that of the *privatio boni* in my
> practical work. Fate would have it, however, that I had to treat
> a patient, a scholarly man, who had become involved in all
> manner of dubious and morally questionable practices. He
> turned out to be a fervent adherent of the *privatio boni*, be-
> cause it fitted in admirably with his scheme: evil in itself is
> nothing, a mere shadow, a trifling and fleeting diminution of
> good, like a cloud passing over the sun. The man professed to
> be a believing Protestant and would therefore have no reason
> to appeal to a *sententia communis* of the Catholic Church, had
> it not proved a welcome sedative to his uneasy conscience.[50]

It should be unnecessary to say that this idea that evil is "nothing," a "trifling diminution of good," is a grotesque caricature of
anything that has ever been generally held in the Catholic Church.
Perhaps there is no doctrine that human perversity cannot seize
upon and distort as a cover for its crimes, or a defence mechanism for its neuroses. It is not, alas, unknown for people to claim
fervent adherence to Jung's own psychology because, they say, it
is so "spiritual" and so free from unpleasant things like infantile
sexuality and anal erotism—a fine escape, too, from their personal problems and misbehaviour into a blissful world of collective
archetypes and other people's mythologies. If the misunderstandings of Jung's patient are widespread, we can only agree that they
are deplorable and dangerous, but it is doubtful if the constant
emphasis on the reality of sin and suffering within the Catholic
Church would permit any practising Catholic to share them. The
privatio boni, as Professor Maritain has said,

> as it is being. And evil works *through* good, since evil, being in
> itself a privation or non-being, has no causality of its own....

What is thus the power of evil? It is the very power of the good that evil wounds and preys upon. The more powerful this good is, the more powerful evil will be—not by virtue of itself, but by virtue of this good. That is why no evil is more powerful than that of the fallen angel. If evil appears so powerful in the world today, that is because the good it preys upon is the very spirit of man—science itself and moral ideals corrupted by bad will.... The whole spectacle of things is that of a procession of things good wounded by non-being and producing by their activity an indefinitely-increasing accumulation of being and of good, in which that same activity also carries the indefinitely-growing wound—as long as the world exists—of non-being and of evil.[51]

It is not very profitable to argue about the meaning of words, and it cannot be said that Jung's polemic has led to anything very constructive. Each side, not surprisingly, tends to beg the question and assume that "evil" means to the other what it means to him, from which it is an easy step to show that his statements about it are ridiculous. One would like to dismiss the rather tedious discussion with the reflection that, as one Jungian has put it:

I have never been troubled by the difficulty which seems to be caused by using the same word "evil" in two subtly different senses. In the statement "evil is the absence of good" evil refers to a state of disharmony or disorder, whereas in "evil is a positive force" the word denotes those activities which cause or reflect this state. Thus evil things, by their positive activity, cause or express an evil state of lack of harmony or wholeness, just as, in an analogous way, a psychological illness can be described in terms of a lack of integration or of the positive activity of an autonomous complex. The argument that there

must be evil in God depends upon an unfortunate reification
of the adjective "evil."[52]

It should, moreover, be remembered on Jung's behalf, that
the conception that evil is *privatio boni* is undoubtedly a product
of conscious reflection, of intellectual analysis, and not of immediate sense-experience. Aquinas himself recognizes that to the un-
reflecting apprehensions of the psyche, the privation which is evil
"habet rationem cuiusdam entis"—has the character of a certain
kind of entity—and is a positive contrary.[53] Furthermore, the psychological apprehensions of, and reactions to, evil are very positive
psychological realities, and it is with these, naturally enough, that
a psychologist is particularly concerned. Darkness may indeed be
a privation, an absence of light, but a child's terror of the dark is a
very real and positive thing.

But the fact remains that the word is used on each side in different senses, and this fact introduces a source of serious misunderstanding, and adds complications to our task of bridgebuilding.
Jungian phrases like "integrating evil" or "accepting the shadow"
are apt to sound to Christian ears something like an approval of
sin, or at least a compromise with wickedness, notwithstanding
Jung's frequent assurances that they mean nothing of the sort.
His talk of good and evil as "equivalent contraries," each equally
"parts" of reality, of the psyche, and even of God, and of "relativizing" good and evil, suggest all too easily to one who holds the
traditional conception, an uncommitted tolerance of the terrible
privations of good—psychological, physical, moral and divine—
which are mankind's calamity. It is not always easy for him to realize that the words are being used in a sense different from that
to which he is accustomed. On the other side statements emanat-
ing from Christian sources, expressing a detestation and rejection
of evil, sound no less appalling or absurd to those to whom evil

means some integral constituent of reality, indeed a "part" of God himself. The utter confusion which can arise is illustrated by one disciple of Jung (and a Christian priest at that) who reads Jung's sense of "evil" into the baptismal renunciation of world, flesh and devil, and describes them as expressions of the "hitherto one-sided acceptance of Christ" which must now, thanks to Jung's work, be "overcome"![54]

I must confess that for my part I have great difficulty in understanding just what Jung *does* understand by evil, and how, intellectually, he would have us differentiate it from good. And it is not indeed altogether clear what he would have us understand by "integrating," "accepting" and even "becoming conscious" of it. There is no doubt at all in my mind of the immense importance of these conceptions, or of the experiences on which they are based, but they do appear to be wrapped in certain ambiguities which, even from the therapeutic standpoint, it seems desirable to clarify. And precisely the traditional and Christian analysis of evil seems to provide these needed clarifications.

Fundamental to this analysis is the distinction, familiar in our everyday experience, between *malum rei* and *malum actionis*, the badness of a thing and the badness of its functioning or behaviour. My car does not go properly, it malfunctions (*malum actionis*), but this is due to some disorder in the engine itself (*malum rei*). Both these phenomena are privations of good: in the first case the absence of what I call "good going," in the second case of good order in the works. If I am to correct the bad behaviour, I must correct the disorder in the engine: I must in effect supply its good working order which is absent. To do this I must first know what the disorder is. I may, of course, find that the absence of right order is due to the presence of something else—water in the tank or dirt in the plugs. I may also find that there has been some reciprocal causality here; not only may the faulty behaviour be due to the faulty engine, the faults of the engine may have been made worse by constant faulty behaviour. All this I must discover and in this sense of *knowing* what is the matter, I must "accept" it. But if I "accept" the disorder in the sense of liking it, approving it, willing it, I shall never get around to repairing the car, and it will continue to misbehave. And it is hard to see how I can "integrate" the disorder, for it is itself a certain disintegration. The "badness" both of the car and its behaviour will remain; their "evil" will not be overcome by good—by the restoration of the absent "good order."

In the human context, and in the psyche, *malum rei* becomes *malum poenae*, the evil we undergo or suffer, and *malum actionis* becomes *malum culpae*, the evil we do, our misbehaviour.[55] Discrimination between them is of vital importance. Faulty behaviour, or what I consider to be such, is due to faulty being, and faulty being may be due to faulty behaviour—my own or other people's. A man, truly, is not a machine; he can, to some extent, voluntarily correct his own behaviour. But even this he can do only by changing his own will, supplying the privation of bad will (the absence from his mind of due consideration for the good) which expresses itself in misbehaviour.[56] A fully human act is a conscious and voluntary act, whether it be "good" or "bad." But not all our actual behaviour is such. Fallen man, as theology understands him, is a disordered being. He is in a condition of *non-posse-non-peccare*, of not being able never to sin, and this by reason of the disorder common to us all, which we attribute to original sin, and apart from the particular disorders of particular individuals.[57] Only when his will consents to such misbehaviour, known to be contrary to man's supreme end or objective, and when it is of a serious character, do we have what is traditionally called mortal sin.[58] In modern psychological language this may be described as a conscious and wilful identification of the ego and by the ego with the faulty behaviour, whether externally acted out or only interiorly entertained, in defiance of the known good or goal of the whole. The mortal sinner prefers some partial or passing good (*bonum commutabile*) to his supreme and unchanging good and highest value, namely his God (*bonum incommutabile*) and hence the real goal of his whole personality in time and eternity.[59] Because this partial and passing good is set over and against the whole, it is also evil: it is deprived of the relatedness to the whole which it should have. Only then do we have *malum culpae*, sin, in the strict and fullest sense. To the extent that voluntariness is lacking, we do not have a fully human act (*actus humanus*) though we have an act produced by a human being (*actus hominis*).[60]

By no means all our misbehaviour or malfunctioning is voluntary; though to the extent that it is involuntary it is infra-human, and it is, on that account, often accompanied by a peculiar sense of guilt or shame.[61] Very often the particular disorder from which it comes is in large measure unconscious. The disorder is not in itself sin—it is *malum rei* and not *malum actionis*—though it may issue in misbehaviour, and also arise from, or be increased by, misbehaviour, our own or somebody else's. It is an evil which we undergo or suffer from (*malum poenae*) and both it and the resultant misbehaviour are, as such, not only involuntary but clean contrary to what we will: "the good which I will, I do not; but the evil which I will not, that I do.... Unhappy man that I am, who shall deliver me from the body of this death?"[62] Moreover, in practice we often find we have deluded ourselves as to what is really good and really bad in our behaviour. We often fail to see the evil side— the mixed motives or the harmful consequences to ourselves and others—of the conduct we have accounted "good," and how our "bad" or unwanted behaviour has often been an expression, although a disordered expression, of fundamentally good elements in our personality, and essential to its wholeness and integrity.

On this showing, those psychic contents which Jung calls the "shadow" are not, and indeed cannot be, wholly evil or bad. Their badness is found to result from something which they lack, and of which they have been deprived, and notably consciousness itself. This privation may come from, or be intensified by, bad action, voluntary or involuntary—no psychologist ready to take all the factors of the personality into account will exclude the possibility that unethical behaviour has been a factor in the etiology of a neurosis or in turning a latent psychosis into an overt one. The disorder may arise from actions which the subject has believed to be very good, and perhaps *were* very good. But it may also arise from hereditary, educational and environmental factors, or from perfectly "normal" ego-development in childhood. For the ego cannot develop at all without becoming differentiated from the primordial unconscious wholeness; and it cannot become differentiated without forming some sort of a "shadow," a complex of those psychic contents which the ego has found unacceptable on one ground or another.[63]

These contents, by reason of their privation of consciousness, will also issue in unacceptable behaviour, and may be expressed in spontaneous images, in dreams, phantasies or projections, which present hostility and danger to the ego (for they are the contents which have become the enemy of the ego's aims, ideals and attitudes). They fill it with fear, sorrow, pain, disgust, anger or aggressiveness. To the extent that the resultant behaviour is involuntary, and is on that account sub-human, it may occasion a peculiar sense of guilt or shame. These behaviour patterns may be contrary to accepted moral standards, or they may, as Jung has said, be deplored simply because of their nuisance-value, on grounds of expediency.[64] They are, in either case, accounted "bad" by the ego, and are "disobedient" to its desires and behests. The difficulties of facing and integrating these contents will be enormously enhanced, indeed become psychological impossibilities, if it be supposed that the "shadow" is "evil in itself." *Nullus propter malum operatur*—nobody can act on account of pure evil—expresses an ancient, but still valid, psychological truth. There must be some real or supposed good in its object, or to be got out of it, for action to take place at all. And psychological experience shows constantly that "integration of the shadow" means a progressive recognition that there *is* good—often a vitally important good—contained in the "shadow." Indeed it is usually seen increasingly that its positive contents are *good*; that all that is bad about them are the privations they have suffered from the ego. But correspondingly it is discovered that the ego itself was by no means so wholly good as had been supposed; and it is just this recognition that the ego also had been bad—i.e., deprived of its needed positive attitude to the contents it had rejected—that makes integration possible. As this happens, and the analysant progressively overcomes his negative attitudes and emotions towards the shadow-contents, the nightmarish features of the shadow-images become, like the ogres in the fairy-tales, less hostile and more co-operative. It is increasingly recognized in the course of therapy that there had been good and bad on both sides; and if this is what Jung means by the "relativization" of good and evil, it is thoroughly acceptable, and expresses known psychological facts. But it is often humiliating to recognize that all the good had not been with the ego, nor all the bad with the shadow. And it often demands considerable courage to enter into, without becoming identified with, the shadow's strangely different, and usually diametrically opposite, standards of value. Yet the fact is that the ego had repressed, or too harshly suppressed, the contents of the "shadow" which had, by that very fact, become more shadowy, more compelled to rebel and explode, in the interests of the "self," of the wholeness of the personality. But there is no integration except to the extent that the privations of good on both sides have been supplied. In other words, as we understand matters, integration of the shadow cannot mean—as Jung too often seems to suggest—the addition of evil to good, but the overcoming of evil *by* good. Integrated evil ceases to be evil, its privations have been supplied; it is, to the extent that it is integrated, simply good.

Christ tells us to "resist not evil"[65]; though elsewhere the New Testament bids us resist the devil.[66] Resistance of evil is, however, of two sorts, known to psychologists as suppression and repression:

> Repression is a sort of half-conscious and half-hearted letting go of things, a dropping of hot cakes or a reviling of grapes that hang too high, or a looking the other way in order not to become conscious of one's desires. Freud discovered that repression is one of the main mechanisms in the making of a neurosis. Suppression amounts to a conscious moral choice, but repression is a rather immoral *penchant* for getting rid of disagreeable decisions. Suppression may cause worry, conflict and suffering, but it never causes a neurosis. Neurosis is always a substitute for legitimate suffering.[67]

Without suppression there can be no growth of the personality, no life in society, no psychological differentiation, certainly no following of Christ. It is the negative side of the positive and deliberate choice of any particular good. But what is to be suppressed or rejected is, in the traditional view, the *privation* of some good in what is essentially good. The baptismal renunciation of the world is renunciation of worldliness, or the godlessness of the world, not of the world which God found to be very good,[68] and which he so loved as to give his only-begotten Son.[69] Renunciation of the flesh is renunciation of carnality, the domination of flesh without the spirit, as an autonomous principle which lusts

against the spirit.[70] But renunciation of Satan is precisely renunciation of spirit when it is an autonomous principle at once Godless
and rejecting the God-made rights of the flesh. Herein, in the
Christian view, lies the devilishness of Lucifer, who is not, and
cannot be (as Jung seems to suppose), only evil. Ancient tradition
sees Satan, on the contrary, as the greatest and noblest, the most
intelligent and powerful of all God's creatures, but who is nevertheless the worst because he has chosen to be Godless and set
himself against the Incarnation, the manifestation of God in human flesh.[71] Jung could not misrepresent Christian theology more
seriously than when he presents it as setting a purely "spiritual"
Christ against a fleshly, material, "chthonic" Antichrist.[72] On the
contrary, "Every *spirit* which confesseth that Jesus Christ is come
in the *flesh* is of God; and every *spirit* that dissolveth Jesus is not
of God; and this is Antichrist."[73]

But it is of course true that, in practice, unconscious or half-
conscious repressions get mixed up even with our necessary conscious suppressions. We are apt to throw out the baby with the
bath-water. It should however be recognized that the rites and
teaching of the Church are calculated to prevent unconsciousness,
and consequent repression, of evil. We have seen how the rites
preceding baptism should arouse awareness of evil and the Christian ego's opposition to it—not, it must again be emphasized, opposition to an integral part of reality or of psychic wholeness, but
to privations of it or to forces which would so deprive it.[74] This
anamnesis of evil—archetypal in the forms of world, flesh and devil, personal in the forms of one's own specific failings and inclinations to be made and kept conscious by self-examination and
confession—is encouraged throughout the whole life of a practising Christian.

But there is some ambiguity in the phrase "becoming conscious" (*Bewusstwerdung*) of the "shadow." As we have seen, full

consciousness means for Jung, not a mere knowledge of psychic contents, but also "the *relatedness* of psychic contents to the ego...insofar as they are sensed as such by the ego." We have interpreted this to mean that consciousness implies conation as well as cognition.[75] It is certain that a mere objective knowledge of the contents of the shadow does not usually suffice for its integration: they remain merely an object, unrelated to the subject. It must usually be emotionally experienced to be assimilated, and all the more so because, as Jung points out, the shadow is almost invariably entangled with the subject's "inferior" function,[76] and that function must come into play if the shadow is not merely to be known *about*, but to become actually conscious. Does this mean that it must be loved, and even perhaps willed?

The Jungian answer to this sometimes seems far from clear or quite consistent. But just here the traditional conception of evil as *privatio boni* and the distinctions of *malum culpae* and *malum poenae* become of vital importance. *Malum culpae*, or sin, *cannot* be integrated. It is by definition, as we have seen, the privation of integrity. It is the surrender of the good of the whole to the demands of the autonomous part, and as such is destructive of integrity. It should therefore on no account be willed or loved. But this does not mean that no relatedness of the ego or conation is called for. On the contrary a very definite attitude of the ego is required of the Christian towards sin. It is, however, one not of acceptance but rejection; not a love but detestation; not a *velle* but a *nolle*, a will *not* to *do* evil, and of contrition for having done evil. Father Beirnaert, interpreting baptism in the light of the Church Fathers and liturgies as a confrontation with the shadow, writes that for a Christian:

> To face the dragon, representing sin, is to recognize evil as a
> fact, but what this leads to is total opposition to it, and indeed

its destruction in the waters of baptism. Salvation consists precisely in being delivered from it, having once looked it in the face and known it for what it is. Jung sees perfectly clearly that this is what divides those who have merely experienced the reality of the archetypes from believers as such. For the former Good and Evil are more closely bound together than a pair of twins. The experience of the totality of the "Self" includes all the archetypes, however contrary to one another. For the believer, Good and Evil form an antinomy, and we must decide for the one and reject the other.[77]

This is important and true, if what we understand by evil is *malum culpae* or sin. But the antithesis to Jung becomes less sharp when it is remembered that for Jung "evil" means a positive component of reality while in traditional Christian formulas it does not. A Christian's rejection and contrition fall not on any good which, from any point of view, is in his sin, or in any good which may indirectly have arisen by occasion of it, but precisely on its privation of good, and especially its privation of positive relatedness to the Self and to his Summum Bonum, his supreme value and last end, namely his God.

For all this is not of course to say that no good and no integration can come as an indirect consequence of sin, of willing and doing evil. Indirect, because directly and in itself sin is wholly destructive of good and of integration. But indirectly, good can and has come of it ever since the *felix culpa* (the "happy fault") of Adam, the *certe necessarium peccatum* (the "truly necessary sin") of Adam.[78] Where sin abounds, there does grace the more abound; though we may not sin *that* grace may abound.[79] The neurotic, all too often, is *unable* to sin freely: his very repressions and fear of the "shadow" prevent it, and the same fear can produce an equally compulsive and largely spurious "goodness." Just for this reason, the Christian Gospel and the rites of the Church have no real meaning for him, for they presuppose the experience of sin and the power to respond to them freely. The actual experience of having sinned may (as, according to the Epistle to the Romans, it did for the whole Gentile and Hebrew worlds) enable him to appreciate his need for faith and the healing Christ. But sin remains sin, and the end does not justify the means. Psychotherapists who assure their patients that their sins are no sins, because of the benefits to their health which may come from them, are not only transgressing their professional competence; they are encouraging the accompanying guilt-sense to be repressed into unconsciousness, and hence likely to form another, and even more intractable "shadow."

When, however, we turn from *malum culpae* to *malum poenae*—from the evils we do to the evils we undergo—the Christian programme is very different. Such evils are, of their very nature, *contra voluntatem*: contrary to our wills, our comfort, our pleasure. Here we are bidden to take up our cross, to accept them willingly, even lovingly, though with full awareness that they *are* evils, contrary to what our natures and natural inclinations, quite rightly, desire and hold to be good.[80] These, though privations of genuine goods, are part and parcel of our fallen natures, and their acceptance, conative as well as cognitive, is indispensable to our growth, health, wholeness and holiness. This we may see more clearly when we turn to consider health and holiness in our next chapter.[81]

X.

HEALTH AND HOLINESS

Probably the strongest inducement to divorce soul from psyche arises from the difficulty which is often found in practice to correlate health with holiness, even sanity with sanctity. The practitioner, whether he be pastor or psychologist, can hardly fail to be impressed and sometimes perplexed when he observes that the two by no means always appear to coincide. Dr. Strauss, whose views on soul and psyche we have recorded in the first chapter, leaves us in no doubt that such observations as these have encouraged his own view of the matter:

> There is a comfortable, but superstitious, belief among many
> Catholics, lay and clerical alike, that one could not possibly
> become neurotic or psychotic if one avoided mortal sin and
> went to the Sacraments regularly. Yet, I would contend, there
> have been neurotic, psychotic, and even mentally sub-intelli-
> gent saints. Amongst the many reasons for this popular belief
> is the failure to differentiate between the soul and the psyche.[1]

Elsewhere Dr. Strauss has invoked the late Father Herbert Thurston in support of his contention that many of the saints would nowadays be diagnosed as neurotic or psychotic, and the contention is one that few who are acquainted with the literature of the subject would care to dispute. Another Catholic psychiatrist has told us how he became impressed with the importance of distinguishing soul from psyche by the case of a religious sister among his patients. This unfortunate woman was riddled with scrupulosity, with an overwhelming sense of guilt and the conviction that she was damned. It happened that, during the course of her psychiatric treatment, which resulted in no amelioration of her distressing symptoms, she developed cancer and was told she would die of it. The psychological symptoms at once disappeared, and she appeared to be prepared for death with every sign of tranquillity, joy and confidence in Divine mercy. Contrary to the doctors' prognosis her life was spared, and the psychiatrist had hoped that the psychological recovery would persist likewise. But it was not so. Restored to life, the former symptoms of obsessional anxiety were restored also, exactly as they had been before.

The psychiatrist's conclusion that, while the soul can be all right, the psyche (or, as he preferred to call it, the mind) can be all wrong, and that the one is therefore not the other, is understandable. And indeed if by "soul" we are to understand an exclusively "religious part" of man, or better the supernatural life of grace in the soul, the inference might be legitimate. But we have seen in our first chapter that such a use of the word is novel and perilous. There is no need to invoke such a hypothesis in order to understand that it may be possible to be ready for death and to live in another world without being able to adjust to the prospect of a continued life of mental torture in this world.

But is it possible to recognize that psychological health does not necessarily go along with personal holiness—or holiness with psychological health—without postulating some such distinction of their respective subjects? We do not need to go deeply into either hagiography or into psychopathology to recognize that there does not always seem to be a clear equation between the two. We may recall the "managers and cashiers"—the clergy—of Samuel Butler's *Erewhon*:

They did not please me; they lacked, with few exceptions, the true Erewhonian frankness; and an equal number from any other class would have looked happier and better men. When I met them in the streets they did not seem like other people, but had, as a general rule, a cramped expression upon their faces which pained and depressed me.... I could not help feeling that there must be something in their lives which had stunted their natural development, and that they would have been more healthily minded in any other profession.... Few people would speak quite openly before them, which struck me as a very bad sign.

That was, of course, a jaundiced picture, and is now a century out of date. But it is sufficiently apparent that those among our neighbours who are most eminent for their piety and religious professions, and those who might win the psychologist's approval for their balance and maturity, are by no means always identical. The fact is one that can arouse perplexity and scandal among our contemporaries for whom the psychologist's criteria are decisive, and the more likely to chime in with their own. Without postulating a formal distinction of soul and psyche, and while still maintaining a distinction of the supernatural life of grace in the soul from its purely natural activities, we are still confronted with a very serious problem. For if, as we have maintained, "grace perfects nature," should we not expect an exact correspondence between an individual's holiness and his health, his sanctity and his sanity? Should we not even expect all devout believers to be sane and, from the psychologist's standpoint, fully mature and balanced individuals, and unbelievers to be neurotic and unbalanced in proportion to their unbelief? The fact that this is apparently not so is the commonest and perhaps the most weighty of the objections brought forward against a positive correlation of religion and psychology.

Rather curiously, no such difficulty is commonly felt regarding the compatibility of *physical* illness with personal holiness and moral integrity. It is not usually considered surprising or scandalous that a very holy person should have tuberculosis or polio; or even that he should be mentally deranged provided only that the derangement can be traced to physical, and not to psychogenic causes. Yet to those of us who hold that body and soul are not two separate things, but that man is an ensouled body, and that there is no such thing as a human body or organ apart from its informing life-principle or soul, the co-existence of somatic illness with holiness is hardly less problematic than that of mental illness. Although specifically mental health and illness, and their relation to holiness and moral integrity, present us with special problems, we cannot entirely isolate them from the problem of health and illness in general.

But neither health nor holiness prove on examination to be such simple concepts as is generally supposed. Although a closer scrutiny of them will not at once dissipate all these difficulties, still less plumb all the mysteries of the evils which beset mankind, it should help us to view them with less naivety. Such a scrutiny, however difficult, will be no less worthwhile if it induces us also to re-examine the basic aims and the inherent limitations of psychotherapy, as well as the basic principles of a Christian life. We will therefore first examine the notion of health in general, and then of mental health in particular, from the standpoint of medicine and psychology themselves. We must then ask what Christianity has to say about health and disease, and finally what it has to say about holiness.

Although we use the words "health" and "healthy" every day, and suppose we know quite well what we mean by them, their meaning proves on closer inspection to be very elusive. As Mr. Kenneth Walker has said:

Health cannot be defined in purely negative terms as an absence of disease. It is a positive condition which is worthy of
much more close study than it has yet been given. The truth
is that the medical profession has been so occupied with the
investigation and treatment of disease that it has been able to
spare but little time for the study of health.[2]

He relates that:

A few years ago a representative body of medical men assembled
in a room to find an acceptable definition of the word "health."
After much discussion they reached the conclusion that health
was "a state of complete physical, mental and social well-being,
and not merely an absence of disease and infirmity."[3]

But who, Mr. Walker justly asks, is to be the judge of this state
of well-being? Certainly not the subject himself who "feels fine,"
for there are illnesses in which a patient may be feeling remarkably
well and yet be suffering from some serious disease, such as generalized peritonitis. Moreover, his report on his psychological and
social state is still less trustworthy. The neurotic patient is particularly likely to be biased on this subject, since a neurotic is inclined
to attribute his troubles to his fellow men rather than to himself.
"If only people would not worry me so, I would be well" is his
attitude.[4]

Social and other criteria are even less reliable, and Mr. Walker
concludes that "the representative body of medical men cannot be
said to have arrived at a satisfactory definition of health."[5]

He himself offers as a "possible definition": "the ability to
retain an inner state of harmony and to make quick adjustments
to external changes in the environment."[6] This idea of health as
harmony accords with what may be called the traditional, classical

conception of health. We find it already in Alcmaeon of Croton who, according to Aristotle,[7] was a contemporary of Pythagoras. A fragment from Aetius tells us that Alcmaeon defined health as an equilibrium of powers of functions (*isonomia tōn dynameōn*). Disease correspondingly was a disharmony arising from the predominance (*monarkhia*) of one or some of these at the expense of others, which predominance may arise from either internal or external causes.[8]

> Hippocrates and his disciples succeeded in bringing to full development this fertile idea of Alcmaeon: disease seems to be always and exclusively a disturbance of the equilibrium of the *physis* (nature); and the treatment, the physical regimen (*diaila*) intended to restore the harmony which the *causa morbi* altered. It follows that the physician should be, above everything else, a *physiologos*, a person capable of speaking correctly about the *physis*.... Faithful to this intellectual attitude, the physicians of the fifth century...find the immediate cause of all disease in a disorder of the *physis* of the person affected; and their remote cause in an alteration of the vital relationships between the individual *physis* of the patient and the universal *Physis*.[9]

This conception of health as a harmony of powers or functions has been general ever since, however differently interpreted. It is "the cornerstone of the naturalistic pathology of the Occident."[10] We shall find it, not only among physicians, but also among theologians. Aquinas defines health (*salus*) as a due disposition or harmony of the components of an animal (whether human or not) judged in relation to its capacity for action, but more especially as conformity to its specific nature.[11] And, as will presently appear, it is in these same terms that he understands holiness also.

This view of health, as a harmony of *physis* or nature, implies some kind of anthropology—in the sense of some idea of the nature of man, and also of his place in the universe. Truly enough, even for the ancients, this idea of human nature was not some *a priori* idea to be imposed from without, but was to be discovered empirically in medical practice itself. "The only guiding criterion of the physician should be—as is stated in *De Prisca Medicina*—the impression received through the senses; that is, the sensorial exploration of what is going on in the body of the patient."[12]

Yet it is just these empirical data themselves that make application of the definition in the concrete so difficult. The very fact that man is a living organism forbids us to understand his healthy equilibrium or harmony in any absolute or static sense. On the one side, "Consider the perfect harmony of a living organism which, even in illness, rises to the occasion and battles with the illness in a most intelligent manner."[13] On the other, we see that "adjustment means rest, finality, completeness, none of which are compatible with human existence, whose essence is motion."[14] Man's being is a ceaseless becoming—a coming-to-be and a passing-away—and the very balance which makes his health consists in a certain unbalance. Rest, finality, completeness spell—in this world—not life but death. Moreover the very powers, components or functions which are to be balanced, are not, as in a machine, static "parts," but are subjected to—indeed their very functioning consists in— the ceaseless "metabolic whirlpool," and "these processes go on even in an apparently static constituent like bone."[15] Unlike a machine, a man's "good working order" cannot be estimated by its efficiency in accomplishing a predetermined task, nor by the permanence and indestructibility of his components. Any attempt to impose on him a pattern of "health" which disregards this fact is already to dehumanize him and even to "de-animalize" him. The very harmony of the whole, the life and health of the whole, requires destruction as well as construction, catabolism as well as anabolism.

But this whole is not only a living whole; it is also a dying whole: the components to be harmonized are not only life-giving but also death-bringing.

> Even in the somatic field an uninterrupted process of dying sets in from the very moment of birth; the cells are subject to constant renewal, and increasing age brings with it an increasing deposit of inorganic substances and hardened matter, a process which affects primarily the walls of the blood-vessels, the heart and lungs. There is a progressive diminution of elasticity, of vital resilience and of general mobility, until finally a stage of infirmity (in the literal sense) is reached; all this rendering eloquent testimony to the whole process of somatic dying. The idea that man is designed for health seen as the smooth inter-functioning of the body-soul unit, or for a state not entailing infirmities, is certainly an illusion which dies hard. Even if Adler's theory of organ-inferiority being the focal point in the formation of neuroses does not too often prove true in practice, it cannot be denied that man begins his life with various somatically preconditioned *loca minoris resistentiae*, varying with his own particular disposition; and one cannot maintain that the general picture given above adds up to a pattern of "health" in the commonly accepted sense of the term.[16]

Media vita in morte sumus[17] ("in the midst of life we are in death") is empirically observable fact. It is manifest not only in the investigation of the psyche, but already in "the sensorial exploration of what is going on in the body." Professor Viktor von Weizsäcker gives many other examples. For instance, "Recent research by Roessle shows that the pathology of inflammation

includes, not only a defensive warfare of cells against other cells or
against foreign bodies with the object of self-preservation, but also
and at the same time a veritable cell-suicide."[18] He himself makes
this "solidarity of death in life" the first principle, not only of his
"medical anthropology," but also of his clinical teaching and practice.[19] Living includes dying, and death is the completion of living.
If health means wholeness, and wholeness includes the principles
of infirmity and death, the healer cannot adopt a purely negative
and hostile attitude towards them.

> The doctor's task is not to make war on death, but to make
> a pact with it. The doctor cannot put death to death, but he
> should make peace with it, and in this way try to outwit it for
> a while.[20]

Von Weizsäcker maintains that, even in general medicine, it
should be borne in mind that death is the end of life, not only in
the sense of end-result, but also in the sense of end-intended or
completion:

> Death is always, not merely the antagonist of life, but a part
> of life itself, without which life would not be life. Goethe's
> *Stirb und werde* expresses the same fact more gently but quite
> completely. However, it is not merely a commendable moral
> maxim, but stubborn fact.[21]

If death is an "end" for somatic medicine, it is still more obviously so for psychological. Von Siebenthal writes:

> If we want to find an "end" (*Ziel*) for psychotherapy which
> will apply in all cases, and which should never be lost sight
> of despite our preoccupation with particular complexes,

repressions, frustrated drives and unhappy relationships, we can come to know it only from a total view of what it is that man is—in actual fact and fundamentally. Truly enough, the way to this end will differ in each case; and, on our side, we may have complete success only seldom. And yet the end of man is everywhere the same. It is, in the last resort, neither pleasure nor riches; it is neither satisfaction of the pleasure-principle, nor adjustment to society or to the reality-principle. It is death. If we [psychiatrists] want to take seriously the people entrusted to us, and if the art of psychotherapy is to be more than a routine technique, we have to concern ourselves with their total situation, and bring the end of psychotherapy into agreement with the end of human beings generally. I mean that we have to orientate the people entrusted to us in the direction in which they are in fact orientated, towards the future and the suffering of eventual death. Any other orientation is unrealistic, or substitutes a part of the way for the whole.[22]

If the nature of health in general is problematic and elusive, that of *mental* health is thus no less so, and has received even less critical attention. It is possible to find textbooks on the subject in which no attempt is made to examine, let alone define, the concept. Such textbooks commonly equate it tacitly with social adaptability and extrovert—usually youthful—efficiency. Popularly it is equated with "normality," which in its turn tends to become equated with humdrum conformism. Such "normality," tacitly assumed to eliminate suffering as well as individuality and originality, is sometimes thought to be the goal of psychiatry and psychotherapy. Many psychotherapists will indignantly reject any such aim for, as Jung rightly points out:

To be a normal human being is probably the most useful and fitting thing of which we can think; but the very notion of a "normal human being," like the concept of adaptation, implies a restriction to the average which seems a desirable improvement only to the man who already has some difficulty in coming to terms with the everyday world—a man, let us say, whose neurosis unfits him for normal life. To be "normal" is the ideal aim for the unsuccessful, for all those who are still below the general level of adaptation. But for people of more than average ability, people who never found it difficult to gain successes and accomplish their share of the world's work—for them the moral compulsion to be normal signifies the bed of Procrustes—deadly and insupportable boredom, a hell of sterility and hopelessness. Consequently there are just as many people who become neurotic because they are merely normal as there are people who are neurotic because they cannot become normal.[23]

It may readily be seen that such standards of normality[24] taken as the criterion of mental health, would exclude not only the saints, but also the exceptional, the original, the creative, the individual in every walk of life. Without denying that psychoses and even neuroses are often endogenous (i.e., originate within the subject) and are not purely reactive to the social environment and pressures, the fact remains that the criteria of "normality," thus understood, are more often those of social acceptability than of medical diagnosis. It is well known that in many societies other than our own, those whom we might account psychotic are given an honourable place in the social structure, and this precisely by reason of their closer contact with the abnormal and the unconscious. It is still uncertain how far psychotic "delusions" are due to a "disease entity" which produces abnormal phenomena rather than to an inability of the ego (and of society) to relate to phenomena which are of themselves quite normal or merely paranormal.[25] The one account does not, in any case, exclude the other.

Latterly there has been a welcome reaction from the conception of mental health which finds its norm in majority opinion, and the reaction has come from sociologists as well as from psychologists. The former are represented by such works as David Riesman's *The Lonely Crowd* and the *Solitude and Privacy* of Paul Halmos. Kenneth Burke has said that "people may be unfitted by being fit in an unfit fitness"[26]; Erich Fromm, that there are those who "have accepted the opinion of the majority so completely that they have been spared the sharp pain of conflict which the neurotic goes through. While they are healthy from the standpoint of 'adjustment,' they are more sick than the neurotic person from the standpoint of the realization of their aims as human beings."[27]

It has been suggested that it was different criteria of mental health, and therefore of the aims of psychotherapy, that occasioned the first rift among the depth-psychologists. In the early days of psychoanalysis "what Freud sought to attain was, before all else, capacity for enjoyment (*Genussfähigkeit*) which is bound up on one side with the riddance of symptoms, and on the other with the drive to satisfy the individual's instincts."[28] For Alfred Adler, on the contrary, "the social standpoint was decisive." Organ inferiority rather than instinct-repression was for him the primary factor in neurosis, and it is understood solely in terms of reaction to social demands. "Man is considered exclusively as a social entity, and correspondingly neurosis for Adler means, in a definite sense, 'anti-sociality'—although, of course, the attainment of social adjustment renders possible again the individual's enjoyment of life."[29]

Jung has steadfastly refused to envisage any one single aim for psychotherapy, except the very general and negative one "to reach a state where the unconscious contents no longer remain unconscious."[30] We have already seen that he advocates the greatest variety of different treatments to meet the variety of individual needs.[31] On this account he finds the ordinary medical procedure of diagnosis and prognosis inapplicable in psychotherapy.

> In flagrant contrast to the rest of medicine, where a definite diagnosis is often, as it were, logically followed by a specific therapy and a more or less certain prognosis, the diagnosis of any particular psychoneurosis means, at most, that some form of psychotherapy is indicated. As to the prognosis, this is in the highest degree independent of the diagnosis.... We are not dealing with clinical diseases but with psychological ones. Whether a person is suffering from hysteria or an anxiety neurosis or a phobia, means little beside the much more important discovery that, shall we say, he is a *fils à papa*.... The true psychological diagnosis becomes apparent only at the end. Just as a sure diagnosis is desirable and a thing to be aimed at in medicine, so, conversely, it will profit the psychotherapist to know as little as possible about specific diagnoses.[32]

No "eclectic" has pleaded more strongly than Jung for a "more extensive individualization of the methods of treatment,"[33] and for the elimination of preconceived aims.

> As far as possible I let pure experience decide the therapeutic aims. This may perhaps seem strange, because it is commonly supposed that the therapist has an aim. But in psychotherapy it seems to me positively advisable for the doctor not to have too fixed an aim. He can hardly know better than the nature and will to live of the patient.... Each of us carries his own lifeform within him—an irrational form which no other can outbid.... We must follow nature as a guide, and what the doctor then

does is less a question of treatment than of developing the creative possibilities latent in the patient himself.[34]

Jung forcefully repudiates the popular belief that successful
treatment will rid the patient of suffering:

> Suffering is not an illness; it is the normal counterpole to hap-
> piness....The principal aim of therapy is not to transport the
> patient to an impossible state of happiness, but to help him to
> acquire steadfastness and philosophic patience in face of suf-
> fering.... Behind a neurosis there is so often concealed all the
> natural and necessary suffering the patient has been unwilling
> to bear.[35]

Even the riddance of the patient's symptoms is not always to
be expected as the result of therapy: "If the worst comes to the
worst, he will even put up with his neurosis."[36]

It is true that Jung often speaks of "individuation" as the aim
of treatment; though even this he does not regard as appropriate for all patients, especially not for younger ones.[37] Yet to call
the aim of therapy "individuation" is, for him, precisely to deny
that there is any one fixed and universal aim, or any clear norm
of mental health to be sought. For by "individuation" he understands, not some common aim, but "the process of forming and
specializing the individual nature...as a differentiated being from
the general collective psychology."[38] It is the process "in which
the patient becomes what he really is"[39] and "the individual way
is never a norm."[40] But individuation consists, anyhow in its later
stages, not in eliminating the collective factors (which is impossible, and would issue only in solipsistic individualism) but in the
individual ego's becoming conscious of them, and so freed from
their unconscious power and enabled to be related to them.

For, even while emphasizing the variables in human psyches, the variations of individual personalities, and the impossibility of foreseeing any one single aim to the therapeutic process, Jung has also drawn attention—to an extent perhaps unrivalled by other psychologists—to the evidence for the basic homogeneity of the psyche and for the presence of universal constants beneath the countless variables and variations.

> I am so profoundly convinced of this homogeneity of the human psyche that I have actually embraced it in the concept of the collective unconscious, as a universal and homogeneous substratum whose homogeneity extends even into a world-wide identity or similarity of myths and fairy tales; so that a negro of the Southern States of America dreams in the motifs of Grecian mythology, and a Swiss grocer's apprentice repeats in his psychosis the vision of an Egyptian gnostic.[41]

Individuation itself means, not individualism and the apotheosis of idiosyncrasies, but a positive relation of the individual ego to the collective archetypes, of which it becomes increasingly conscious.[42] In the process the ego itself becomes profoundly engaged and transformed. Without this conscious relation and engagement of the ego, there is no individuation and no transformation of the personality, no matter how rich the emergence of archetypes. Rather will the ego then become overpowered and swamped by the collective in the way which we observe in the psychoses. On the other hand, just because individuation develops the *individual's* relation to the collective, it renders impossible an uncritical acceptance of collective norms: "it is the development of the psychological individual as a differentiated being from the general, collective psychology."[43]

The "common factor" in the individuation process "is the emergence of certain definite archetypes…the shadow, the animal, the wise old man, the anima, the animus, the mother, the child, besides an indefinite number of archetypes representative of situations."[44] But also, notwithstanding the fact that the individuation process "takes the greatest imaginable variety of forms in different individuals,"[45] it has itself an archetypal character, as Jung has abundantly shown. The hero has a thousand faces,[46] and a thousand different names in as many myths, stories and dreams, yet, despite the diversity of the adventures which befall him, his way is invariably a way of intense suffering and courageous struggle, of departure from the agreeable and the familiar, of confrontation with terror and the unknown, of radical transformation of his personality, before the treasure or the goal can be obtained. We find a similar pattern in countless religious dramas and initiation rituals,[47] in the so-called fertility rites of spring,[48] in fairy stories,[49] in the processes of the alchemists,[50] in the Christian Way of the Cross.[51] In the individuation process, as observed by the psychotherapists today as an "empirical fact,"[52] the like pattern repeats itself. It is never a matter of the riddance of suffering, of the elimination of guilt or of the death-wish, of the reinforcement of the familiar ego-attitudes or conditioning to contented acceptance of the prevailing cultural pattern or values. On the contrary, it means an intensification of suffering, struggle and conflict, and a learning *how* to suffer, an experiencing of guilt and of personal and even cosmic disintegration. So far from eliminating death, it knows of no life except through death—through confrontation with the death-dealing powers of the psyche[53] and the actual accomplishment of successive "deaths of the ego." Without willing renunciation of familiar forms of conscious life, the life of the whole, of what Jung calls the Self, is not realized. "Abdication of the ego" is the first condition of individuation—as distinct from a sterile succession of unconscious images in which there is no participation of the ego. In individuation:

> The patient becomes increasingly aware that the personality is not controllable by consciousness, which is only a part and not even the centre of a transpersonal inner psychic reality. At first this fact is only vaguely appreciated by the ego, which gradually abdicates from its illusion of dominance; as this happens, the transpersonal archetypal forms, laden with affect, come more into the field of consciousness as fantasy images; if the ego relates to these adequately a development begins and progresses in a fairly regular way…it culminates in the emergence of symbols of the Self.[54]

Psychological experience shows that this "abdication of the ego" demands, not weakness, but great strength on the part of the ego.[55] Otherwise psychosis ensues—indeed psychosis may be understood to consist in the weakness of the ego relatively to the power of these unconscious forces.[56] To die, as a positive voluntary act as distinct from passively permitting death to have dominion over us, or from a fatalistic gesture, demands strength, not weakness; and "whosoever will save his life shall lose it." But the ego-abdications of the individuation-process, with their results in newer and higher forms of conscious life, already "orientate us to the end to which we are in fact all orientated"—the dying and death of the whole, seen not as an unfortunate accident, but as the very completion of earthly life as we know it, and always immanent in it. Moreover, these psychological "dyings and risings" already accustom us to *Hope*—the last gift left in Pandora's box amid all the ills and woes of mankind.[57] If these partial dyings bring about life more abundant, it becomes less incredible that the dying of the whole is a gateway to life everlasting in which death is finally overcome. But nor is it surprising that such an achievement requires a strength of the ego which is beyond human capacities, and that it is only in and through the complete, self-sacrificial dying of a God-Man that such a resurrection of the whole could be accomplished.

But although the experiences of the individuation-process thus give our Christian hope a certain plausibility, to the extent that they already accustom us to the pattern of life through death, of the gaining of life or *psyche* through losing it, they cannot of course establish it. Complete, unquestioning hope in God and for God can be established solely on the power, mercies and promises of God himself. As faith is concerned with the humanly unknowable but the divinely known, so hope is concerned with the humanly impossible but the divinely achieved.[58] Though psychology may study intimations of immortality in this life, it can neither achieve nor promise it, and its own field of inquiry and activity is closed with the death of its subject-matter. But as the aim of depth-psychology is the making conscious of what is unconscious, and the aim of individuation, in particular, is the making conscious of the "self"—our own individual way of being whole—their aim is in fact that of human life generally, namely death. For it is death which, in one way or another, finishes and completes us; and the dread of death—the "sickness unto death" of which Kierkegaard wrote so movingly and so profoundly, and which so often lurks behind our trivial but agonizing phobias[59]—is the dread of our failure to become "finished" personalities. As Jung says:

> Death is the great Finisher (*Vollender*).... In death, supreme-
> ly, is completion attained—in one way or another. Death is
> the end of the empirical, and the goal of the spiritual, man....
> Everyone who is not yet where he should be, and has not
> yet brought to pass what should have been brought to pass,

experiences dread (*Angst*) about his end, his final account.
Man evades so long as he can becoming conscious of those
things which are still wanting to his completion, and so hin-
ders becoming conscious of his true "self," and thereby his
readiness for death.[60]

The *horror vacui*—the dread of nothingness and of the end
of ego-consciousness—dissipates with ego-abnegation, sacrifice
and the consequent growth of awareness of the timeless archetypes and of the ego's possibilities of transcending itself. For in the
conscious attainment of completion the primary task of ego-consciousness itself is fulfilled, and it has no more to do: death is swal-
lowed up in victory.

But it is clear that such a consummation is beyond the powers of the ego, and still more so beyond the powers of psychology. Psychology can only draw attention to the facts, and indicate
whither they may lead.

It need hardly be asked how these psychological findings square
with traditional Christian teaching about, and attitudes towards
health, sickness and death. It has, however, been alleged that those
teachings and attitudes have been by no means consistent through
the centuries, and that the triumphant optimism of the first Christian centuries has given place to a resigned defeatism. In recent
centuries there has certainly been a tendency to present health and
sickness as matters purely for medical science, and about which religion has little to say and less to do. The priest and the pastor is to
be called in when the doctor can do no more; the anointing of the
sick, it is alleged, so far from being an efficacious sign of hope and
of health, has become the signal of "no hope" and the equivalent
of a death warrant. Medical science having failed, all that remains
is "spiritual consolation" which is to consist for the most part in
exhortations to passive resignation to the inscrutable will of God,

with the implication that disease and death are his good pleasure, if not his own creation. The crucifix dominates the sick room and the death-bed of the devout Catholic, and he has been taught to "accept death as an act of homage and adoration to the Divine Majesty, and as the only means of coming to his first Beginning and his last End, in union with the death of his dear Redeemer."[61] The devout Anglican is, or was, to be told that "whatsoever your sickness is, know certainly that it is God's visitation" and to "take in good part the chastisement of the Lord."[62]

It is not suggested that the sentiments are disreputable; but they have been contrasted sharply with those of the Bible and the early Church, even though the difference may be mainly of emphasis. For the Bible, the Living God is the *fons vitae*—the source of life—the author of health and wholeness. Death and disease are ascribed solely to his "adversaries," the devil and sin. Man's original, prototypal state, as he issued from the hands of his Creator, was an immortal one where sickness had no place. Already in the Old Testament:

> Healing is one element in the salvation of God which is to be revealed in the last times, for salvation involves both God's rescuing of his people from their oppressors, and their restoration to "wholeness" in every aspect of their lives. Ezechiel pictures the living water flowing out from the restored sanctuary of God for the healing of the nations. He and Jeremiah link their visions of the age of blessedness with the healing of stricken Israel, and Micah speaks of the collective healing of the nation as part of the saving activity of God "in that day." Healing, as part of God's salvation, is therefore eschatological. It is an object of hope....
>
> In the New Testament the healing of mankind remains an eschatological concept. It is still, as Rev. 21 would suggest, an

object of hope. It belongs to the Kingdom of God for whose
coming the Christian prays. Like other aspects of the Kingdom, however, it is already present by anticipation in the ministry of Jesus…. Sin is forgiven, disease is cured, and men are
restored to wholeness….We must never forget that the miraculous healings of Jesus are *signs*. Both in the synoptics and the
Fourth Gospel, this is the primary significance of the "mighty
works."[63]

The same convictions were certainly uppermost in the pre-
Nicene Church.[64] Here again life and health are all from God,
death and disease all from his adversaries. They were not something to be embraced as dubious gifts of God, but to be overcome
in the power of God and his Christ. The figure of the incarnate
and risen Christ presented a new vision of the possibilities open
to man. The risen, rather than the crucified, Christ was the relevant, transforming symbol. Death is still "the end" of our mortal
pilgrimage, for in the Lord's first coming the eschatological hope
is indeed revealed and anticipated, but not yet accomplished on
a cosmic scale: the devil and all his works are not yet everywhere
overcome. But it is purely incidental to the attainment of the immortal completion revealed in the risen Lord. Death has lost its
sting, for "to live is Christ, and to die is gain."[65] What in contemporary eyes was remarkable and indeed unique about the Christian martyrs was not that they suffered excruciating torments for
their beliefs (that was not uncommon), but that they made so
little account of them and even embraced them joyfully, thereby
manifesting the triumph of the Christ-life in and over death itself.
So little was the extinction of mortal life regarded that, as Dr.
Frost says, "the word 'death' itself becomes transferred to the vital
and catastrophic separation from God through sin which severs
the Christian from the regenerate life, or to the equally vital and

catastrophic events which sever the sinner from his old life, that from the waters of Baptism he may rise with Christ in newness of life."[66]

For Aquinas, summarizing the reflections of subsequent centuries, holiness (*sanctitas*), health (*sanitas*), completeness (*perfectio*) and wholeness (*integritas*) are, in principle, virtually synonymous. His one word *salus* does duty for our two words "health" and "salvation." He has, indeed, a keener realization than had some in the early Church, and some of his own contemporaries, that the nature, the *physis*, of man is corruptible and mortal; and though sin is still at the root of his involuntary suffering and mortality, this cannot be because it has introduced some positive poison, but because it has withdrawn man from the supernatural activity of the living God which had prevented the natural seeds of corruption from taking effect.[67] Man's original, prototypal state is one of *integritas*.[68] It was a state of wholeness or rightness; of equity (*iustitia*) in the sense that every part and function of man was given its due, no more and no less, and without expense to that of others. It was a wholeness which arose precisely from the fact that man, so far innocent of sin, was given sanctifying, i.e., holy-making, grace.[69] This brought about, firstly, a harmony of the individual within himself, because all his components, with their variety of functions, are subordinated to and co-ordinated with his understanding and will (his reflecting consciousness), which in their turn are subordinated to and co-ordinated with the mind and will of the Creator.[70] From this came a social harmony of man with man,[71] and a harmony of man with his environment, both in the animal kingdom and in the rest of creation.[72]

The primordial sin, because it was the rejection of sanctifying grace, destroyed man's centredness in God, and is precisely disintegration. For original sin is essentially:

a certain disordered disposition which arises from the dissolution of that harmony in which the original equity had con-
sisted, as bodily sickness is a certain disordered disposition of
the body which arises from the dissolution of that equilibrium
in which health consists. Hence original sin is called a sickness
of nature.... And just as a bodily sickness has a privative element—because the equilibrium of health is taken away—and
a positive element—namely the disordered parts—so original
sin is at once an absence of the original equity, and with this a
disordered disposition of the parts and functions of the soul.[73]

Psychological disorder, in the broadest sense, is thus "normal," and indeed universal, for fallen man, that is to say, for empirical man as we know him. His nature is not destroyed: none of his
essential parts are eliminated, but they *are* disorganized. And like
a machine, though all his parts may be present, and even individ-
ually in good shape, he cannot function as he should when those
parts are not co-ordinated. So fallen man is unable to behave even
as his nature in its integrity requires, let alone do what he can only
do as a "holy" man with God's help and in his grace.[74] Moreover,
once the centre of his cohesion is lost, countless forms of disorder, arising from countless causes, may supervene. A whole and
integral jug is of one shape: once broken it may fall into countless
pieces of different shapes and sizes. Still more do the living parts
and faculties of human nature, deprived of their centre and the
power of grace which bound them equitably together, tend to fly
off in different directions, and at each other's expense in innumer-
able different ways.[75] While not all these may be, by psychiatric
standards, pathological, some may very well be so. Original sin, as
the absence of the original integrity, is not the cause of particular
ailments; but particular ailments with their particular causes would
not exist except for the disorganization, the sickness of nature,

which is common to us all. This is, in Jungian language, the failure, common to us all, fully to realize the archetypal "Self."

Sanctifying grace is, by God's mercy, still available to fallen, disintegrated man. And, on this Thomistic showing, its function is still to perfect, and to bring health and wholeness to human nature, and this precisely by restoring its centre of cohesion in God. Baptism brings forgiveness and the rebirth of the life of grace which the original sin had lost. But it does not automatically restore the prototypal integrity. It is empirically evident enough that, as the Council of Trent pointed out, baptism does not straightway cure the disorder of desires, the disintegration of tendencies which results from the loss of the original innocence and equilibrium.[76] Still less does it eliminate the particular causes of particular disorders, nor is it directly concerned with them. They remain the specific province of medicine, whether somatic or psychological. The suggestion, still too common in some "religious" quarters, that grace and the means of grace—sacraments and prayer—will automatically cure these specific disorders is as unsound theologically as it is medically. It may indeed be a "comfortable" superstition for those who proffer the advice "that one could not possibly become neurotic or psychotic if one avoided mortal sin and went to the sacraments regularly." But for those who receive it, it is a cruel one which will usually bring nothing but disappointment and an additional inducement to utter despair.

For sanctification, since the fall, is no longer a given *fait accompli*, but a process.[77] Just because sanctifying grace perfects nature, and nature as it actually is in its disintegrated condition, it must progressively integrate the whole of it, and this includes its sicknesses and mortality. The integration of death, and of the death-dealing elements, is now an essential part of holiness, as it is of wholeness and health. It must be a painful process, the way of the cross, the integration of the evil which is precisely the

privation of the original wholeness and of the particular disorders
which are consequent on that privation. Following the example
set supremely by Christ, the consequences of sin and of history,
direct and indirect, are now the very condition of sanctification,
the stage on which the drama must be played. The presence in
the souls of the righteous of those consequences, among which
neuroses and psychoses are certainly to be included, even their
exceptionally conspicuous presence, should therefore occasion no
surprise. (This does not of course mean that neuroses and psychoses are necessarily an indication of sanctity—though they may
well offer exceptional opportunities for sanctity just because, as we
have seen, they may be a summons to a yet unrealized wholeness.)
They are positively to be expected, and in their most virulent
forms, in those whom canonization has singled out as exceptional
souls of heroic stature.[78] Wholeness, in the sense of complete re-
integration, is indeed finally the work of grace. But it is still eschatological; something to be hoped for from God rather than fully
achieved in this life. Just because our mortal life is a combination
of living *and* dying, deathless life finally conquers death only when
death has finally conquered mortal life. Although it may be true
that latter-day piety and preaching have damped down too much
the triumphant note of the early Church in the face of sickness and
death, it was always true that crucifixion and purification through
suffering is the only way to resurrection.

All this is, of course, theology: it is not empirically verifiable.
The very existence of grace is a matter of faith, even though psychologists record experiences with their patients of which "you
may safely say: 'This was the grace of God.'"[79] For theology also
the presence of grace—even in ourselves, let alone in others—
cannot be empirically observed or known with certainty. All that
can be said is that certain psychological phenomena, such as the
perception of one's own delight in God or unawareness of having

committed grievous and unrepented sin, enable us to conjecture its presence.

> For the source and the object of grace is God himself, who, on account of his transcendence, is unknown to us... Hence its presence or absence in us cannot be known with certainty.[80]

Grace depends entirely on God; and though the presence of certain psychological phenomena may indicate its presence, their absence does not permit us to affirm *its* absence. Still less does the presence of any involuntary affliction or disorder, whether of soul or body, whether organic, toxic or purely functional and psychogenetic. And even though such a disorder may bring about involuntary disordered attitudes and behaviour, we have no right on their account to suppose that the sanctifying processes of grace are absent, even though the disorders may prevent their outward manifestation. It may well be that it is in and through those disorders that the life of grace is operative, and that the very disorders contribute to the sanctification, whether they be due to a virus, to bacilli or to a father-fixation. There seem to be no grounds whatever for asserting that the tuberculosis of St. Thérèse of Lisieux was a means to her sanctification, a part of her wholeness, but that her attacks of scrupulosity were not.

But, although not empirically verifiable themselves, these theological insights do, I would submit, fit the psychological facts. And they form an indispensable background to any intelligent and realistic discussion of the interrelation of religion and mental health which is not to become sidetracked into irrelevancies. But they will not directly allay the misgivings and answer the practical questions with which this chapter opened. Can it be said that religion is always and everywhere conducive to mental health, even as we have tried to describe it? Or can religion be (as is, after all, commonly suspected) a positive obstacle to mental health and growth and, for that matter, to wholeness and even holiness? Does depth-psychology throw any light on the matter which might be instructive to pastors of souls and to religious people generally? To these questions we must turn, and with as little prejudice as we can, in our final chapter.

XI.

RELIGION AND MENTAL HEALTH

In our last chapter we indicated that mental and emotional disorder is by no means incompatible with personal holiness as theology understands it. Man is still *in via*, and his way is the way of the Cross, whether or not he willingly bears it, and even if he attempts to avoid it. The final triumph over disease and suffering, although revealed in the risen Lord, is still for most of us an eschatological hope rather than an accomplished fact. A Christian is not immune from the common psychic disintegration which theology attributes to an original sin, and indeed his very Christianity presents him with possibilities of conflict and guilt-sense from which others are spared.[1] Nor is he immune from those countless particular causes of particular disorders which afflict humanity.[2] He has, it is true, unique resources at his disposal to enable him to suffer creatively rather than destructively, and to attain—by God's grace—what theology will call a greater Godlikeness, and psychology might call a greater maturity and integration. But it cannot always be asserted that the failure to avail himself of these resources is necessarily due to a deliberate and conscious fault on his part. It *may* indeed be so, and perhaps more often than purely mechanistic psychologists are prepared to allow. But moral and religious earnestness, and even the Word and Sacraments, will not always avail—and neither are they directly intended—to make personal unconscious contents conscious, nor even to adjust and strengthen the ego to recognize them. While "in some cases a religious experience stabilizes a profoundly disturbed person, as can be seen from the lives of such men as John Bunyan, George Fox, Jeremiah and St. Paul...in other cases, severe psychoneurosis adulterates religious experience, reducing it to exceedingly immature and neurotic forms."[3] A man's personal religion may be infected by the general disorder, and so, until itself radically changed, be unable to overcome and integrate it. Indeed it may happen that sincere but misguided efforts to utilize the resources of religion to deal with unconscious complexes will, by strengthening the ego-defences, increase rather than mitigate the disorder. The Biblical story of Job presents us with just such a case. The immensely devout but anxiety-ridden Job intensifies his religious piety, offers sacrifices "continually" and reiterates his protestations of trust in God.[4] But until healed by the final vision, he succeeds only in aggravating its unconscious opposite—the blaspheming "shadow" which he had projected on to his children—and suffers a complete breakdown. The pattern is distressingly familiar to those who have been called upon to deal with the mental and emotional disturbances, and especially the anxiety-neuroses, which sometimes are to be found among the devout.

We have suggested that, although popular conceptions of health and popular conceptions of holiness differ widely from one another, and may sometimes appear to conflict, both conceptions will, if thought through, be found to merge. This is not, however, to say that *religion* is conducive either to health or to wholeness—or indeed, for that matter, to holiness. We have not yet examined the widespread suspicion that "religion does more harm than good," both to the individual and society, and that it induces psychological conflicts and retards psychological maturity. Although an immense amount has been written in recent years on the practical bearings of religion on psychology and of psychology on religion, there doubtless is—and for many more years will be— much more to be said. It is of some importance that we begin by defining our terms. We have, we trust, said enough of our under-standing of health and wholeness; it remains to ask what is to be meant by religion. It may be helpful to use, as a frame of reference, the classical account of religion as we find it summarized and ex-pounded by St. Thomas Aquinas.[5]

For Aquinas, we have seen, holiness is wholeness, and both of them are health—in the most comprehensive sense of that word. But he tells us, rather more surprisingly, that religion is holiness too.[6] His argument for this assertion is not, it must be admitted, based on the factual evidence we might reasonably seek, nor does it take the slightest notice of the factual evidence which suggests the contrary. His thought, we may consider, moves in a tranquil sphere of pure ideas, unsullied by disagreeable facts like the statis-tics for juvenile delinquency of those who have attended denomi-national schools, the prevalence of inhibitions and guilt-complexes among the devout, the horrors and crimes which men have com-mitted in the name of religion and which have led succeeding generations to re-echo Lucretius's "Tantum religio potuit suadere malorum."[7] Indeed, the argument rests on nothing more solid than some questionable etymology, and need not detain us.

But there is more in the treatise *On Religion* of Aquinas than this, and which may be more helpful to our purposes. On first reading, this may seem not to be so. We may feel that, throughout the treatise, the saint's mind moves in a realm of ideas and ideals far removed from the facts of what is called religion in our soci-ety, or even in the annals of religion generally. And it is true that he is not concerned with empirical *Religionswissenschaft*, and his method is not inductive, notwithstanding his occasional reference to religious phenomena by way of illustration. He is, quite openly, concerned with what religion ought to be rather than with what in fact often bears its name. This is evident from the context in which the treatise is set. It occurs in that Second Part of his *Summa* whose declared subject-matter is man viewed as the image of God, and capable of directing his actions to the realization of that image or deviating from it.[8] The setting is thus a moral setting, and within that setting religion is considered as a class of human activity which should promote the attainment of that end. Aquinas is well aware that there is false and harmful religion as well as true and beneficial religion, though he will not dignify the former with its name. In this moral context, idolatry, superstition and the various forms of magic are not types of religion, but precisely sins against religion, and he stresses their harmfulness to man. This approach to the subject will seem foreign to those accustomed to a more empirical approach. But it should not be valueless to the practising therapist who seeks to understand the correct functioning of an organ if he is to treat its irregularities and disorders, and who has come to appreciate that his patients' religion—or pseudo-religion or irreligion—is a psychological factor which he can neither ignore nor amputate. While we would not ask him to accept this classical "philosophy of religion" uncritically, it may perhaps stimulate him to reflections which a purely empirical or statistical treatment fails to provide. We shall suggest that he, in return, has much to offer the pastor, the religious educator and religious people generally in their own concern with the practical workings of religion.

Religion, then, as Aquinas and the ancients understood it, is a human activity. An unpractised religion is no more religion than looking at a painting is painting. It *is* a practice, not a theory. Even though it may be said to presuppose a theory—at least that if the existence of the Divine and man's dependence upon it—that theory is seldom, if ever, worked out theoretically and then acted upon. Man seldom proves the existence of God intellectually, and then worships him. Rather does the reality of God and human dependence become realized in religious practice itself. It is in and through his religious practices that he will find his theophanies,

his images and conceptions of Divinity, and although these practices may be accompanied by verbal instruction and intellectual
apprehensions, his understanding of them will normally be conditioned by his actual religious experiences. Nor is theory about
religion itself religion. Talk about it, even understanding it and its
psychological mechanism, are no substitute for it, any more than
understanding justice or courage is any substitute for being just or
courageous. Yet discussion and understanding of religion can help
us to understand what we are doing, or are supposed to be doing
and perhaps failing to do, and what it is we are doing to ourselves.
For—and Aquinas will let us make no mistake about it—religion
is of no benefit to God, but only to ourselves.[9]

Nevertheless, religion differs essentially from magic, however much, in actual fact, the two may be mixed. Magic seeks to
harness superhuman powers to human use, to the aims, good or
bad, of the ego.[10] To "sell" religion for its psychological benefits
is to run a grave risk of destroying religion and turning it into a
species of magic. Religion, on the contrary, is the ego's expression
of subjection to, and dependence upon, superhuman power. It is,
according to a definition of Cicero echoed by Aquinas, "the virtue which brings reverence and awe to the higher nature which is
called 'divine.'"[11] It is a willing bringing (*afferre*) of reverence and
awe, not a mere passive being overwhelmed by a numinous experience; although, doubtless, it will commonly presuppose some
such experience, whether it occurs privately in the individual psyche or is communicated in the ritual of the group. Religion has,
as Aquinas explains it, a certain likeness to justice. For as justice
is the bringing to another fellow-human of what is due to him,
so religion may be considered as the bringing of what is due to
almighty God, to the unknown and unseen Mystery behind the
universe and on which, it is assumed, our own existence and well-
being depend. But strict justice is possible only between equals,

for only between equals can dues be paid at parity (*aquum*). What we "owe" to our parents or our country, what is "due" to them from us, can never be a strictly just *quid pro quo*, since they are "the sources of our existence and of our upbringing," and for these we incur a debt which we are unable to repay either in kind or equivalently. Nor, though to a lesser degree, can we adequately repay what we owe to governors and teachers. To all of these we owe, not the strict justice which is due to equals, but some measure of honour or reverence—honour being precisely that which is due to those who, in one way or another, excel us. *Pietas* was the name given, at least since Cicero, to the honour due to the parents and fatherland; *observantia*, to the honour due to governors and teachers. *Religion* is what is due to God alone.

> Man is a debtor to different objects differently, corresponding to the different ways in which they excel him, and the different benefits he receives from them. God is supreme in both respects, for he transcends all, and is the First Source of our being and government.[12]

Our dependence on God is total, his claim on us is limitless and strictly unpayable, his Lordship is absolute. By religion the ego consciously and willingly expresses its actual situation of creatureliness and dependence, and it expresses it in service (*servitus*). Being a total dependence, it is expressed in forms of service which differ in kind, and not merely in degree, from those which can be given to any fellow-creature, even the most venerable. It is *latreia* as distinct from *douleia*.[13] Thus religion is, or should be, a virtue in the sense of a disposition which benefits the subject and his activities.[14] The activities which we call religious are beneficial because they express a conscious and willing recognition of man's place in the universe: they benefit him because they impress him with this recognition and enable him to live in accordance with the realities of his situation. Some of these activities are specifically and exclusively religious—adoration, prayer, sacrifice. We do not find them apart from religion. These are all labelled with the general name "*cultus*"—they are a *colere*, a cultivation of the Divine. But religion should govern (*imperare*) all human activities. All that a man does, can and should be done as an act of creaturely reverence and service to God. It is in this sense that "religion clean and undefiled before God and the Father is this: to visit the fatherless and widows in their affliction and to keep oneself unspotted from this world."[15] But what gives any action a religious quality, whether or not it be itself specifically religious, is the underlying will to give oneself and one's actions to the service of God—a conative act which Aquinas calls *devotio*, but which we should render as self-consecration or devotedness rather than as devotion. It is, as such, a matter purely of will and intention, which may or may not be accompanied by "devout" emotions.

Religion is not, in the technical sense, a "theological virtue." Unlike faith, hope and charity, its immediate object and concern is not God himself, but this *cultus* of God. God is that *to* which (*objectum cui*) religion is directed, but its immediate concern (*objectum quod*) is not the Creator but these creaturely recognitions of the creature's situation before the Creator. It is not, as such, supernatural, though by grace, faith, hope and charity it may be supernaturalized. In itself it is quite natural; it is consequent upon man's recognition of his dependent place in the world, his subordination to higher powers, and supremely to the Author of all. Religion may, indeed, come more "naturally" to some than to others: to some it may mean a comparatively effortless and unreflected response to numinous experience, to others it may mean tedious and perhaps bored endeavour. To all it means a certain playing of a role: a performance which achieves no immediate utilitarian end

outside of man himself. But the role is a reasonable and realistic
one, precisely because it puts the ego in its place, and not merely
in theory but in actual practice. Worship, praise, prayer, sacrifice
are all acted-out recognitions that, as Jung puts it:

> ...even the enlightened person remains what he is, and is nev-
> er more than his own limited ego before the One who dwells
> within him, whose form has no knowable boundaries, who
> encompasses him on all sides, fathomless as the abysms of the
> earth and vast as the sky.[16]

The acting-out[17] is, in the Thomist view, of great importance.
Truly, "God is a spirit, and they that adore him must adore him in
spirit and truth."[18] The interior, mental and voluntary element in
religion is essential and primary; without it there is no intelligent,
voluntary submission to God, and the external performance will
become a meaningless, perfunctory and perhaps hypocritical routine. But the whole man being God's creature, his religion should
be expressed by his whole being, soul and body. Appropriate bodily posture and gesture, in which mental and physical attitudes are
harmonized, will also be required "in order that," as Aquinas puts
it, "the mind of man may, by signs and symbols, be stirred to those
mental acts whereby he is joined to God."[19]

It may be urged that this Thomist picture of religion is an
unduly ideal and sophisticated one, inapplicable to much that can
be called genuine religion and to many earlier stages in its growth
and development. It must be readily conceded that it describes a
fairly fully-fledged and adult religion which is not to be found or
expected among primitives or children. It presupposes, even while
it helps to establish, a differentiated ego and a personal will such as
hardly emerge before adolescence. There can be little doubt that a
magical phase commonly precedes anything that approximates to

what we have described as religion, and that this phase is an important and a normal one in establishing the ego. Mrs. Eve Lewis has drawn striking attention to the magical character of children's thought, play and ideals during the latency period of middle childhood; but she also points out the necessity for the sacrifice of the "inflated ego of middle childhood" in early adolescence, and how the spontaneous outpouring of phantasy and play which comes in pre-adolescent years symbolizes the putting away of these childish things.[20] It is, however, precisely with fully-fledged religion as an aim and a standard of appraisal that we are here concerned.

It may still be objected that our picture is a purely Occidental one, and that to analyse religion in terms of Graeco-Roman ideas of justice is inappropriate to religious phenomena outside the European tradition. Elsewhere, it may be said, and to a very large extent among both mystics and simple people in the West itself, religion is more a matter of ecstatic identification with the God through ritual or inner experience, in which the ego is eliminated or absorbed, than a conscious moral obligation of the ego itself towards what completely transcends it. Whether or not we call such identification by the name of religion is largely a matter of words. But for Aquinas also, contemplation or meditation of some sort is indeed an indispensable preliminary to and accompaniment of religion.[21] Since will follows upon thought, there can be no willing service of God without thought of God. Thought and meditation, he recognizes elsewhere, do indeed tend to that obliteration of the subject in the object which he calls ecstasy.[22] But the thought which prompts religion, he continues, will be not only about God, religion's "object," but also about its "subject," our own needs and dependence upon God. Such thought, however, though an indispensable cause of religion, is not itself religion, which remains essentially conative rather than cognitive. Thus understood, religion is in no way an obliteration or suppression of the ego, nor an escape from the ego into the purely archetypal or transcendental, but a conscious, rational and ethical relationship of the ego to what transcends not only the ego but the whole cosmos.

Whether or not we may derive the very word "religion" from *religare* (to "tie up" or "bind together"[23]), it is hardly disputable that religion, understood and acted out in this way, will function automatically as an integrating function of the whole personality, and of any society in which it is established as a norm of behaviour. It will combine and co-ordinate the whole range of human functions and activities, interior and exterior, mental, emotional and physical, in a single unity of aim. This it will do, to the extent that it is uncontaminated by magic, not by subordinating the non-ego to the ego, but contrariwise by subordinating the ego to the absolutely Other—*das ganz Andere*. This will not (as Jung occasionally seems to fear) depotentiate the ego, for it will not unconsciously project its own power onto the other, thus alienating from the ego its own energy and transferring it to the Divinity, but rather find its own power in its own positive relation of dependence on the Omnipotent.[24] At the same time, religion should ensure that psychological functions, though co-ordinated through their subordination to what lies wholly beyond them, are duly activated and differentiated from one another. The ego is absorbed neither by the "self," nor by the archetypal generally, but precisely differentiated from them by religion's own establishment of a conscious relationship to them, and should thus be preserved from those psychological disorders which the Jungians call "inflation."[25] On the other hand, the ego is delivered from those unrealistic assumptions of isolated autonomy and supremacy which theology calls *superbia* and which psychology finds at the root of most neuroses. In specifically religious activities, such as worship, praise and sacrifice, the "persona" plays a role which is no longer—as inevitably in "profane" life—a mask which hides the authentic individual in response to social demands, but one which expresses the attitude both of the worshipping individual and the worshipping community of which he is a member.[26] Moreover, every known form of religion appears to have some ritual or method to activate the "shadow" and to deal with it, whether by transference to a scapegoat, a ritually-induced experience of rebirth, detailed confession and absolution of personal sin, or some other form of collective or individual purification. This is so notwithstanding the fact that the specification of *what* is to be considered to be evil, shadowy or disintegrating differs widely from group to group and, among more highly individualized peoples, even between individual and individual, in spite of certain common norms. The "anima," the "feminine principle" in the psyche, is likewise activated by religion. What St. Augustine called "that part of the soul which is, as it were, an image or type of woman in every soul"[27] is that which is able to express the religious attitude of the creature towards God. It is that which, as St. Augustine explains, was tempted in Eve and which consents as maiden, bride and mother in Mary and the Church.[28] Although religion is a willing activity of the ego, the activity of the ego and the will is here precisely that of consent to the subordination of the "anima" to the Divinity.[29]

The psychological function of religion, at once integrating and differentiating, becomes clearer when we reflect upon these specifically religious activities themselves. Prayer, understood in the simplest way of asking God for what we want, involves a forthright acknowledgment of human wants. Stoics in Europe, and Buddhists in the Far East, have seen that human desires are the cause of all human misery and wickedness, and have devised techniques for their elimination. But to want is human, and inseparable from finite existence, and to cease to want is to cease to be human. The Stoic, for all his magnificent ideals, tended to become a little god at other people's expense and that of his own common humanity.

The Buddhist frankly recognizes that the final extinction of want is also the final extinction of human existence in Nirvana. Psychology shows that while conscious wants, especially when unrelated to the needs of the whole personality and of society, can be harmful enough when recognized, unconscious wants are still more damaging both to the individual and to society. By prayer, if it is genuine and not only a parrot-like repetition of other people's formulas, a man is led to recognize *that* he wants and to formulate *what* he wants, and not to repress his wants as an evil to be eliminated, but to see them as an essential element of his condition as a human creature. Particular wants, by being related to God, cease to function autonomously, but are consciously related to the whole, the "self." So far from being incompatible with religion, they become material for his recognition of his dependence on the Author of all, as well as the motive for his own secular strivings. Aquinas sees that prayer, so far from being a magical means for the attainment of egotistic aims, is automatically a practical recognition of the sovereignty, power and bounty of God.[30] Thus a child by asking its mother for what it wants not only seeks to obtain it but, by the very fact of asking, acknowledges in a concrete and practical way that she is the giver and its own dependence on her. Magic seeks to effect what the ego wants. Prayer, Aquinas explains, is not an effective cause which itself produces what we want, but a "dispositive" cause which disposes us to receive it as a gift of the Author and Giver of all. Prayer thus integrates the ego's wants and desires, whether for daily bread or for spiritual riches, with what utterly transcends it and all finite goods. The ego's autonomy over and against the "self," and even against the cosmos, is progressively overcome by disposing it to receive the fulfilment of its wants from the Lord of all.

Prayer, in this primary sense of petition and intercession, may be purely interior, or may be also expressed exteriorly in words and posture. Sacrifice, on the other hand, is essentially an external act, though it expresses and promotes an interior attitude: the attitude of complete self-giving and the renunciation of every egoistic claim which recognition of the all-embracing sovereignty of God requires. Jung came early upon the motif of sacrifice in the dreams of modern and "irreligious" people as an archetypal symbol of psychological transformation, and the indispensable condition of psychic growth and individuation. It was his final chapter, that on "The Sacrifice" in his *Symbols of Transformation* in 1912, that first marks his most radical departure from the ego-centred orientation of early psychoanalysis and his revaluation—his "Copernican revolution"[31]—of the interrelation of the ego and the unconscious. In his *Transformation Symbolism in the Mass*,[32] which reached its final form forty years later, he has given us a more profound analysis of the psychological function of ritual sacrifice generally, and of the Mass especially.[33]

From this picture of ideal religion we have omitted all specifically Christian characteristics; for example, the spirit of joy, peace, patience and the rest which St. Paul ascribes to Christian practice.[34] We may have had the good fortune to have known people who are "religious" in the way described, whose eyes are single and whose whole lives are a harmonious service of God, stabilized, integrated, differentiated and matured through their specifically religious observances. But we shall have to admit that such people are rare and, understandably enough, they are never seen professionally by psychiatrists and psychotherapists. They need no physician, and will trouble neither the psychologist nor the pastor of souls.

Far more troublesome to both is the celebrated "failure of religion" in the modern world. By this we may understand not only the alienation of vast numbers of people from any sort of recognized religious practice, public or private (a phenomenon unprecedented in the history of mankind), and the fact that many appear to do quite nicely without it, but also the "lapse" or "loss of faith" of a considerable percentage of adolescents and young people who in home or school have had a careful religious upbringing. To this we should add the apparent failure, in many cases, of the religion of professedly religious people to function as a wholesome psychological factor, even when it does not, to all appearances, function rather as a source of, or pretext for, psychological retardment or disorder. This "failure of religion" has of course, and notwithstanding some increases in church-attendance in recent years, been a matter of anxious inquiry and interesting experimentation among religious leaders and educators. Christians, in particular, can hardly ignore it without ignoring their obligation to evangelization. But little attention seems yet to have been paid to the contributions which depth-psychology might make to the understanding of the problem, and perhaps towards its at least partial solution. The depth-psychologists themselves have, in very large measure, had to concern themselves mostly with the problems of those already estranged from religious practice and profession. Their very craft has come into existence as a "secularized cure of souls"[35] to cope with problems brought about, as many of them recognize, by the breakdown of old-time religion as a primary factor in social and psychological hygiene.[36] They have on that account little to say directly on the problem as it confronts the religiously committed. But it seems that their findings are often highly relevant. Although their findings will not permit us to make dogmatic and generalized assertions about all the causes and cures of the "failure of religion," they do at least suggest certain working hypotheses for investigation; hypotheses which have been to some extent confirmed by some of us who have had occasion to work with concrete cases of "religious failure."

It is, of course, possible to attribute this "failure of religion" simply to a moral failure, a failure of will. According to this view the adolescent who "lapses," who "loses his faith" and abandons religious observance after leaving school, does so only through his own fault. Similarly the adult who fails to make his life a unified service of God, and who neglects the resources of religious observances, simply fails in that willingness to give himself to the service of God which Aquinas calls *devotio* and which, as we have seen, is the mainspring of an adult and mature religion. Those who—it may be further alleged—although regular and even keen churchgoers, nevertheless appear to make of their religion a departmentalized factor which makes for disharmony and immaturity, have only themselves to blame for having failed in that total self-giving which the service of Almighty God requires. This simple diagnosis of the "failure of religion" as due to a blameworthy moral failure is not, however, always confirmed by experience, and it is a judgment which it might be wise to leave to the Judge who alone knows all the secrets of the heart. We cannot indeed leave this moral factor out of account; especially if we are to hold, as we have done, that adult religion is a moral obligation and not merely a compulsive, automatic reflex to given stimuli. The Luciferian *non serviam* (I will not serve) is a powerful impulse in us all; and it cannot be denied that irreligion or inadequate religion can and does sometimes arise from a moral failure of will. But, as Mrs. Eve Lewis points out, the transformation of the "magical" attitude of middle childhood to the religious attitude demanded of adolescence—as indeed is the transition from childhood to adolescence generally—is not an easy one.[37] It is, as she says, all the more difficult in our modern Western civilization with its absence of puberty rites, and hence "no clear-cut break between childhood and adult life as there has always been for primitive man." The difficulty is enhanced where there is no impressive rite like Confirmation to mark the transition and inculcate symbolically a sense of adult responsibility, or where the rite is anticipated in childhood years when it is, however supernaturally efficacious, symbolically and psychologically premature and meaningless. Dr. H. C. Rümke, while maintaining that "unbelief [he seems rather to mean irreligion] is an interruption in development," nevertheless also points out the fears which must be overcome, the apparent threats to the ego, which religious surrender to God demands.[38] The possibility of irreligion, of not serving, must at least be faced and considered before religion as voluntary choice can come into being. Childhood conditioning, and the perpetuation of the magical attitude which the adolescent finds no longer to work in real life as he now begins to experience it, may often prevent such a choice from ever being even entertained. In many cases, it would seem, there has been no moral failure of will; the moral choice has never arisen. The choice, so far as there has been any conscious choice at all, has been between the continuation of a collective childhood pattern of behaviour, inculcated by and inseparably associated with the collective behaviour of the family or the school, together with magical thinking now outgrown, and abandonment of the whole business of religion as irrelevant to life as now experienced, and inconsistent with its new demands for self-reliance.

Psychology cannot of course pronounce whether the decision should be for or against religion. It can only observe its presence or absence, the forms that religion or substitutes for religion take, and mark their effects on the personality as a whole. It can also observe that certain religious forms and images are efficacious, and that others are not, and to some extent account for their efficaciousness or inefficaciousness as psychological factors and determinants. It must however point out that religion and irreligion are not wholly a matter of will—and nor are faith or unfaith. Will cannot operate in a void: the field of conation is limited by the field of cognition. It must have an object. Faith also cannot operate in a void. We have seen that, even from the theological standpoint, *fides qua*, the gift of faith by which we believe, requires *fides quae*, *enuntiabilia* or *credenda* which are ultimately mediated and expressed in experienced images and symbols.[39] We should not lightly charge with deliberate unbelief or loss of faith those who may only have suffered the frightful loss of a world-picture, a set of childish images, which no longer ring true to inner and outer experience, and the demands of a more responsible life. They have not necessarily wilfully abandoned faith in the *prima veritas*, in ultimate truth, or submissive receptivity to the mind of the Creator. On the contrary, it may be that loyalty to truth itself appeared to them to demand the abandonment of presentations of it which no longer expressed it. To state matters in Thomistic terms: will follows upon intellectual apprehension, and what is not intellectually apprehended is outside the range of will, choice and personal decision. Intellectual apprehension, according to the same account, is in its turn dependent upon images—it is an *abstractio a phantasmatibus*—and what is not imaged is not apprehended and consequently not capable of being willed, of being an object for choice and decision. In the "energetic" terms of Jung's psychology, will is "that sum of psychic energy which is disposable to consciousness.... A psychic process, therefore, which is conditioned by unconscious motivation, I would not include under the concept of will."[40] On this Jungian account also, consciousness presupposes imagery, and it is only by symbolization that unconscious contents become conscious and psychic energy (*libido*) becomes disposable.[41]

Furthermore, an image or a set of associated images, which is to function as a principle of integration, must present no partial system or dissociated complex, but must be capable of constellating the whole personality and of reflecting its own potentialities of development and growth. A fixed image, like an *idée fixe*, evokes only a fixed stare, and so long as it is emotionally adhered to as a model for the personality, or as demanding its total allegiance, it will inhibit development and growth. A veritable symbol, which is both living and psychologically efficacious, must constellate both conscious and unconscious contents, and can therefore never be a deliberate construction of conscious apprehension alone. If, finally, it is to present what demands the total service of religion, it must also have a collective archetypal character. It must make present to consciousness what can claim such total surrender. Such surrender cannot be without sacrifice of whatever may hinder it, but may not be given to what restricts or injures the genuine possibilities of the personality and the fulfilment of its destiny. Theologically speaking, total surrender (*latreia*) to anything less than the Infinite is idolatry, and the effect of idolatry, as Old Testament prophets remarked, is to limit and degrade the idolater to the likeness of his idol. Neurotic disorder in the form of a fixation may be expected if the whole personality is surrendered, or pretence is made that it surrenders, to an object whose image positively excludes actual or potential parts of it. Two (or more) mutually exclusive images or sets of images will correspond to mutually exclusive autonomous complexes, and to the extent that one or all of them are unconscious and emotionally charged, the conflict between them is likely to be disintegrating and neurotic. At best the one will be a mere compensation for the other, and if the one is associated with "religion" and the other is not, the "religion" may become, so far from integrating, a source of psychological dissociation and, in all probability, of alternations of "religious" and highly irreligious behaviour. There are certainly many worse things, from the point of view of mental health and balance, than a purely compensatory religion—the hour's Sunday "service" which "makes up for" the rest of the week devoted to quite other and unrelated services—provided that there is no self-deception that it is any more than it is. But compensation is not integration, and it seldom permanently satisfies the psyche's need for wholeness, any more than it satisfies the Almighty's demand for total service—to say nothing of his "chief commandment" to love him with all our heart, mind, soul and might. Psychologically as well as theologically, a purely compensatory religion is still a "failure of religion."

A recapitulation of some of the contentions in our previous chapters may suggest ways in which the findings of depth-psychology might assist us in understanding and remedying these various "failures of religion." We maintained in our first chapter that a dichotomy of soul and psyche—the first understood as the domain of the theologian and pastor, the second as the domain of the psychologist and psychotherapist—is untenable alike from the standpoint of an integral theology and that of an integral psychology. Such a dichotomy can only foster an immature religion which positively excludes large parts of the personality from a religious integration, even if it does not also encourage a neurotic split of the personality. We then saw that psychology, to the extent that it is concerned with the health and wholeness of the personality, has found it increasingly impossible to exclude problems of *Weltanschauung*, of man's place in the universe, of the aims of human life and action—all of them concerns of religion—from its own domain. At the same time, depth-psychologists have drawn attention to, and studied, those basic psychological factors which Jungians call primordial images or archetypes. Their importance to theologians and pastors lies in the fact that they are shown to be the raw material of religion, the endopsychic, "built-in" determinants and patterns of religious behaviour. We have indeed had to question some of Jung's interpretations of these data; in particular his exclusion of affirmations of divine transcendence from psychological consideration, his disinclination to distinguish the God-imago from symbols of the "self," and especially the Trinity from the quaternity. We have also had to bring some qualification to his view of the psychological function of dogma in general and of some dogmas in particular, and to suggest some correctives to the distortions which his conceptions of good and evil impose on some religious doctrines and practices. But these questions and criticisms, though of considerable practical consequence, leave his empirical findings intact, and their importance in the practical functioning or malfunctioning of religion should be immense. It seems to be established beyond doubt that these archetypes are operative in all religions, and that all religious forms result from their interaction with various forms of social or individual consciousness. Whatever the uniqueness of Christianity, its differences from, and even opposition to, other religious forms, it is, in this respect, no exception. In the archetypes, the theologian, the pastor and the religious teacher may find that point-of-contact, the *Anknüpfungspunkt*, between the Word of God and the "natural man" which has been the subject of much theological discussion in recent decades. This discovery is not altogether new. Tertullian, in his *De Testimonio Animae*, long ago indicated that such primordial images of the "untutored soul" form the common ground between Christian and non-Christian, and provide the material with which the Christian revelation has to do.[42]

There can be no doubt that, in past ages, external religious images and forms corresponded closely to archetypes. By religious images we are of course to understand not only visual images, painted or sculptured, but also the image of the Divine evoked by myth and story, hymn and doctrine, sacred drama and dance. By religious forms we may here understand all those activities whereby men have expressed their attitudes to their God or gods. Widely as these have differed from one another in different cultures and among different peoples, and great as are the changes they have undergone, they were the more or less direct expression of what we now call archetypes. Indeed they are one of our principal sources of information about the archetypes themselves, and a principal term of reference for the method of "amplification" employed by analytical psychologists today.[43] Hebrew and Christian religion, it is true, convey a message which can never be derived from the archetypes alone, but that message was never independent of them, let alone alien to them. We have accepted, at least as a plausible hypothesis, Jung's contention that even the doctrine of the Trinity corresponds to an archetype, while recognizing (as he also does) that its statements about the Three in One are quite unique. In the God-Man also we find an archetype, although outside Christianity there is never presented so absolute a union of extreme opposites as does the Nicene and Chalcedonian doctrine of the unmixed union of the Infinite and the finite, each retaining its own integrity.[44] We have found an illustration of the conformity of Christian forms with archetypal patterns of psychic development in the ancient pre-baptismal rituals. Such illustrations could be multiplied indefinitely. As Dr. Austin Farrer has shown, Christianity meant not an abandonment, but a transformation, a rebirth of the primordial images.[45] The central New Testament rites of Baptism and Eucharist, as had been the Old Testament rites of circumcision, Passover, scapegoat and animal sacrifice, were not new forms, but old forms given a new and, we may say, a perfected significance. The early Church in the Graeco-Roman world, for all its opposition to paganism and idolatry, took over the archetypal forms already familiar to that world, as Father Hugo Rahner has shown in detail.[46] It understood, with Justin Martyr, that "Christ is the Logos in whom the whole human race participates; and all who lived in accord with this Logos were Christians, even if they were considered to be atheists as were Socrates and Heraclitus."[47] For Clement of Alexandria this use of "pagan" images was deliberate policy: "Come, I will show you the Logos and the mysteries of the Logos, and I will show them to you in the images which are entrusted to you."[48]

Is this altogether the case today? Of course the mysteries of the Trinity and the Incarnation retain their revered position in catechetical instruction, but perhaps are hardly presented as living images or images for our own living, and may be even too revered to operate efficaciously as psychological dominants. But we might ask what, by and large, are the images which are conveyed to our Christian children in actual fact in their homes, churches and schools. How do they correspond with their actual psychological needs and with the archetypal processes which, it is established beyond doubt,[49] take place in them? To answer such questions satisfactorily requires more experience than we can claim, but the findings of depth-psychology suggest that they deserve investigation. Some experience with adult "failures of religion" does, however, indicate that the inappropriateness of the "holy images" given to children (and not only to children!) is a frequent cause of subsequent "lapse" and of religious and psychological conflicts which can take neurotic forms. We may suspect that the ecclesiastical artist and hymnographer, and those who supply their wares to our infants and early teenagers, carry a responsibility which is insufficiently recognized. The images associated with religion, and which are presented in childhood, have a remarkable persistence, and when inadequate can inflict a lasting damage which merely intellectual correction can do little to repair. A picture of God or Christ which is presented only or mainly as forbidding this, that or the other, will operate psychologically as a purely forbidding or repressive factor, and will not easily develop into a comprehensive and integrating one. On the other hand a picture which expresses only gentleness and sweetness will hardly integrate growing experience of the brute facts of life and its challenges to firmness and struggle. Against the claims of each to total allegiance the growing ego must itself struggle if it is to survive, just as physical growth demands that outgrown clothes be discarded. When such images are not discarded, they may, and sometimes do, constellate complexes which come into conflict with other factors in the personality. It may be urged that our forefathers succeeded in bringing up their offspring in godliness without assistance from child-psychologists. But neither do they appear to have made special provision for them in some illusory belief that they understood their children's special needs. It is only comparatively recently that we have thought fit to offer our children the insipidities of "children's corners," the sentimental doggerel of those hymns which are labelled "For Children," or the saccharine "holy pictures" on the walls of denominational schools. These, too often, leave a permanent impression of what is authentically "religious" or "Christian" with which the fleeting words of even the wisest catechist or teacher can hardly compete. Our present knowledge of psychology suggests that such images more often represent the adult's compensating projections rather than anything that corresponds to the child's own needs or archetypal experiences. We do not deny that many children may *like* such pictures, though perhaps more often they merely feel they *ought* to like them in deference to adult expectations. They also like sweets, but cannot live on them throughout their lives. The Christian child of earlier ages had to make do with the same pictures as his elders. He was not, in any case, under the same social pressures as is the modern child not to be "soft" and "sissy" in everything *except* religion. But in the awesome figure of the Pantokrator over the apse he would, we may suppose, be presented with an image conveying to him that sense of mysterious, stern but benevolent *power* which, as has been shown, is the primary concern of middle-childhood years, and which would never lose its validity. In such a Christ-figure he would find the supernatural, miracle-working hero who could wholesomely claim all his allegiance, and whom he would find no occasion to abandon with the changing demands and attitudes of later years. He will not be almost forced, as are many modern children, to seek provision for these archetypal needs in miraculous supermen and space-travellers wholly unassociated with what is presented to him as religion.

Professor Eliade may be right in principle when he finds that the uniqueness of Hebrew-Christian religion lies in its abolition of the division between the sacred and the profane, the archetypal and the historical.[50] But paradoxically enough the impoverishment of sacred images and their isolation from profane ones seem to have been carried to unprecedented extremes in latter-day Christendom. The dance, the drama and nearly every rhythmic expression, together with most other forms of symbolization, have been progressively excluded from divine worship and secularized. Even among Catholics, for all the greater richness of imagery with which they are surrounded, much has been lost and banished from association with the "sacred." The portrayal of "shadow" figures in devils and gargoyles, of "secular" activities on misericords, have been eliminated from the sacred precincts; and even the portrayal of Old Testament heroes, villains and events, usual in medieval churches, is seldom found in modern ones. The full light of the New Testament blazes at once without any *praeparatio evangelica*. Our Christian ancestors, for all their ignorance of methodical psychology, had more insight than we into the immense varieties of the needs of individual souls, and into their varying capacities and degrees of religious growth and understanding. Not only the human race, but also the human individual, needs a graded pedagogy if he is to be led to the fullness of Christ. Modern psychology confirms that the religious teacher or leader can damage the soul or psyche both by giving it too much too soon, or too little too late: meat to babes or an enforced milk-diet to the mature. Aquinas recalled an ancient, but now largely forgotten, insight when he pointed out that the Old Testament of written law enforced by fear, and the interior law of the New Testament "whose entire power consists in the grace of the Holy Ghost through faith in Christ"[51] represent not only stages in the general *Heilsgeschichte*: they also represent stages in individual religious development, whether the individual happened to live before Christ or afterwards.

> For there were some, under the conditions of the Old Testament, who possessed divine charity and the grace of the Holy Ghost, and who were principally intent upon God's spiritual and eternal promises. To the extent that they did so, they already belonged to the New Law. Similarly there are some in New Testament conditions who are still materialistically minded, and have not yet attained to the perfection of the New Law. On this account they require to be persuaded to good works by fear of punishment and by the incentives of temporal promises.[52]

As these are unready for the fullness of New Testament standards of the interior life of the Spirit, and the full liberty of the sons of God, so there are others for whom detailed prescriptions sanctioned by threats must be soul-destroying and unendurable. Aquinas echoes Augustine's complaint about "those who load even *our* religion with enslaving burdens, and to such an extent that the condition of the Jews was more tolerable, notwithstanding the fact that God's mercy has willed our religion to be free, and to consist in the simplest and fewest possible observances."[53]

Much earlier still, Origen drew particular attention to the need for a great variety of images to meet individual needs and capacities. The incarnate Logos himself has enumerable facets, *epinoiai* or *theoremeta*—Wisdom, Word, Truth, Life, Light, Shepherd, Healer, Master, King, Vine, Bread, Door, Alpha and Omega, Lamb, Consoler, Priest, Prophet, Messiah, Rock. Not each of

these is meaningful to everybody; and "as there are so many sides
to his personality, Jesus can manifest himself to men in different
ways, according to their capacity for seeing him…and he reveals
his mysteries to them only by degrees."[54] It was, in Origen's view,
an important task of the Christian teacher or *didaskalos* to present the appropriate images according to the individual disciple's
needs or capacities. Like the Good Shepherd, he knows each of
his sheep by name, and goes all the way to seek those that are
lost. This insight is lost when the religious images become unam-
biguously "realistic," and many of the aspects of our Lord, or his
Mother, are not represented at all. The disappearance of representations of Christ triumphant, the almost exclusive representation
of him as evoking sympathy—whether as agonized on the Cross
or exposing a bleeding Heart—can surely be spiritually impover-
ishing when it is balanced by no presentation of Majesty, Power
and Mystery. Similarly, the mature and often stern Theotokos of
the old ikons, and of the figures of Mother and Child of the dark
and early middle ages, have given way to white-clad, pink-faced
adolescents.[55] Images which could function as symbols, reflecting
unconscious and numinous, as well as conscious and intelligible,
apprehensions, have been replaced by more or less "realistic," and
therefore psychologically superficial, portraits. This departmental-
ization and impoverishment of images has, of course, its own psychological cause, for they are themselves a product of the psyche.
But it should not surprise us if investigation were to show that
their psychological and religious effects were harmful and at the
root of much of the contemporary "failure of religion."

But depth-psychology also shows us that, while images are
necessary for the psyche and its religion, they also can become
harmful or, more exactly, can be consciously or unconsciously
misused to the psyche's hurt. The psychologist is accustomed to
speak of projections of, or on to, the image. The term is admissible

if it be understood as an attachment of a sum of psychic energy on to the image and its consequent detachment and dissociation from the ego. This familiar process, which is essentially an unconscious one, will mean the loss of that sum of energy to the ego and its consequent weakening or depotentiation. The image will, in effect, cease to be a symbol, and become a mere object unrelated to the subject, and the content which it "presents," so far from aiding the subject's consciousness, will be automatically dismissed as belonging wholly to the "other." This loss of energy, and at the same time of consciousness, may well become psychologically stultifying and inhibiting. The widespread suspicion that religion is weakening, and that the atheist or agnostic "humanist" may find within himself the power and the responsible awareness which the religious man transfers to his gods, is probably rooted in the supposition that religion does in fact mean projection of this sort. But theology must agree that such a use of images is wrong and harmful to the soul: it is in fact, though unconsciously, idolatrous. In Christian teaching, man himself is the image of God, and while external images are needful as his servants in the formation of the Divine image which is himself, he may on no account serve them, or transfer to them his own responsibilities as the image of God in this world. They are means, not ends, symbols not objects, reflections not substitutes. But we have already indicated that it is necessary to distinguish between this unconscious projection, and conscious, willing and mature faith, and that faith rightly understood is never in the image as object but only in the unknown and unseen which the image (if it is truly a symbol) presents.[56] Aquinas insists that even the human form of Christ has a place in religion, not as its ultimate object, but only as a means to total dedication to the unknown God.[57] Moreover, this God is, according to Christian teaching, not "outside" the worshipper and unrelated to him, but a Power and a Love and a

Wisdom who indwells him and is available to him "to use and enjoy" as his own possession.[58] Here assuredly is no projection, dissociation or depotentiation of the ego. There is no doubt that, in concrete fact, conscious faith and more or less unconscious projection can become mixed together, but they should not in principle be confused. The simple believer who consciously transfers his theological and archetypal concerns to the teaching Church is not, in this technical sense, projecting, or losing needed psychic energy, or sowing the seeds of a neurosis. On the contrary, his libido is freed from undue bother with such burdens, and thus unencumbered is capable of being directed into the practical concerns of life in a thoroughly wholesome fashion. When, however, he begins to view his Church—or his crucifix or his Madonna, or even the humanity of Christ "according to the flesh" but without the spirit—as an object unrelated to himself and a substitute for his own energies and responsibilities, troubles may well ensue.

But the particular and unique demands which Biblical and Christian religion makes on its adherents should not be overlooked in this matter of the "failure of religion." Even in the heyday of triumphant Jewish theocracy, of the medieval synthesis of Church and State in a "sacral" society, of established national churches, this religion was always that of an "elect," a "peculiar people," a "gathered" Church even though it claimed to be the religion of everybody. In the Old Testament it is that of a chosen people set aside from the gentiles, in the New that of the "called" set aside from "the world." It could never be, as are most pagan religions, a form of "the world," of the normal social structure—however much, since the conversion of the Roman Empire, Christian responsibilities and political considerations have tended to make it such. Adherence to it must therefore always be a source of tension between the "two cities," the reign of God and the values of "the world." In a simple pagan community, or in

any authentically "sacral" society, the reconciliation of adaptation
to the religious fellowship with adaptation to the secular society
presents no serious problem, for they are in fact one and the same
thing. In a pluralist society such as our own it is bound to create
acute tensions, which will be religiously and psychologically deleterious to the extent that they are unconscious and glossed over
by religious education. The tension is valuable and creative when
consciously recognized and when the struggles it entails are accepted; but when ignored or repressed—when the Christian images and values are retained but the peculiar demands which they
make are disregarded—psychological and social confusion is likely to result. The very fact that Christian doctrines present the archetypes in their "hitherto most perfect form" makes them all the
more demanding. The Holy Trinity, taken as the prototype of the
mens, the reflecting psyche, presents an intensity of consciousness which is unmatched in any pagan or philosophical triad. The
unmixed unity of God and man in Christ presents a union of
extreme opposites of the Infinite and the finite, of humanity unmixed with Divinity and of Divinity absolute and unadulterated,
unparalleled by any anthropomorphic deity or semi-divine human
hero. It demands the utmost of purely human "historical" living,
unmixed with the eternal and the archetypal patterning; and, at
the same time, of divine living with "conversation in heaven" uncontaminated by compromise with worldliness. Transubstantiation, as Jung suggests, by insisting on the completeness of the
Divine transformation of the elements, the breadlike and winelike
signs alone remaining, presents and demands a completeness of
personal transformation unequalled in any other of the countless
forms which archetypal symbols of transformation assume.[59] In
the sphere of conduct, Christ's descriptions in the Sermon on the
Mount of life under the reign of God are demanding beyond anything found elsewhere, and indeed totally impossible if codified

as legally binding directives for the natural man. Yet to the extent that this description has become part of our heritage, failure to live up to it becomes an occasion of conflict and guilt-sense of an intensity unknown to the "innocent" pagan. The requirement to be perfect as our heavenly Father is perfect is not, after all, possible to beings who, according to orthodox theology, have become incapable of abiding even by the laws of their own nature.[60] The Christian symbols and Christian ethics presuppose the active presence of the Holy Spirit and, where that is not accepted, they increase rather than decrease the possibilities of mental and emotional disorder in our Christian and post-Christian era. For it is the Spirit who gives them life and makes them life-giving. Without the Spirit—the "Third" in the prototype of full consciousness—they are the mere "letter" which is not only dead but killing.[61]

It has been said that modern psychological investigation has confirmed the view that man is naturally, and indeed incurably, religious.[62] Though his god may be his belly, or sex, a political abstraction, a hero-figure, a scientific method, or health or wealth or truth—or a polytheistic Olympus of such gods at odds with each other—and whether he calls them gods or not, and whether he is conscious of it or not, every man is serving and seeking and honouring something or somebody. It is this "devotedness," however unwilling, that makes him tick, and patterns his behaviour. The discovery of this fact can be a shock to those who suppose themselves free of religion. But no less a shock awaits those who, with or without psychological analysis, discover that the gods they actually serve, the images they actually revere and which determine their behaviour, are not always those of their religious professions, and of whose very existence and potency they had been blissfully unaware. Thomas Carlyle once wrote:

It is certain, whatever gods or fetishes a man may have about him, and pay tithes to, and mumble prayers to, the real "religion" that is in him is his practical hero-worship. Whom or what you do in your very soul admire, and strive to imitate and emulate; is it God's servant or the Devil's? Clearly this is the whole question. There is no other religion in the man which can be of the slightest consequence in comparison. Theologies, doxologies, orthodoxies, heterodoxies, are not of moment except as subsidiaries towards a good issue in this: if they help well in it, they are good; if not well or at all, they are nothing or bad.[63]

Carlyle left the criterion of good and bad in the air, and thereby his pragmatic test is practically valueless. But not the least service that psychology, and especially depth-psychology, can render to religion is its test of the genuineness of our professions. We cannot afford to contemn it on the grounds that it can tell us nothing of religious truth, but can concern itself only with how religion works, or fails to work. For religious truth is, after all, a truth that is supposed to work, and indeed to bring healing to the nations. If psychology can tell us anything of how it does so, or fails to do so, it has something to offer the modern religious preacher and teacher, and indeed the modern churchgoer generally, which he can ill afford to neglect. This book has far from exhausted its possibilities in this direction; but it has also attempted to go further, and to commend the findings of depth-psychology to the attention of both believers and unbelievers. For depth-psychology has already gone far, as we have seen, to offer us a better understanding and appreciation of the workings of our very "doxies," and of their healing relevance to the inmost needs of our soul—or psyche.

Appendix I

TWO OTHER TREATMENTS
OF THE SOUL AND PSYCHE PROBLEM

Two other approaches to the soul-psyche problem, and to the respective roles of the pastor and the psychotherapist, merit consideration.

In an essay on "The Nature of the Problem" between religion and psychology, Dr. D. Stafford-Clark has written as follows:

> C. S. Lewis has given us a most helpful analogy.... He has likened the mind and body to a radio set, itself a complicated, delicate but highly vulnerable piece of mechanism, tuned to receive a programme a very long way off. In conventional terms the set, even in its most complicated and intricate design, is essentially "material"; the programme, on the other hand, is essentially "immaterial." Yet the programme provides the ultimate justification for the existence of the set, and it is to receive and give expression to this programme that the set has been designed and built. None the less, if the set becomes damaged or decayed, it is quite likely to distort the programme even to the point at which interference renders it no longer recognizable at all. At this point the set needs attention, although it may appear to the superficial listener that it is the programme which has gone wrong.
>
> I have developed this analogy in my own words.... In this use the psychiatrist must assume the role of the radio technician, and may be able to restore the set to something like

working order; and in this sense he is working in harmony
with the general purpose implicit in the full reception and
reproduction of the programme, but he is not necessarily in
better touch with the programme or its source than anybody
else. A radio technician who takes upon himself the status of
programme director or critic is clearly mistaking the limits of
his own capacity, at least in so far as these are bound up with
his trade.[1]

The analogy is helpful up to a point. It should impress the
Christian psychiatrist with the importance and responsibility,
though also with the subordination, of his own function with respect to the welfare of souls. The analogy, however, presents some
difficulties. For while the working order of a radio receiver is un-
affected by the quality, character and content of a programme,
that of the *human listener* may be seriously affected. They act on
his mind, his emotions, and even on his nervous system. To the
extent that the psychiatrist can confine himself to the "material"
and "mechanical" aspects of the receiver—to drugs and surgery
and the functioning of glands and of the autonomic and central
nervous system connections—the analogy is useful. The neurologist, more especially, might validly be likened to the radio technician who indirectly improves reception and selectivity by repairing
faulty connections and replacing worn-out valves. For the psychologist and the psychotherapist, however, matters are not so simple.

Dr. Stafford-Clark is a psychiatrist, although, as his *Psychiatry Today* bears witness, he is a psychiatrist with wide understanding and deep appreciation of psychology and psychotherapy. But
the psychologist and the psychotherapist are, as such, concerned
precisely with the "immaterial" phenomena. The psyche, as "the
sum total of human experience," is clearly not merely a device for
the mechanical reproduction of signals transmitted from outside.

Even in this capacity, it is more like the listener than the receiving-set. It reacts to such signals with pleasure or pain, understanding or boredom, anger, delight or indifference; and also with the ability to switch on or off or over to another wave-length. Moreover, by no means all its "programmes" originate wholly from outside. More importantly still, it is impossible for the psychologist to make this distinction between the programme and the set: the psyche, which is his field of operations, *is* the programme, and the character of the programme and the working order of the set are inseparable and indistinguishable. However much he may wish to be no more than the humble technician, the psychotherapist cannot avoid concern with the programme and forming judgments about it from the standpoint of the well-being of the whole psyche: its adequacy or inadequacy, its beneficial or harmful results, for the patient's requirements. And this is so, even when the programme seems to be transmitted from outside: from lectures, sermons or books. Though he may not wish to be a critic, and must avoid being a director, he can no more avoid passing judgment on what his patient receives (when it is manifestly relevant to his health or sickness) than the physician can avoid passing judgment on what he eats. Attractive though Dr. Stafford-Clark's analogy is, and perhaps valid for the "physical" psychiatrist and neurologist, it provides no escape from the "predicament of the psychologist."

Another interesting, and not altogether dissimilar, solution of the soul-psyche problem is offered by Père André Godin, S.J., in an essay on "Therapeutic and Pastoral Work."[2] Père Godin begins by emphasizing, as we do, the unity of the human personality, and that "it cannot be split into two parts." He wisely puts us on our guard against easy but unrealistic solutions:

It is tempting to say that, during a psychoanalysis, the moral and religious values, in which the personality of the subject was living before the beginning of the treatment, cannot be reached or disturbed in themselves, since they do not depend upon psychic mechanisms, nor on the affective genesis of the mental structure of the subject. It is tempting to say this, because easy. All the same, in reality, the disturbance which the affective structure must undergo in the course of treatment, owing to the transferential relationship which comes into play and develops with the personality of the psychoanalyst, this disturbance does not reach a *part*, but the *whole* of the subject; were it only to do the former there would be no real healing in psychoanalysis. It is not here merely the question of a slightly different use which his free will has to make of psychic gifts modified by the treatment: it is in fact that free will itself which is brought into play, questioned, invoked, raised to a degree of maturity which up to then, in consequence of the neurosis, it was not able to attain.[3]

But all this, Père Godin continues, "does not prevent us from searching for a proper ground for distinguishing two ways of approaching it"—namely the pastoral and the therapeutic. So far, of course, we are in full agreement. But then Père Godin appears to propound, not merely two ways of approach, but just such a dichotomy in the subject as he has deplored. This he is enabled to do by postulating in Freudian fashion, "a field of psychic forces which is largely, if not totally, subject to determinism." This field alone is the concern of psychotherapy. "The determinations, scientifically discovered in psychism, are not opposed to freedom, rather are they the *matter* on which it is exercised, on which it depends and in which its decisions are embodied." Père Godin admits that many of these determinations have not yet been discovered, but he looks (with rather surprising equanimity) to the day when psychoanalysis will be more completely "a scientific technique (however complex and delicate) to obtain results from a starting-point, following determined procedures." This will be (and already to a large extent is) "a technique to transform *not* the whole man, not even his psychology" (in the broader sense of this word, including the deliberate attitudes, decisions and behaviour), but only the psychic "terrain" in man: mental mechanisms, affective dispositions, customs, all together forming the point of departure from which man can and must orientate his life." Translating all this into Thomistic terms, Père Godin maintains that psychic life, thus understood, is "the dispositive material cause (only) of our human, moral or religious acts...the *cause from which* we take the point of departure for our human decisions or lines of human conduct."[4]

This theory—which seems, after all, to be a variation of the soul-psyche dichotomy—should be welcome to those who are prepared to assume both that the "field of determined psyche forces" is a closed system, and that the "causal-reductive" treatment of them is therapeutically and scientifically adequate. But it is just these assumptions which the Jungians, and most other post-Freudian depth-psychologists, have found themselves obliged to reject in the light of further experience and reflection.[5] It is of course agreed that these determinations (though they are also patient of functional and teleological interpretations) are indeed the "matter" on which freedom is exercised, and the "cause from which" our decisions must be made. But the evidence seems overwhelming that the causality is reciprocal, and that the supposed "dispositive material cause" is itself determined to a large extent by "our human, moral and religious acts." In other words, there is, objectively, no such distinct "terrain," only an abstract concept of causal-determinism in which certain psychic phenomena can be included, though not confined.

We do not, however, need to subscribe to this theory to see the important truth in Père Godin's conclusion about the "two ways of approach." "The priest, as a spiritual adviser, is the intermediary between Christ and the soul. The psychotherapist, confronted with the neurotic, is supposed to restore the material psychic dispositions as far as he can, but he is not concerned directly with their use or meaning."[6] What remains unquestionably true in Père Godin's theory is that the psychotherapist *begins* with determinations, in the sense that compulsive or at least unwilled and unwanted symptoms bring the patient for "treatment." The priest or pastor, on the contrary, *begins* with the assumption of the possibility of free "spiritual" response to Word and Sacraments. But the psychotherapist, as we have seen especially in Chapter II, cannot restrict himself to these determinations; and, even with regard to these, he *must* be concerned with their "meaning," and though he may not direct, he cannot be indifferent to their "use." Similarly the priest, to the extent that Word and Sacrament—and indeed Christ himself—are embodied in images and symbols, cannot avoid applying and employing (whether he knows it or not) psychic determinants. Whether he likes it or not, some "psychological engineering" is inseparable from his ministry, as our subsequent chapters should have abundantly shown. This is so, notwithstanding the fact, which Père Godin rightly emphasizes, that "the grace of God does not depend directly on psychic dispositions, and can perfectly operate the sanctification of the neurotic man *before*, *during* and *after* the treatment."

Appendix II

SOUL AND PSYCHE IN RELIGIOUS INSTRUCTION

T he purpose of the exposition in our first chapter has not only been to try to clear the ground between the professional theologian and the psychologist. It seems to raise questions of the utmost importance for our society, to which those especially who are occupied in religious education should give serious attention. For the question should be asked whether the idea of the soul shared by most contemporary Christians resembles that which we find in the New Testament, in the early Fathers of the Church, in St. Thomas Aquinas, in the Council of Vienne. We do not expect to hear from the average Christian the same formulas, but is their idea of the soul anywhere near co-extensive with that of their fathers in the faith? Must it not be said that such pictures of their own "souls" as they may possess are far nearer those of the psychiatrists and theologians whom we have criticized than those of Aquinas, of the Church Fathers and of the Evangelists and Apostles?

Short of instituting a methodical inquiry among a cross-section of average Christians, such questions are difficult to answer with precision. But certainly it is a fact that the Thomist idea of the soul comes as quite surprising news to many of them when they hear and understand it for the first time.

But we do have documentary evidence of what is taught them. Since charity and criticism begin at home, and since Catholic teaching may reasonably be expected to be more in line with tradition than that in newer denominations, we may fairly take authorized Catholic catechisms as our example.

The *Catechism* authorized for use among British Catholics has this about the soul on its very first page:

Q. Is this likeness to God in your body, or in your soul?
A. *This likeness to God is chiefly in my soul.*

Q. How is your soul like God?
A. *My soul is like to God because it is a spirit and is immortal.*

Q. What do you mean when you say that your soul is immortal?
A. *When I say that my soul is immortal, I mean that my soul can never die.*

Q. Of which must you take most care, your body or your soul?
A. *I must take most care of my soul; for Christ has said, "What doth it profit a man if he gain the whole world, and suffer the loss of his own soul?"*

Q. What must you do to save your soul?
A. *To save my soul I must worship God by Faith, Hope and Charity....*

And that is all. Now these statements are, given Catholic beliefs, unimpeachably correct. They are also of the utmost practical importance for leading a Christian life: far more so than any amount of philosophical reasonings, philological inquiries, or psychological constructs. But, we have to ask, what do they *teach*? What is a child or an adolescent expected to *learn* from them? For a catechism is not just a collection of correct and sublime statements, but is supposed to be an instrument of instruction and education: this *Catechism* is "chiefly intended for the use of children in Catholic schools."

It is a first principle of good teaching that it must begin, not necessarily with what is most important, but from what the learner already knows and falls within his own experience. And it is axiomatic that all knowledge begins, not with more abstract predicates, but with concrete images or "phantasms." It is also known that the first images formed by children have a strong persistence into later life.

What sort of image of the soul can these catechism answers convey to a child or an adolescent? It is, he is told, a "spirit," which he can hardly picture except as some gaseous vapour, some sort of phantom or ghost; anyway as something with an existence and life of its own, quite independent from *him*. It is "immortal," and since he knows that *he* must die, must he not presume again that this soul is something else, and quite apart from himself? He must take more care of his soul than his body. Splendid: but could he ever guess from these words that it is he himself through the powers of the soul which must take the care, and must he not picture soul and body as two separate entities, and suppose that "he" is a third entity who must care for both? His soul, as he must picture it, is something else that *he* must save. Could he ever for a moment guess that he *is* this body and soul, that the soul of which he should take care is the very life of the body without which it would be a lifeless corpse and no human body at all?

And where does all this touch his intimate everyday experience? Can he have an inkling that this soul, which is like God and immortal, and which should worship God by faith, hope and charity, is his own very life? Could he possibly suppose that it is this selfsame soul which hungers and thirsts, laughs and plays and weeps, loves and hates, dreams and daydreams, thinks and feels, sees, hears, smells? What could such a "soul" have to do with terrors and nightmares, or with...*deep inside in that silent place where a child's fears crouch?*[1] What, somewhat later on, can he suppose that it could have to do with the business of growing up, achieving personality? What with the problems and the new worlds of experience—sexual, cultural, social—which in countless different forms are opened up in adolescence? What can his "soul" be except some misty, pious ghost, wholly occupied with religious exercises and an after-life, and with nothing to say to life as actually known and experienced—except perhaps to condemn it?

For all that such young people have heard about it, the Fathers of the Church, St. Thomas Aquinas and the Council of Vienne have laboured in vain. The formulas that have been given them are, so far as they go, orthodox and important enough; but the impressions and ideas which they may be expected to receive from them are, if not actually heretical, utterly at variance with those of the Bible, the Fathers and Councils of their Church.

Matters will be further confused, rather than elucidated, for the student of the *Catechism* when he comes to declare (in Questions 29 and 30) that "the three powers of my soul are my memory, my understanding, and my will" and that these are "the likeness to the Blessed Trinity in my soul" because "in my one soul are three powers." He must naturally suppose that the soul has *only* three powers—since there are only three Persons in the Trinity! Even an experienced and subtle theologian must have extreme difficulty in making sense of this statement. It seems to be a botch of the very abstruse ideas of St. Augustine's *De Trinitate*. But what Augustine calls "memory, understanding and will" are precisely not "powers" but *acts*,[2] and they are not said to be "of the soul" but of the *mens*. The "*mens*" for Augustine is not the whole soul, but its "*pars superior*" which, being capable of self-reflection, is independent of bodily organs, and differentiates the human from other animal souls. "Memory" for Augustine is the "*thesaurus inscrutabilis*" of our knowledge, by no means confined to past events. It is more like Plato's "reminiscence" than anything that is likely to be understood by the word "memory" by children in schools. These acts of memory, understanding and will are said by Augustine to be like the Trinity inasmuch as they are not three lives but one life, not three *mentes* but one *mens*, and because understanding proceeds from memory, and will from both, and are distinguished not in substance but by relationship.[3] Augustine's ideas about the *soul* are not easily summarized and are sometimes obscure. But it was certainly for him the life-principle in general[4] which has countless powers, activities and passions besides those of memory, understanding and will.

The psychological effects of this division between the religious and the secular fields, between "soul" and the entirety of experienced life, could be disastrous. It should be a matter of profound concern to all who are disturbed by the psychological and social state of religion in our times. It is well known that preachers are forever denouncing the departmentalizing of religion, its confinement to a small section of life, its divorce from the everyday living of the individual and society. But it seems inevitable that their words fall on deaf ears so long as, from the very beginning of their religious instruction, their hearers have been conditioned to picture religion and life as belonging to two distinct entities. It is well known also that immense sacrifices are made (especially by Catholics) to ensure the religious education of their children, and that there is widespread anxiety about the big percentage of them who abandon religious faith and practice soon after leaving school. Yet, if such be the ideas of the soul with which they leave it, it can hardly be surprising. It is certainly not always that they wish to have nothing to do with religion. Rather it may be that they not unreasonably suppose that religion has nothing to do with them: with either inner or outer life as they have come to experience it.

Appendix III

ARCHETYPES: FAD OR FICTION?

The term "archetype," coined (or, more exactly, revived and redefined) by Jung, has become regular English currency. Like other words he has put into circulation and which have generally "caught on" (e.g., "complex," "extroversion," "introversion') it appears to have met a widespread need which previous language failed to supply. It is, however, a remarkable fact that, while it has become accepted currency in educated circles generally, and especially in literary and artistic circles, it is seldom even mentioned in English-language works on scientific psychology and psychiatry outside confessedly Jungian circles. Indeed it is probable that the majority of British and American professional psychologists and psychiatrists, while they can hardly ignore the phenomena which Jung treats of under this name, would confess to scepticism regarding the very reality of archetypes. If they have read Jung's works at all, they will often confess to being quite baffled by the subject. This seems to be due, at least in part, to the very proliferation of Jung's statements about archetypes which are as varied (some would say contradictory) as they are frequent. Matters are complicated by the fact that, in his efforts to make himself understood, Jung frequently describes archetypes in terms borrowed from other disciplines—biology, optics, nuclear physics, crystallography—and by correlating them with philosophical concepts taken from Plato, Kant and Schopenhauer. Phenomena, postulates, hypotheses, theories, models, analogies and metaphors are not always too clearly distinguished from one another, and the very quantity and variety of descriptions are not at all easy to correlate, and may suggest a certain vagueness and lack of precision to all but the most patient and leisured reader.

It would be outside the scope of this book, and beyond the capacities of its author, to deal adequately with the subject. Since, however, much of this book presupposes that archetypes are real psychological factors, something should be said about the position as the author understands it.

To avoid some common misunderstandings, it is necessary to distinguish several different questions: (1) *That of archetypal or primordial images*; (2) *that of archetypes, properly so called*; (3) *that of their origin; and, closely allied to this*; (4) *that of their physical cause or concomitant.*

(1) *Archetypal or primordial images* (sometimes confusingly abbreviated to "archetypes") is a class-name for a group of psychological *phenomena*. These, and these alone, are observed empirically. Their distinguishing characteristics are that they are *transpersonal* (i.e., not traceable to the memory or personal unconscious of the subject), archaic (i.e., "in striking unison with familiar mythological motives"), and collective (i.e., "at least common to entire nations or epochs: in all probability...to all times and races"). In common with other images (in the psychological sense) the archetypal image is "a presentation (*Vorstellung*) which is only indirectly related to the perception of the external object [and] depends much more on phantasy activity, and as the product of such activity it appears more or less abruptly in consciousness." It may, however, be not only visualized, but also expressed in artefacts, dance, drama, play, "acting out," etc. Such images are, moreover, not only static forms (the Wise Old Man, the Eternal Child, the Quaternity, etc.) but also processes (the Night Journey, the

Search for the Treasure, the Combat with Demons, Sacrifice, etc.). To the extent that the image "presents" (i.e., makes present to the ego) what is essentially unknown as well as what is known, it is also a *symbol*. However, "whether a thing is a symbol or not depends chiefly upon the attitude of the consciousness considering it." To the extent that it seizes upon the subject in spite of himself and fills him with a sense of awe, it is *numinous*. The similarity of such images permits a certain sub-classification into groups, but they are altogether too protean and intermixing to permit such precision as is possible in botany or zoology. In Jung's view, "the primordial image is the preliminary stage of the idea, its maternal soil.... The primordial image has advantage over the clarity of the idea in its vitality."[1]

These archetypal images are found notably in (a) dream material; (b) active imagination (an introverted relaxation of consciousness whereby images are allowed to function autonomously); (c) the imaginative activity of children[2]; (d) the dreams and hallucinations or delusions of psychotic patients. In addition "the contents of consciousness, it is evident, contain mythological products from the unconscious which intrude themselves from time to time." An immense literature has in fact grown up displaying archetypal motifs in novels, poems, fairystories, rituals, strip-cartoons, scientific methods, etc. These, however valuable for "amplifications," are considered unprofitable by more cautious Jungians as sure evidence for purely archetypal images since "language and education provide consciousness with a mass of mythological motifs which, however, by no means prove their previous unconscious existence."[3] This criterion of assessment is irrelevant to the purposes of this book, since its purpose is not to prove anything about the previous existence of these images or to isolate them from all learning processes. It is enough for our purposes that they exist and function in fact, whatever hypotheses may be offered to explain them.

To avoid a common misunderstanding, it should be said that there is no question of these *images* being inherited as such. On the contrary, they appear discontinuously.

(2) We are not conscious of whence these images appear; hence their source is unconscious. They "happen" or "appear"; they are not consciously devised or constructed. *Ex hypothesi* their unconscious source is not personal—i.e., not repressed experiences of the individual psyche. On this account Jung *postulates* an "objective" or "collective" unconscious, and archetypes properly so called to denote its positive contents. These contents are not directly observed, and are, *ex hypothesi*, not directly observable. But as a result of his observations and reflections on the primordial images and their behaviour, Jung finds himself "led to believe that there are certain collective unconscious conditions which act as regulators and stimulators of creative fantasy activity and call forth corresponding formations by availing themselves of the existing conscious material." These conditions he calls also "formative principles," "dominants," or simply "archetypes."[4] Elsewhere Jung describes the archetypes merely as "possibilities," "potentialities" or *Vorgänge* of the empirical presentations. It is not altogether clear whether he regards them as real psychological (or, as he later preferred to call them, *psychoid*) entities (or forms) *inferred* from the empirical data, much as Aristotle inferred potency from act, matter from form, *intellectus possibilis* from intellection. He certainly often speaks of them as if they were existent entities, while at the same time emphasizing that they lie beyond consciousness, and thus are not knowable.[5] It seems more cautious to regard them, not as inferences, but as "theoretical contrivances," akin to waves, corpuscles, electrons, and possibly also instincts, in other sciences.[6] It should be noted that this "belief" that *images* are to some extent preformed in the human psyche does not contradict

the ancient view that the human *intellect* begins as *tabula rasa*, nor does it in any way commit us to "innate *ideas*." Also that, although the "archetype" provides us with a conceptual tool for dealing with certain phenomena, it in no way "explains them away" since, even if it be allowed that archetypes are "real entities," we do not know what they are. Religious and other representations are thus in no way invalidated by being classified as archetypal.

In this book this conceptual tool or "contrivance" has been accepted and used as such, and we leave open the question of their "existence."

(3) "In establishing the generality of the primordial images and postulating the unconscious archetype as their source, Jung defined a field of study which has occupied him for the rest of his life. There is no necessity for him to investigate their origin but it would strengthen his position if he did so."[7] Unfortunately his efforts to explain their origin has often had the effect of weakening his position, since no satisfactory hypothesis about the origin of archetypes seems yet to have been found. Jung himself has frequently attributed the archetypes (*not* the images directly) to heredity. This, as Dr. Fordham points out,[8] is open to serious objection from the biological standpoint and raises the question of...

(4) The physical or somatic basis or concomitant of archetypes. It seems that, if such there is, it has not yet been discovered. It also raises the very difficult question of the relationship of psychological archetypes to biological instincts.[9] It may be that, as Fordham says elsewhere, "the nuclei of activity co-ordinating on the basis of a whole brain may one day bring the archetypes within the range of experimental study"[10]; and Mr. Crawford Knox, in a yet unpublished manuscript, has suggested that the neurone networks of

the cerebral cortex may be found to supply a "physical" basis for culturally determined image-formation, such as cannot be easily explained either by instinct or heredity. But no satisfactory causal and physical explanation has yet been found. Most hypotheses that have so far been offered, while they must pay due regard to the fact that archetypal images are not only "natural" but apparently culturally determined and determining, appear to presuppose the continuity of human history and biological evolution. This further underlying hypothesis is doubtful in the extreme.[11] The reality of the archetypal images, and the usefulness of the postulated unconscious archetype, can be maintained independently of all these hypotheses regarding their origin and physical basis, as we endeavour to do in this volume.

APPENDIX IV

WHY CHRISTIANITY IS "CATHOLIC," ACCORDING TO AQUINAS

The following is a quotation from St. Thomas Aquinas, *Expositio super Boetium De Trinitate*. It occurs under the heading, "Whether the Christian faith and religion are fittingly called catholic or universal."

"Faith, like other mental acts, has two subjects; namely those *who* believe and *what* they believe. The Christian faith can be called catholic or universal from both these points of view.

"From the point of view of those *who* believe, because, as the Apostle says in Romans 3, the true faith is that which has as its witnesses the Law and the Prophets. But in the time of the Prophets different peoples worshipped different gods in different ways, and only the people of Israel gave due worship to the true God. So, since there was no single universal religion, the Holy Spirit foretold through them that the worship of the true God should one day be the task of everybody. Thus, for instance, he foretold through Isaias, 'Every knee shall bow down to me, and every tongue shall acknowledge me' (Isaias 45:24). This prophecy is brought to pass in the Christian faith and religion. Hence they are deservedly called 'catholic,' inasmuch as they are to be received by every sort and condition of men. Hence also, all those who have fallen away from this faith and religion—which is promised to and to be received by all generally—are not called catholics but heretics, inasmuch as they are separated from the universal fellowship.

"But also from the point of view of *what* is believed in Christian faith, we find a truth which is rightly called catholic. In older times there were different arts and methods whereby different particular human requirements were supplied, or alleged to be. Some of these supplied only man's material needs, such as wealth or position or pleasure. Others met only man's spiritual needs, for instance, moral virtue or intellectual culture. Some people thought that the gods were to be worshipped only on account of material benefits in this life; others, only on account of rewards after this life. Porphyry claimed that, for certain superior people, there could be a catharsis of the imaginative part of the soul, though not of the whole soul. He said, according to Augustine (*De Civ. Dei*, x), that there had not yet arrived one sect which supplied a universal method for the liberation of the whole soul. But this has now arrived in the Christian religion, as Augustine points out. For it teaches that God is to be worshipped not only on account of eternal benefits but also on account of temporal ones, and it directs man not only in spiritual matters but also in the use of his body and of material things, and it promises bliss both for soul and body. Hence its standards are called universal because they include and orientate the whole life of man, and everything which belongs to it in any way whatever.

"It is true that some sects claim for themselves what belongs to the Christian religion, but they cannot accomplish all they claim; so the attribute of universality does not strictly belong to them....

"The Christian faith is not called catholic or universal because it embraces each individual of every kind, but because it embraces every kind of individual, for some have adhered to it from among every sort and condition of men."

APPENDIX V

JUNG ON JOB

If ever there were grist for the Jungian mill it was, one might suppose, the Book of Job.[1] It can be read almost as a paradigm of a "mental breakdown" followed by an "integration process" such as Jung himself has often described it.

Job, we are told in the first verse, was "simple and upright, and fearing God and avoiding evil." Seemingly he has never even experienced evil, and abounds in cosy piety and worldly prosperity. He has, as Satan points out (verse 10), a "fence about him, and his house, and all his substance." It is not difficult to be "good" in such narrow, sheltered confines as these, but it is not the way to be a grown-up man, let alone a hero, a prototype of the way of healing and salvation through crucifixion and resurrection. And clearly all is not well with Job. His avoidance (the Hebrew means "turn aside from," "ignore") of evil seems to amount to repression of his "shadow"—the diametric opposite of his conscious piety. He appears to be driving his children to drink, and he is ridden with anxiety that, while in their cups, they will precisely "curse God" (verses 5, 6, RSV). He is trying to ward off this anxiety with sacrifices which he offers "continually," which looks somewhat like an obsessional ritual. A psychologist can hardly avoid the impression that he is projecting his "shadow" on to his children.

Any psychologist should know he is heading for a crash. Any theologian should know that such easy and complacent virtue cannot continue long in this post-lapsarian world. Job's professed

love for God—and God's for him—must grow up from this agreeable but infantile and unconscious, auto-erotic phase. Job's idol of
a merely intelligible and amiable God must be smashed; he must
learn the lesson which the New Testament writers were to see it
was the function of the Old Testament heroes to teach: that man's
righteousness before God is not wrought by moral works without "faith in the Absurd," the Unseen and the Unknown. So the
psychologically and theologically inevitable happens: Job's fences
are down; evils rush in. His sufferings are truly frightful, but they
are also symptoms; and the loss of his domesticated animals and
his children (concerning whose youthful high spirits he had been
inordinately anxious), the chidings of the *anima* (his wife), and
the psychosomatic eruptions (his boils) add up to a clear clinical
picture. He cannot cope. He retires to the dunghill, the libido is
introverted and he is in the grips of intense neurotic depression
and conflict.

The conversation with the three "friends" begins, and goes on
and on. Job suffers, they say, *ergo* he is morally guilty. Job knows
he has not sinned, and morally he has not; but unconsciously he
has disregarded the natural laws which require that a man must
grow up, and that his psychological and spiritual growth should
keep pace with his physical growth. He has forgotten (or has not
realized) that the Author of moral commandments and legal covenants is also the Author of man's physical, animal and psychological nature, and that its laws and demands cannot be disregarded
with impunity. He oscillates miserably between confidence in Jahwe and ironic blasphemy (God is just not what he had supposed);
he is overwhelmed with perplexity and self-pity. Job and his friends
are all right, and all wrong: the problem is simply insoluble on the
conscious levels of rational argument about moral merit, and on
the supposition that God is nothing but an indulgent Daddy or an
equal party in commutative justice. This conversation is typical of

what happens when unconscious, existential guilt is mistaken for conscious moral guilt.

Then comes Elihu, the *fourth* friend (this surely should have appealed to Jung). He is young, inferior, hitherto silent and repressed; yet he claims to have (what the talkative three had quite overlooked) the *Spirit* of the Lord. He is something of an intuitive, a poet. He is sick of all this argument without issue, and must break down its fatal assumption of the competence of consciousness to resolve it. Like any skilful analyst (though certainly he preaches overmuch) he indeed grants what he can of the conscious convictions and values of his hearers; but he opens to them gradually another point of view: he stresses the vastness and incomprehensibility of God and the limitations of the conscious human standpoint: he "will not level God with man" (32:21). He silences the rationalistic and moralistic chatter by recalling that "there is a *spirit* in man; and an *inspiration* of the Almighty gives him understanding" (32:8). There are ways of God that are beyond wordy explanations (33:13); but "by a *dream*, in a *vision* by night, when deep sleep falleth upon men, and they are sleeping in their beds, then he openeth the ears of men, and teaching instructed! them what they are to learn, that he may withdraw a man from what he is doing, and may deliver him from pride" (33:15–17). It is from the unconscious and its "royal road" that deliverance must come, and sure enough it does. The emotional tensions are transformed, in typical Jungian fashion, into the terrible, numinous but healing symbol of Jahwe in the whirlwind: a mandala of dynamic spirit. The amiable, comprehensive maker of covenants with Israel, the intelligible author and rewarder of the moral law, is *also* the *mysterium tremendum*, the Lord and Creator of the irrational and brute creation as well as of man's high ethical aspirations. In the vision Job also beholds Behemoth, the clumsy, mighty irrational brute power beneath which he had squirmed; and he learns that precisely this "evil" is "the chief of the ways of God." So the vision unites the opposites, for former evil is integrated into the totality of the Self; the "captivity" of Job is "turned," he emerges from the ordeal the adult man God had repeatedly urged him to be, and "with twice as much as he had before."

It has all gone according to schedule: one might almost think that the author had consulted Professor Jung's psychological treatises before writing it. And one might suppose that Jung would be very pleased. But he is not pleased at all. In his *Answer to Job* he gives us a reading of *Job* not unlike that of Bernard Shaw's *Black Girl*. Jung identifies himself wholly with Job in his sufferings and with his sense of being treated abominably and insanely. His sufferings are just cruel suffering and in no wise a symptom; only Jahwe is to blame for them. When Elihu appears, it is not at all as a mediator of the unconscious, but just as one heartless idiot more to maintain that Jahwe cannot, in spite of reason and experience, be wrong. (Yet this "absurdity" is, after all, Job's own deep conviction also; without it there would be no opposites, no conflict, no tragedy.) There is no transformation of the libido into the symbol, and no transformation of Job—he merely submits, with his tongue in his check, to *force majeure*. The story has no denouement at all: "Jahwe abruptly breaks off his cruel game of cat and mouse.... Job's torments suddenly come to an end." Anyway, they have been "pointless," "to no purpose." Job's harrowing experiences have profited him nothing; the only lesson to be drawn is that God is a beast. Jahwe in any case has nothing to teach Job; he is "unconscious," "at odds with himself," contradictory, irritable, irrational, unstable, childishly hungry for love and admiration; in short "a prehistoric menagerie." On the contrary, it is Job who "shows himself superior to his divine partner both intellectually and morally," and it is Job who will, and does, teach God. Jahwe is a slow learner, but after further graded instructions from Ezechiel,

Daniel, the Sapiential writers and Enoch, he himself becomes man: not, however, *propter nos homines, et propter nostram salutem* (for us men and for our salvation), but for his own self-improvement. Unfortunately, however, he incarnates only his "light side," to the neglect of the "dark," in the guiltless Christ who "did no evil." So the last state is worse than the first: evil is more repressed and unconscious than ever and threatens a terrible revenge. The coming of Christ heralds the reign of Antichrist: the triumph of almighty evil through atomic fission. There are, however, signs that God is learning better the dark, feminine side of his all too masculine nature: there is the Woman of the Apocalypse, and there is the papal definition of the Assumption: hints of a coming and more satisfactory rebirth of the God-Man.

The summary of the argument is of course unfair, but no more astounding than many pages within it. Psychiatric journals appear, on the whole, to have received it with discreet silence. But the *bien pensants*, if not also the genuinely devout, could hardly restrain their complaints of impiety and blasphemy. Protestant divines were particularly censorious: they seem not to have read the preface addressed *Lectori Benevolo*. But Jung hardly invites their benevolence. Such a *reductio ad impossibile* of the private interpretation of Scripture, when it really succeeds in cutting loose from all tradition and every *consensus fidelium*, must seem a cruel caricature. Nor can it be pleasing to be told that the Pope's definition of the Assumption is thoroughly enlightened and up-to-date, while at its critics (the Anglican Archbishops included) is hurled the supreme insult of being obscurantist and behind the times—as well as of being deaf to the Holy Ghost! Catholics will welcome Jung's insights into the psychological and cultural significance of the definition and of contemporary Marian devotion generally; but they will be hesitant to open their arms to this gift-bearing Greek. For Pius XII and C. G. Jung seem hardly to be talking about the same thing in their affirmations of the Assumption. According to the latter, while the visionary figure of Apocalypse 12 is "an ordinary woman, not a goddess" (for all that she is apparently the monstrous titaness Leto who begat Apollo by leaning against a mountain!), the mother of Christ, being an immaculate virgin, is "different from all other mortals": hardly flesh and blood at all.

But the bizarre ideas in this volume will astonish educated Christian readers less than the naïve misunderstandings and misrepresentations of elementary doctrine. Can Jung really suppose that sacrifice and worship are for God's benefit rather than man's? Or that the commandments are or could be directives for divine behaviour as well as human—or would he subject God also to the laws of gravitation or thermodynamics? Has any Bible-reader really supposed that "Christianity burst upon world history as an absolute novelty"? How does he charge a religion, which puts the Cross at its centre, with repressing consciousness of evil ? How has he missed the very essence of the Christian's situation which is to be at once a child of God by baptism and a child of wrath by inheriting a grace-deprived nature? He quotes St. John's "He that is born of God commits no sin," but ignores his reiterated "If we say we have no sin we deceive ourselves...make him a liar." Thereby he misses the conscious duality in John—and in grown-up Christians generally.

But when we have read Jung's preface ("I beg of you, dear reader, not to overlook it," he writes) we must see that all such questions and observations are largely beside the point. Nor will a Catholic, firm in the security of his faith, "answer" the book by drawing from his treasure things new and old and showing how they sort out and dispose of the countless points which the book raises. Jung has remarked elsewhere that there must be continual misunderstanding between the theologian and the empirical psychologist over their use of the word "God"; for "the theologian will naturally assume that the metaphysical *Ens Absolutum* is meant," while the empiricist "just as naturally means a mere statement, at most an archetypal motif which performs such statements." It appears, then, that Jung employs names like "Jahwe" and nouns like "God" to function not as signs but as things (to adopt modern terminology): as second, not first, *intentiones* (to adopt scholastic terminology). Such usage is legitimate, though perhaps unusual even among empiricists, but we must allow Jung to use words in the way he chooses, and (difficult though it may sometimes be to construe some of his sentences in his own way) try to understand them accordingly. Thus it emerges from this preface that in statements about "God" or "Jahwe" he is talking about endopsychic images considered as psychological phenomena and not as signs for what they merely represent. He is "quite conscious that...none of my reflections touches the essence of the Unknowable." He is talking all the time of the interaction between archetypes and ego-consciousness, personifying the former because of their seeming autonomous behaviour. When, for instance, the book says that Jahwe is unconscious, or that aspects of him become conscious, we should understand it to mean that he (or it) is unconscious to the human ego, or that aspects emerge into human consciousness—the only consciousness which the rigid empiricist, who rejects the validity of inference, will recognize. We have suggested, in our *God and the Unconscious*, that for Catholic theology also "progressive revelation" consists precisely in such an enlargement of human consciousness, and it might be expected that Jung's book could be read as a contribution to the history of that process. Read from this standpoint, it certainly offers several illuminating and exciting insights. But generally speaking it cannot be so read. For Jung deliberately reads the Scriptures through a pair of highly distorting spectacles. Although he is not writing of God but of God-images, he is not writing even of Job's images of God, but rather of his own images of Job's images. This method effectively obscures an objective and dispassionate reading of the Scriptures against their own authentic historical background: it is an interpretation of "God" at several removes. Its aim is "not to give a cool and carefully considered exegesis that tries to be fair in every detail, but a purely subjective reaction": to present "the way in which a modern man with a Christian education and background comes to terms with the divine darkness which is unveiled in the book of Job." Jung will "not write in a coolly objective manner, but must allow my emotional subjectivity to speak if I want to describe what I feel when I read certain books of the Bible.... I shall express my affect fearlessly and ruthlessly." What he offers us is the highly feeling-toned reaction of "a layman and a physician who has been privileged to see deeply into the psychic life of many people." It is an angry book, but it is an anger born of experience and compassion for mankind in its contemporary quandary, and in the disastrous inadequacy of its supposed Christian education to enable it to come to terms with contemporary realities. The preface is headed with the text, "I am distressed for thee my brother": and we recall Jung's declaration which, if it cannot win our approval, must yet command our respect:

> I do not write for church circles, but for those who stand *extra Ecclesiam*. I associate myself on purpose and deliberately with those who are outside the Church.... The Church is my Mother, but the Spirit of my Father draws me away from her into the wide world and its battlefields.

Even an instructed Christian may expect an explosion when an adult, whose religious development has become fixated at the kindergarten level of bourgeois morality *plus* "a Friend for little children above the bright blue sky," becomes confronted with the

realities of life, of the ways of God both in the Bible and in contemporary events. It is understandable that he feels a close kin-
ship with the disillusioned, tortured Job. Yet it is a fact that the
acquaintance of millions of our contemporaries with Christianity has not reached beyond this stage. The violence of the abre-
action is understandable, but its infantile quality may still amaze
readers who are unfamiliar with abreactions. We might suppose,
for instance, that the text, "Whom the Lord loveth he chastised,"
might call a halt to the tantrums, and even induce the author to
reflect that his grievance is hardly adult. But the only reaction is
that of the spoiled child: "It would be quite understandable if
the Laodiceans did not *want* too much of this 'Love.'" Other
remarks about Christian ideas of love and goodness, otherwise
unintelligible or merely abusive (e.g., "To believe that God is the
Summum Bonum is impossible for a reflecting consciousness")
become clear commonsense if they be understood as the reactions
of a consciousness which, religiously speaking, has become fixated
at the oral phase, for which "love" means the egotistic "I want,"
and "goodness" only an elementary *bonum delectabile*—perhaps
just "good luck." "Reflecting" or not, such a consciousness is a
primitive one which has as yet scarcely differentiated religion from
magic, which has never heard of the logician's niceties about the
analogical predication of *bonum*, or come within miles of experiencing the saints' joy in God: St. Paul's "All things work together for good to those who love God," or St. Julie Billiart's "How
good the good God is!"

"One would be very ill advised," Jung remarks in quite another connection, "to identify me with such a childish standpoint."
Nobody who has read his more "objective" books or who has
noted the deep insights in this book—let alone anyone who knows
him personally—could make such a mistake about one of the most
mature and advanced spirits of our time. Why then, we must ask,

does he identify himself with such childish standpoints here? To this there seems no answer except his distress for his brother, his deliberate identification with those *extra Ecclesiam*. This book should be neither laughed off nor should it provoke anger or disgust. It does not belong to the large and worthless library written by cranks who wrest the Scriptures to prove some crackpot theory. Its depth and tragedy we can only guess from the fact that it calls upon, not other men, but the hallowed names and symbols of God to carry the projection of the criminal and pathological persecutor. A Christian reader should hear, beneath all the provocation, behind the seeming mockery of much he holds most sacred and most dear, a profoundly moving cry of anguish, a reproachful signal of distress.

But he should also observe that, destructive and childish as much of this book seems to be, its aims are eminently constructive, and that its challenge to ourselves and our contemporaries is imperative and urgent. We must regret that the author seems so often to bark up the wrong tree; but we should see that his attack is essentially directed on Victorian, liberal, diluted, one-sided pictures of God and his Christ which are utterly inadequate to the tasks which our age imposes upon humanity. We can only agree with Jung that these obsolete and insipid idols must be destroyed if a new realization of the God-Man in his wholeness is to be born in human minds and hearts, and humanity itself is to survive. But this precisely is the constant lesson to be drawn from a dispassionate reading of holy Scripture itself, and it is seldom more explicit than in the Book of Job itself. It is also the lesson of the history of the Church, whose task is to carry on and develop "what Jesus began to do and to teach"—what Jung calls the "continuing incarnation of God which began with Christ." We too await another coming of Christ, not in meekness only, but in the full exercise of his power and majesty, and for "the *hieros gamos*, the marriage of the son with the mother bride." The pity is that in his violent re-action against an emasculated version of Christianity, he has failed to see that he is, in spite of himself, on the side of the Bible and of authentic orthodox Christianity. Blake wrote of Milton that he was on the devil's side without knowing it; we may say of Jung that he is on Jahwe's side even when he seems to mock at him.

In the very last sentence of the book, when all its *Sturm und Drang* have subsided, Jung leaves us in no doubt that he has known the answer to Job all along:

> Even the enlightened person remains what he is, and is never more than his own limited ego before the One who dwells in him, whose form has no visible boundaries, who encompasses him on all sides, fathomless as the abysms of the earth, and vast as the sky.

What is this if not—though couched in more modern lan-guage—the answer to Job; precisely Jahwe's answer to Job in the Book of Job?

APPENDIX VI

THE "FEMININE PRINCIPLE"

Readers may challenge us to define just what we mean by "the feminine" and the "feminine principle." The addiction of some clergymen and psychologists to generalizations about "Woman" and "Women" can arouse a resentment which, in this author's view, is thoroughly wholesome and often justified. Even when these descriptions of what women are, or ought to be, are not unrealistic, patronizing and contradictory (as they sometimes are), the mere fact that "woman"—unlike "man"—is treated as an *object* which needs to be described and can be circumscribed is rightly felt as arrogance by anyone who knows herself to be, first and foremost, a human *subject* with unlimited possibilities. Not only, in our view, is it impossible to formulate a highest common factor of woman's "infinite variety," it is also illegitimate to lay down any objective formula which would restrict what a woman may become. It is curious that no similar addiction is shown by such writers to describe and restrict the male of the species. The explanation may lie in the fact that, by the authors concerned, it is taken for granted that men are subjects, and not other objects—the observer is not observed. For the male as male, and even for the woman who has adopted or introjected male attitudes, woman as woman is eternally the "other," and to that extent object, while to herself she is subject. But even as object, she is an object about which it is difficult for the male to be objective without projecting his own desires, needs or fears. Jung recognizes these limitations when he writes:

> How is a man to write about woman, his exact opposite? I
> mean, of course, something accurate, that is beyond the sexu-
> al programme, not contaminated by resentment, and beyond
> illusion and theory? Where is the man to be found capable of
> such superiority? For woman stands just where man's shadow
> falls, so that he is only too liable to confuse her with his own
> shadow. Then, when he wishes to repair this misunderstanding,
> he tends to overvalue the woman and believe in her desiderata.[1]

Jung is, of course, describing tendencies in male psychology.
Yet even Jung seems to condemn her to be eternally the male's
"exact opposite," whereas most spirited women know better—and
can prove that almost "anything he can do she can do better," or as
well; and that she has an immense amount in common with males,
and things of greater value to her than the alleged oppositions.

Males and females are not, as such, distinct species capable of
being precisely defined by a common genus and distinctive *dif-
ferentia*. Neither, in any species, is the one merely a function of
the other. However far the concept of sexuality be extended, no
human person can be defined and described solely in terms of
his or her maleness or femaleness. Masculinity and femininity, it
seems, represent not two different sorts of *beings*, let alone opposite ones, but a distribution of *functions*, in some respects opposite
and complementary, among the same sort of beings.

If we attempt to describe this differentiation of functions by
induction or generalization from actual specimens of members of
the two sexes, we run into all sorts of difficulties. Physiologically
and biologically, the distinction, and even the oppositeness and the
complementarity, are clear enough. Each is uncompleted, sterile,
and indeed meaningless, without the other. But beyond the purely
physiological and biological realm, it becomes very hard to determine what is characteristically masculine and characteristically

feminine outside a particular culture-pattern. Dr. Margaret Mead, in her outstanding book, *Male and Female*, has shown that what are considered to be typically "masculine" or typically "feminine" functions and characteristics differ vastly in different societies. In some societies, including our own, they differ considerably in different strata of the same society.

> Whether we deal with small matters or with large, with the frivolities of ornament and cosmetics or the sanctities of man's place in the universe, we find these great varieties of ways, often flatly contradictory one to the other, in which the roles of the two sexes have been patterned.
>
> But we always find the patterning. We know of no culture that has said, articulately, that there is no difference between men and women except in the way they contribute to the creation of the next generation; that otherwise in all respects they are simple human beings with varying gifts, no one of which can be exclusively assigned to either sex.... However differently the traits have been assigned, some to one sex, some to the other, and some to both, however arbitrary the assignment must be seen to be...it has always been there in every society of which we have any knowledge.[2]

The universality of the patterning already suggests some archetypal preformation. The variety and contradictoriness of the distribution of functions and characteristics between the two sexes suggests that it has little to do with purely rational or utilitarian apprehensions. Dr. Mead does indeed claim to find amid the variety certain constants which she attributes to some "basic regularities in sex development" which no society has yet eliminated, and which tends to orientate the female to stress the values of *being* and the male to stress those of *becoming* and *action*.

Whether women like being women or deeply resent it, they will teach their girl-children that they belong to the same sex, whether that sex is regarded as fortunate or unfortunate, and their boys that they belong to a different one. This fundamental regularity is tied up with lactation, and with the carry-over into social patterns that because women breast-feed children, they are also the ones to care for them. If breast-feeding were completely superseded as a form of feeding infants—always a possibility in our mechanical-orientated society—and fathers and brothers were to take over an equal responsibility for the child, this biological regularity would disappear. Instead of girls learning that they simply were, and boys that they must become, emphasis would shift to such matters as relative size and strength; the preoccupation of the developing child would alter, and so might the whole psychology of the sexes. At present, the by-products of lactation still hold universally, for in all societies the care of infants is believed to be more women's work than men's, and we have therefore no way of telling whether or not the male drive towards assertion of maleness through differentiation from female through achievement has any other base beyond this earliest one. Cultures like the Arapesh show how easily, where parents do not discriminate strongly between the sexes of their children and men take over a nurturing role, this drive in the male may be muted. But this muting on the whole seems expensive enough so that it makes one question whether there are not a number of other, perhaps more phylogenetically determined, roots for assertiveness in the human male. However that may be, the mother-child situation at present provides a perfect learning context in which girls learn to be and boys learn the need to act.[3]

But many psychologists and other observers will question even this much. According to Dr. Erich Neumann:

> Man's original hermaphroditic disposition is still largely con-
> served in the child. Without the distributing influences from
> outside which foster the visible manifestation of sexual differ-
> ences at an early date, children would just be children; and
> actively masculine features are in fact as common and effective
> in girls as are passively feminine ones in boys. It is only cultural
> influences, whose differentiating tendencies govern the child's
> early upbringing, that lead to an identification of the ego with
> the monosexual tendencies of the personality and to the sup-
> pression, or repression, of one's congenital contra-sexuality.[4]

This is probably true, but still leaves unexplained why active features are called masculine and passive ones feminine, and
why cultural influences are always differentiating. For Neumann,
as a Jungian, the "explanation" of course lies in the archetype,
as we shall presently see. It is remarkable that Dr. Mead, for all
her personalistic and Freudian bias, also invokes "phylogenetically determined" (Jungians would say "archetypal") roots for the
universality of the patterning. She later attributes to women an
exceptional (though not exclusive) "ability to recognize difference
from the self" in contrast with men's "ability to project the self
in building a construct or a hypothesis." Hence, she claims that
the "greatest intuitive gifts will be found among women"—gifts
which have "lain fallow, uncultivated, uncivilized." This, which is
consistent with her "being-doing" antithesis, she however attributes to woman's actual or potential experience of maternity rather than to any "phylogenetic roots."

But here we are back to generalizations about psychological
differentiation between men and women, which are very hard to

substantiate since they are found to admit of many exceptions which hardly prove the rule. On this subject much has been written, but it is by no means always even consistent, and is usually based, if not on projections, then on data provided by a single culture.[5] Jungians, as is well known, tend to contrast the psychological make-up of men and women sharply: the ego, persona and shadow being represented by the same sex, the "soul-image" ("animus" or "anima") being "usually figured" by an image of the other sex.[6] We think that "usually" (too often transmuted into "always") should be heavily underlined. All depends, we believe, on the extent to which the ego is identified with, or differentiated from, the biological or cultural sex-characteristics of the subject. While certain statistical regularities may be observed in the respective psychologies of men and women within a given culture, it seems doubtful if they are of universal validity and are to be ascribed to "nature" rather than a specialized "nurture." Given that masculinity and femininity present an archetype, we must beware of regarding them as a mere abstraction or generalization extracted from actual men and women. The projection of this archetype on to living men and women, in such wise as to identify them with it, can be as ruinous to objective empirical psychology as it can be to interpersonal relations.

The evidence, of which a vast quantity will be found in Jung's books alone, that "masculinity-femininity," concretized as "male-female," is archetypal seems overwhelming. For this reason (see Appendix III) this "pair of opposites" defies definition in conscious and conceptual terms. It is a *phenomenal* pair of opposites whose "source" may be postulated, but can never be conceptually grasped; though it can be to some extent "intuited," since intuition is "perception by way of the unconscious." It must be doubted, however, whether this intuition can ever in practice be unmixed with the "learned" associations which the terms male and female evoke in a particular culture. But, if truly archetypal, it is equally doubtful whether the meaning of "male-female" can ever be gathered only from experience of actual men and women. Consistently with his view that the archetypes are inherited (see Appendix III), Jung holds that:

> Every man carries within himself an eternal image of woman, not the image of this or that definite woman, but rather a definite feminine image. This image is fundamentally an unconscious hereditary factor of primordial origin, and is engraven in the living system of man, a type ("archetype") of all the experiences with feminine beings in the age-long ancestry of man, a deposit, as it were, of all the impressions made by women; in short, an inherited psychical system of adaptation. Even if there were no women, it would be possible at any time to deduce from this unconscious image how a woman must be constituted psychically. The same is true of the woman; that is, she also possesses an innate image of man.[7]

This presupposes the inheritance, not only of acquired characteristics, but even of acquired experiences. It also seems to presuppose that the archetypal image can be acquired from experiences of actual women. And it leaves out of account that the male-female archetypal images appear in the psyche of both men and women, whatever the differences in the ego-attitude towards them. Elsewhere Jung has said:

> This primordial pair of opposites [man and woman] symbolizes every conceivable pair of opposites that may occur: hot and cold, light and dark, north and south, dry and damp, good and bad, conscious and unconscious.[8]

This also raises difficulties: to say that one set of *phenomena* symbolizes another set of *phenomena*, and is primordial, appears to be a purely subjective assessment conditioned by the observer who gives priority to one rather than the other.

It seems less hazardous, and more consonant with Jung's own more mature conception of archetypes (see Appendix III again), to postulate an unconscious archetype of complementary contraries of which the images male-female are one manifestation—an important one because anthropomorphic (or theriomorphic) and capable of associating many others as well as many (though variable) conscious experiences. Other manifestations would be, not only the pairs which Jung names in the above quotation, but many other images and even concepts which are found to be widespread and frequently in conjunction. Examples are the Chinese Yang and Yin, the Creative and the Receptive, the Firm and the Yielding, the Light and the Dark; the Hindu Purusha and Prakriti, Rajas and Tamas; the alchemists' Sol and Luna; our own Being and Doing, Action and Passivity; Logos and Eros; Dynamic and Static; Act and Potency; Light and Dark, etc.

It is in this archetypal sense, though without excluding acquired associations, that "masculinity and femininity" are understood in this book. We may make our own the declaration of Erich Neumann:

> We use the terms "masculine" and "feminine" throughout the book, not as personal sex-linked characteristics, but as symbolic expressions...which must not be reduced to biological or sociological terms. The symbolism of "masculine" and "feminine" is archetypal and therefore transpersonal; in the various cultures concerned it is erroneously projected upon persons as though they carried its qualities. In reality every individual is a psychological hybrid. Even sexual symbolism cannot

be derived from the person, because it is prior to the person. Conversely, it is one of the complications of individual psychology that in all cultures the integrity of the personality is violated when it is identified with either the masculine or the feminine side of the symbolic principle of opposites.[9]

It may be assumed that "primitive bisexuality" (if it is a fact) is unable to overcome the duality of the archetype, or to picture masculinity except as the complementary opposite of femininity (and vice-versa). Thus each is incomplete, and only both together constitute wholeness. The Jungian eagerness (and that of the untutored unconscious) to deify the feminine may be similarly attributed to this inability to transcend the duality, or to conceive God as transcending the *coincidentia oppositorum*. God, on this understanding, must indeed be masculine *and* feminine. For Christians, and most rational theists, he is *neither* masculine *nor* feminine, but transcends this duality and all contraries. But inasmuch as, for Christians, he is revealed as Trinity in Unity, and the Unity is conceived by us as the source of the processions and of the Trinity of Persons, he may be figured as Being and Doing, Mother and Father, Feminine and Masculine, etc. But the dogma corrects any impression this might suggest of duality, for it insists that the Essence and the Persons are identical. God is the uncreated prototype of the contraries which permeate and differentiate creation, but in him they are not contraries but absolute unity. In him the duality is overcome or, more exactly, has not yet become dual. The *duality* and *contrariety* of "divine pairs" (gods and goddesses) thus do not present him, but rather misrepresent him. Male and female "otherness" is thus not to be found *in* God, but only in the relationship of the "utterly Other" to the creature—prototypically, and in supreme perfection, in the relationship God-Mary (or Ecclesia).

APPENDIX VII

SIDELIGHTS ON THE THEOLOGY OF THE MASS FROM PSYCHOLOGY AND COMPARATIVE RELIGION

In an article in *The Life of the Spirit* (June 1957) we attempted to correlate the traditional theological conceptions about the Mass with some of Jung's views about its psychological function as a symbol of transformation, together with some findings of comparative religion and anthropology. We here reproduce it with the Editor's permission.

The Editor asks me to write on "the nature of sacrifice, showing how the Mass is a sacrifice." It sounds quite simple. It is as if I were asked to speak on the nature of Buttercup, and show that the flower you have picked is a buttercup. I can get a dictionary description of Buttercup, show you pictures of the species of *Raminculus* called Buttercup, compare your specimen with these descriptions and pictures, prove to you that there is no difference whatever between them, and conclude without a shadow of a doubt that you have picked an authentic, genuine sample of the class "Buttercup."

We might proceed in the same way with this present assignment. We might look up the word "Sacrifice" in a standard dictionary, or start from some good definition of "Sacrifice" from some Doctor of the Church. Then we could take a good look at what happens at Mass, show how it fits the definition, and conclude that Holy Mass is undoubtedly a genuine specimen of the class "Sacrifice." Or we could do some original research of our own: take a look at all the strange rites and ceremonies, the bloody butcheries and slaughters, the cruel burnings and knifings as well as the noble self-denials or trivial losses of income, which men have called "sacrifices," then find some sort of common denominator of the lot, and finally try and fit Holy Mass into whatever sort of idea of "sacrifice in general" we have managed to extract.

Some theologians have, in fact, gone about matters in some such way. But it seems to be a very mistaken way. It may perhaps be the right way to go about comparative religion. But it is not theology, and to mistake it for theology can have some odd results.

It is not theology, because to the man of faith just what sacrifice means is not shown in any dictionary nor by any general conception obtained by induction from any number of pagan or even Hebrew rites. The nature of sacrifice, the meaning of sacrifice, is shown to him in the unique event of the sacrifice of Jesus on the Cross, his dying for our sins, and rising for our justification. Calvary is not just one specimen (not even the best specimen) of the class "sacrifice." The man of faith (and the theologian, whose job it is to elucidate his faith) may not judge whether or how what Jesus does is a sacrifice by comparing it with Old Testament or pagan standards, or with *a priori* definitions. Jesus on the Cross is himself the standard whereby other sacrifices, or definitions of sacrifice, are to be judged: it is illegitimate to make *them* the criterion of what *he* does. "Sacrifice," we see, is not a class of objects like "buttercup" in which the authenticity of one can be judged by comparison with others or by generalized definitions or descriptions. On the contrary, to the man of faith, the right of other "sacrifices" to be called such must be judged by the measure in which they approximate to, or resemble, or seek similar results to, what Jesus Christ does on the Cross and in Holy Mass.

But, for the very reason that these "sacrifices" do approximate to, resemble, or seek similar results to what Jesus does on the

Cross and in Holy Mass, they serve to illustrate, and help us to understand better, what it is that Jesus does. This is the method, the underlying thought, of the Epistle to the Hebrews. This epistle does not set out to show that Jesus is one specimen of the class "priest" who performs one specimen of the class "sacrifice," but on the contrary that these priests and sacrifices (here of the Old Testament[1]) enable us to understand better what Jesus is and does "once for all," subsuming and transcending them all and thereby rendering them obsolete.

So, it may be said that modern studies in comparative religion, anthropology and depth-psychology about priests and sacrifices may enable us to understand better what Jesus does on the Cross and in Holy Mass; and also what we are to do, and he does to us, at Holy Mass. Truly, these researches do not tell us anything new about the Cross or about Mass that theologians and preachers have not constantly taught us, but perhaps they can help us to see better what the theologians and preachers mean.

But before we illustrate this, a parenthesis is perhaps necessary. It is, or should be, axiomatic for Catholic theologians that the sacrifice of the Cross and the sacrifice of the Mass are one and the same sacrifice. The Council of Trent is very clear about this (Session 9, chapter 2): "The same Christ who offered himself by shedding of blood on the altar of the cross, is contained and bloodlessly sacrificed in the divine sacrifice which is performed at Mass.... The victim is one and the same, and the same is he who now offers through the ministry of priests, as he who once offered himself on the cross: only the way of offering (*ratione offerendi*) is different." We do not then have to look in the celebration of the Mass for something which will make it a sacrifice *apart from* the sacrifice of the Cross, for it is *not* a sacrifice apart from the sacrifice of the Cross. The Council of Trent does not tell us what the "different way of offering" is; but only what it is *not*: it is *without* blood-shedding. But it implies that it is a *ritual* and *symbolic* way: the body and the blood are offered in the symbols of bread and wine, and "through the ministry of priests."[2]

"In every sacrifice," wrote St. Augustine, "there are four things to be considered: *to whom* it is offered, *by whom* it is offered, *what* is offered, *for whom* it is offered."[3] In Christ's sacrifice, St. Augustine continues, it is "one and the same Mediator" who is every one of these four, uniting them all in his one person who is both God and man and also the head of his body, the Church. And it may be said that all other sacrifices, whether Old Testament or pagan, are so many attempts, and also so many inevitable failures, to achieve this identity of all these four elements.

Although by universal consent a "sacrifice" is offered *to* some divine being, there seems to be a universal ambiguity (outside the sacrifice of Christ) as to *by whom* it is offered: is it *by* human or divine beings? It almost seems that sacrifices are something which human beings find themselves *obliged* and yet *unable* to make. Miss Levy, in her *The Gate of Horn*, has indicated that, down to the time of the Hebrew prophets, sacrifice was thought to be primarily of God, to God, and *by* God. Sacrifice was not viewed as a human act, but the enactment of a *divine* act, whether of creation, or of the origin or deliverance of a people, or of the annual renewal of nature, the source of the people's continued life. The priest-king was the embodiment of a god; and so also "the victims were by their nature holy—God to God. Their blood was poured on pillar or earth as a physical bond of union."[4] And (as Professor Mircea Eliade has shown to be characteristic of all non-Biblical religion) the participant is there, not as a human being, but "in full ceremonial action, he abandons the profane world of mortals and introduces himself into the divine world of the immortals."[5]

C. G. Jung has shown the psychological reason why this had to be so. Every sacrifice is a self-sacrifice; yet purely human self-sacrifice is humanly impossible. This is so because sacrifice is not any sort of giving or offering but implies the complete surrender of every selfish claim. An offering "only becomes a sacrifice if I give up the implied intention of receiving something in return. If it is to be true sacrifice, the gift must be given up as if it were being destroyed. Only then is it possible for the egoistic claim to be given up."[6] Otherwise it is no sacrifice, no act of worship of God and of recognition of his supreme dominion, but either an act of magic (a seeking of divine power to accomplish our own egoistic ends) or a blasphemous refusal to recognize that God's claim is to *all* that we are and have, which can be met by no partial offering. There must be complete alienation of the gift from our own possession and use. To "sacrifice" means to "make sacred" or wholly other and *tabu*.

But (as Jung also points out) it is just this total self-giving and total renunciation which is humanly, psychologically impossible. For we can give only what we possess, and we only possess that of which we are conscious. Our actual claims to "me and mine" always exceed the bounds of our conscious awareness: this is proved by the spontaneous and unconscious resistance with which we meet any threat to "me and mine." We do not fully possess ourselves, and therefore cannot sacrifice ourselves. "The offering of so significant a gift at once raises the question: Does it lie within man's power to offer such a gift at all? Is he psychologically competent to do so?"[7] Jung, as a psychologist, answers no. And he also knows that "the Church says no, since she maintains that the sacrificing priest is Christ himself. But since man is included in the gift...the Church also says yes, though with qualifications.'

"Yes," because to sacrifice is a human need and obligation. "With qualifications," because it is a human impossibility, and only the Lord, Possessor and Disposer of all, *can* sacrifice. Yet, at the same time, if *man* does not sacrifice, the performance is wholly

out of this world, ethically worthless and irrelevant to human behaviour, attitudes and history. Moreover, sacrifice remains an obligation of the creature in recognition of his creatureliness, and one
which neither obliges nor befits the Creator.

The Hebrew prophets saw this, in what Miss Levy calls "The
Revolution" in the history of religions.[8] Israel was called, as no
other people was called, to realize that sacrifice was something
which their God required, not merely or primarily in the sacred
precincts of the temple by his priestly representatives, or by the
people when periodically carried "out of this world" by the ritual. It was to be by and of the people themselves in everyday life
and in the vicissitudes of "profane" history. To sacrifice meant
not merely or primarily a periodic retirement from the "profane"
and the personal into the "sacred" and the archetypal; but (as the
Psalmist says) *propter te mortificamur tota die*—on *thy* account *we*
are immolated all day and every day. Already in the earliest reign,
Samuel tells Saul that "obedience is better than sacrifices and to
hearken rather than to offer the fat of rams" (1 Kings 15:22). The
later prophets will stress more and more the need for the interior
and ceaseless submission of a broken and humbled heart as against
the external periodical ceremonials. "Incense is an abomination to
me; the new moons and the sabbaths and the other festivals I will
not abide; your assemblies are wicked.... I am weary of bearing
them.... Cease to do perversely. Learn to do well. Seek judgment.
Relieve the oppressed. Judge for the fatherless. Defend the widow...." (Isaias 1:12ff.). Sacrifice can no longer be only of God to
God, but of man to God, and so find expression in everyday relationships, man to man.

Did this mean that divine, ritual sacrifice is now to be *replaced*
by human, interior acts of self-sacrifice or external expressions of
altruism; and become only a matter of conduct and ethics? But
just this, we have seen, is humanly impossible. The claim to be

able to sacrifice ourselves implies the claim to possess ourselves; and it is just this egoistic and illusory claim which sacrifice surrenders. To *substitute* human, ethical self-sacrifice for divine sacrifice is not to recognize, but precisely to deny the all-sovereignty of God. It is not to make sacred (*sacrificare*) the "profane," but to profane the sacred; and atheistic or satanic moral autonomy is the logical outcome of such presumption.

Only a God-Man could resolve the dilemma. We may apply to sacrifice what St. Anselm says of satisfaction: "Only God *can* make it, only man *should* make it; so it required that a God-Man makes it."[9]

Jung has shown clearly how, from the psychological point of view, the action of the Mass resolves the dilemma:

> In the utterance of the words of consecration, the Godhead intervenes, itself acting and truly present, and thus proclaims that the central event in the Mass is its act of grace, in which the priest has only the significance of the minister. The same applies to the congregation and the offered substances.... The presence of Godhead binds all parts of the sacrificial act into a mystical unity, so that it is God himself who offers himself as a sacrifice in the substance, in the priest and in the congregation, and who, in the human form of the Son, offers himself as an atonement to the Father.[10]

It is indeed the God-Man himself who intervenes audibly at Mass, amidst the human prayers and ceremonies, with "This is *my* body...*my* blood." The merely human priest is priest only because he "acts by the power of Christ," and only "lends Christ his tongue and gives him the use of his own hands."[11] And though Christ is God, and his Godhead gives his sacrifice its all-sufficiency and efficacy, it is as man that he is priest and mediator.

But why the "external signs symbolic of death," since the death was real enough, and the self-offering on Calvary all-sufficient? The *res*, the thing signified, is already accomplished; why the *sacramentum*—the sacred sign? Why the *Mass*? Catholic theology and liturgy have always insisted that God accommodates his actions to our sense-bound natures, in order that "we may be led through visible things to the invisible," and to engage our bodily senses no less than our spiritual understanding.[12] Modern psychology helps us to understand that the sense-symbol is no mere pedagogical device which can be discarded when intellectual understanding has been attained. It is the indispensable carrier and transformer for psychic functions besides those of thought; the bearer not only of conscious and voluntary contents but also of those which lie outside consciousness and voluntary disposition. The symbol, moreover, does not only convey ideas: it *does* things. St. Augustine remarks somewhere that a handshake not only expresses but also promotes friendship. Sacrifice, to be whole (and if it is not whole it is not sacrifice), *must* find symbolic expression and representations: not indeed for the benefit of the divine sacrificer and sacrificed, but for the benefit of the human. It must not only be thought or felt, but *done* by us. Without the Mass, not only is Calvary not really and sensibly present to us, but it is not at our disposal here and now, to offer and to be offered. The symbol alone can focus and contain the *whole*: that which is within the scope of human volition and disposition as well as that which infinitely exceeds it; that which is conscious and subject to human perceptions and understanding, as well as that which is unconscious, mysterious and infinitely transcends them.[13] And the symbol must be divinely established, and a divine act:

> Since man, in the action of the Mass, is a tool (though a tool of
> his own free will), he is not in a position to know anything of the

hand that guides him…. It is something outside, something autonomous, which seizes and moves man. What happens in the
consecration is essentially a miracle, and it is meant to be so….
It is necessary that the transubstantiation should be a cause of
wonder and a miracle which man can in no wise comprehend.
It is a *mysterium fidei*, a "mystery" in the sense of a *dromenon*
and *deiknumenon*, a secret that is acted and displayed.[14]

The data of anthropology and comparative religion enable
us also to view non-Christian sacrifices as approximations to the
identification of those *for whom* they are offered with *that which*
is offered, as well as with the offerer and the God to whom the
offering is made. Miss Levy has pointed out that "the whole body
of ritual…was a harmonious aggrandizement of the theme: divine
power, animal, man"[15] and that the victim was always regarded
as voluntary, itself participating willingly in the ritual slaughter.
Following Levy-Bruhl, Jung writes of the *participation mystique*
between the offerers and the offered, and explains this in terms of
the familiar psychological mechanism of projection, or identification with the symbol.[16] Dr. John Layard, writing of "Identification with the Sacrificial Animal" among the primitive Malckulans,
tells how for the participant the animal "fulfils the function of
an *alter ego* which…he first rears as a woman would rear a child,
then consecrates, cherishes and adores it, thereby investing it with
his own most secret and cherished desires."[17] Too often we talk
presumptuously of "sacrificing" things which we certainly do not
cherish or adore, and which we may even despise and are quite
content to do without, and with which, more obviously still, we
do not identify ourselves. Layard points out how the Malckulan
brutally slaughters precisely the animal which "up to this moment
has been cherished and cosseted and communed with and…has
occupied the position of his most cherished companion."[18] In the

Mass, it is precisely our dearest, adorable and best Beloved whom we offer.

But Jung has long ago remarked how, even from the psychological standpoint, Christ's sacrifice and ours transcends the old animal sacrifices, however great their participants' identification with the victims:

> The relation between Mithra and his bull is very close. But it is the hero himself in the Christian mysteries who sacrifices himself voluntarily.... The comparison of the Mithraic and the Christian sacrifice shows wherein lies the superiority of the Christian symbol: it is in the frank admission that not only are the lower wishes to be sacrificed, but the whole personality. The Christian symbol demands complete devotion; it compels a veritable self-sacrifice to a higher purpose.... The religious effect of these symbols must be considered as an orientation of the unconscious by means of imitation.[19]

Or, as the Epistle to the Hebrews puts it: "If the blood of goats and of oxen and the ashes of an heifer, being sprinkled, sanctify such as are defiled to the cleansing of the *flesh*, how much more shall the blood of Christ who by the Holy Ghost offered himself unspotted to God, cleanse our *conscience* from dead works [as though we could sacrifice ourselves] to serve the living God?" (9:13, 14). Human sacrifice, the slaying of the priest-king himself, was a horrible attempt in this direction, which the substitution of the animal never wholly satisfied. The urge to suicide still often shows itself as a misunderstood manifestation of the sacrificial urge.

Correspondingly, our identification with the offering and the offered is to be not less but more than in the old rites. Not that we are able to contribute anything whatsoever to the intrinsic worth of the sacrifice. Pope Pius XII in his *Mediator Dei* has found it necessary to emphasize that our Lord's self-offering on the Cross and at Mass is all-perfect and efficacious, quite apart from our participation. Nothing is added to his self-offering, nor to what is offered, nor again to those for whom he offers, whether they be present or absent, or perhaps present in body but absent in mind. For here the identification is not primarily and essentially a psychological one, nor dependent on any psychic mechanism of our own, nor yet dependent on our volition, intentions or active participation. Rather do these identifications presuppose an identity which the Lord himself has wrought. It is in no sense our achievement, and in the Mass the claim even to that achievement, or any contribution to it, is surrendered. "*God* was in Christ reconciling the world to himself" (2 Cor. 5:19): it is all God's work and in no wise ours. It is Jansenist heresy to set any limits to those *for whom* Christ sacrifices himself; and we to whom he has "given the ministry of reconciliation" (2 Cor. 9:14) cannot, by our restricted "intentions" and "applications," restrict his. St. Paul saw no occasion to distinguish between the physical, the sacramental and the mystical body of Christ.[20] For St. Thomas, the mystical body (i.e., you and me and all "in Christ") is the *res tantum* of the Eucharist, that which it ultimately signifies and fosters.[21] And there is a profound sense in which, when the celebrant says on Christ's behalf, "This is *my* Body," it is also true that it is his own body, and yours and mine, because Christ has made his own body to be his and ours.

So again we ask: why the Mass, why the "symbolic mode" of offering? It adds nothing, it seems, to the offerer, the offered or to their identity with those for whom the offering is made. Indeed, does not the God in Christ on Calvary show us that there is nothing in the way of sacrifice that we *can* do, but only have faith alone in the blood shed once for all, which rendered all merely human attempts at sacrifice vain and even ridiculous? Is it not shown that the Anglican thirty-nine articles are right when they proclaim that the "sacrifices of Masses...were blasphemous fables and dangerous deceits"?—blasphemous as implying that we can still add something to the work of Christ on the Cross, deceitful because such a claim is a lie?

The conclusion seems inescapable if any such claim were made. But we have not told the whole story. Although "God in Christ" does all, the "*ministry* of reconciliation" is still required and *we* are "beseeched" to "be reconciled to God" even though *he has* reconciled us (2 Cor. 5:18, 20). Even though Jesus Christ discharges our obligation to sacrifice (because we cannot) yet it remains *our* obligation; and although he discharges it, he does not abolish it. We may even say he cannot do so; for the obligation arises out of our very nature as reasonable and free *creatures*,[22] and even God cannot make his creatures not to be creatures, or annul the obligations which arise from the fact of being creatures. And if *we* do not offer, how is *our* obligation discharged? And if we do not offer ourselves with his offering of us, how is his offering of *us* meaningful and true, and not an empty sign without significance?

So *he enables us* to offer: that is, as Pius XII explained, voluntarily to unite ourselves with the offerer and the offered, drawn thereto by the symbol, by the "sacramental mode" of offering.[23] We add nothing to him, to the offering or to the victim: we in no way make even our identity with the victim, we only identify ourselves with the identity he has already accomplished. And even that identifying of ourselves is made possible and actual for us only by his grace. It can be a mental identification only, a "spiritual communion," or the mental *and* physical reception of the body and blood in the symbol.

So *he* does *all* and what he does is all-sufficient and of unlimited worth: yet what he does profits us not at all without our participation. St. Thomas holds that though the sacrifice of the Mass is in itself all-sufficient, its efficacy to those for whom it is offered, and also to those who offer it, depends on the measure of their devotion.[24] And by "devotion" he understands the basic expression of religion whereby we submit ourselves and all we have totally to God.[25] This is what the external sacrifice itself signifies and promotes, and without which it is an empty formality so far as we are concerned. But, on the other hand, we have already indicated that such interior "devotion" is psychologically impossible without the symbol. Calvary is indeed all-sufficient, and the symbolic mode adds nothing to the sacrifice; but it seems that without the symbol our own voluntary and psychological and even physiological identification with the identity there achieved would not be possible.

Possible or not, this "symbolic mode of offering" is what our Lord in the Last Supper has in fact given us. When we say that the Eucharist is both sacrament and sacrifice we should not mean that, so to speak, God has killed two birds with one stone, has ingeniously arranged that one rite should serve two different and unrelated purposes. The living Bread which we eat is the living Bread which we have broken; and whenever and however we communicate, it is of the sacrifice we partake.

Yet holy communion is not communion only with the body that was offered, but with the body which is now risen and glorified. It is characteristic of sacrifices, as opposed to magical rituals, that although (or because) they seek no reward and surrender every claim, they are returned, transmuted and divinized, to the sacrificer. And as God showed his acceptance of the sacrifice on Calvary by raising Christ from the dead, restoring his body glorious and immortal, so now he shows his acceptance of our participation in his sacrifice by giving to us, and transforming us into, the body of him who was slain, but who is now the immortal conqueror of death, who lives and reigns in us forever and ever.

Appendix VIII

THE POLEMIC ON EVIL, CONTINUED

Chapter Nine was completed before the publication of Dr. H. L. Philp's *Jung and the Problem of Evil* (1958). It is entirely devoted to the "polemic" to whose earlier stages this chapter referred. A particularly interesting feature of this volume is the correspondence which it contains between the author and Professor Jung. But despite the evident goodwill and plain speaking on both sides, and their sincere desire to understand one another, the two parties never seem to find any common ground or agreed premises, and their assertions and counter-assertions issue in complete deadlock. Armed with dictionaries and works on theology and philosophy, the author relentlessly belabours Jung with his theological and metaphysical "truths," comparatively indifferent to what or how they "work." Jung sticks obstinately to his "facts" and the manner of their "working," and refuses to admit any other "truths"—unless it be that of his own scepticism, concerning which he could hardly be less sceptical or more dogmatist. Since his "facts" are "psychological facts," and these include fancies (sometimes uncommonly high-flown), and since both are indisputable "truths," Dr. Philp is evidently baffled by Jung. Jung seems to be no less baffled by Dr. Philp's pernicketiness with dictionaries, definitions, expert authorities and logical consistency in the face of human misery, wickedness and catastrophe.

Dr. Philp, although a psychologist himself, chooses to work almost entirely within the framework of theology and traditional philosophy. This means, of course, that he has many good and sound things to say. And when he succeeds in enticing Jung on to his own ground, he has no difficulty in cornering him. But he seems quite unable even to see the ground from which Jung is operating, or to be very concerned about the pressing human perplexities and sicknesses which Jung—however incoherently—is trying to tackle. Nor does he tackle them himself. He is prevented from coming to grips with Jung's problems about the origin and function of evils by his astonishing conviction that " 'good'...is not something which is capable of producing evil, or it would not be good" (p. 109f.). (It is not surprising that Jung later expresses his despair of help from theologians, apparently regarding them as idealistic verbalists, blissfully sheltered from the facts of life!) The author never explains how, on this premiss, he logically avoids the alternatives of Manichaeanism, Jung's good-evil God, or the un-reality of evils. All these he firmly repudiates, but offers nothing to take their place. For traditional theology, as well as for everyday experience, it is of course elementary that good (and indeed only good) can and does produce evils, and sometimes by reason of its very perfection (*Summa*, I, 49, 1). The good God, the Summum Bonum, also produces evils, and by reason of his very goodness, "tam in naturalibus quam in voluntariis"—incidentally (*per accidens*), it is true, but none the less effectively. These God-produced evils are, certainly, *mala rei* and not *mala actionis*, yet even moral evil presupposes *malum rei* (see J. Maritain, *Problem of Evil*, pp. 20ff.).

Dr. Philp's admitted "optimism" and his vindications of God's morals play, all too successfully, the irritant role of a Job's comforter to Jung's anguished protests and questioning. But Jung's own contribution to the discussion is hardly more constructive, and even less conciliatory. More than once, he evades criticism by denigrating his critics. When the author quotes Dr. Erich Fromm's challenge to his idiosyncratic identification of "fact" and "truth," "Mr. Fromm" is implicitly charged with "power-drive," "hubris," "arrogance," and being not "scientifically minded" (p. 10). When Dr. Philp quotes our suggestion that Jung's own "assimilation of the shadow" implies the supplying of a privation, he is informed that "What Victor White writes about the assimilation of the shadow is not to be taken seriously. Being a Catholic priest he is bound hand and foot to the doctrine of his Church and has to defend every syllogism" (p. 20). It is disappointing, but not surprising, that discussion conducted in this fashion gets nowhere at all.

◆

NOTES

All references are given in full, except the following: Books of the Holy Bible are usually given their customary abbreviations. Biblical quotations are usually taken from the Douai Version unless otherwise stated. RSV = Revised Standard Version.

The *Summa Theologica* of St. Thomas Aquinas is referred to simply as *Summa*. Roman numerals (I, I-II, II-II, III) refer to the "Parts" of this work; the first Arabic numerals refer to the number of the "Question"; the second Arabic numerals the number of the "Article"; "ad" followed by an Arabic numeral refers to a reply to an objection within that "Article." For example, I, 49, 2 ad 2 = First Part, question 49, article 2, reply to 2nd objection.

For quotations from and references to works by C. G. Jung, *The Collected Works of C. G. Jung* have been used as far as possible. This is the edition edited by Sir Herbert Read, Michael Fordham and Gerhard Adler, and translated by R. F. C. Hull, which began to appear in 1953, but is not yet complete. It is referred to in these notes simply as *CW*, without repetition of the author's or editors' names. Works by Jung which had not, at the time of writing, yet appeared in the *Collected Works*, are referred to by their full titles.

PG = Migne's *Patrologia Graeca*.

PL = Migne's *Patrologia Latina*.

Denzinger–Bannwart = Henrich Denzinger et Clemens Bannwart, S.J., *Enchiridion Symbolorum Definitionum et Declarationum de Rebus Fidei et Morum*, editio 14a, Friburgi Brisgoviae, 1922.

CHAPTER ONE

1. For discussion and criticism of this claim, see especially Igor Caruso, *Psychoanalyse und Synthese der Existenz* (Vienna, 1952), pp. 157ff.

2. There is another reason why Jungians must find a divorce between soul and psyche unacceptable. For them, the therapeutic process is no mere analysis of the material provided by the "psychic apparatus," but "is in itself dialectic, as a process which, by confronting the contents of consciousness with those of the unconscious, calls forth a reaction between these two psychic realities"; and is thus itself "an activation of the ethical function." (J. Jacobi, *The Psychology of C. G. Jung* [1942] p. 67). Thus, not only can all the ethical values, "disposable libido," religious attitudes, free decisions, etc. (which, by general consent, pertain to the soul) not be excluded *a priori* from the clinical picture, they are also essential to the psychotherapeutic process itself.

3. Vernor Moore, O.S.B., *The Driving Forces of Human Nature* (New York, 1948); J. H. Vanderveldt and R. P. Odenwald, *Psychiatry and Catholicism* (New York, 1952); J. F. Donceel, S.J., *Philosophical Psychology* (London, 1955).

4. Aquinas (*Summa*, II-II, 81, 4) distinguished usefully between activities which are "elicited" by, and peculiar to, religion, and those which are, or should be, "governed" by it—but are not on that account any the less religious. Examples of the former are sacrifice, praise, etc.; the latter should include all the activities of life to the extent that they are performed in reverence for the Creator. See above, pp. 210ff.

5. Gregory Zilboorg, *International Journal of Psycho-Analysis* (1939), p. 480, quoted by Marjorie Brierley, *Trends in Psycho-Analysis* (1951), pp. 199f. In fairness we should add that we have been unable to check this quotation, and that Dr. Zilboorg has assured us personally that, while he continues to vindicate St. Thomas's importance in the emancipation of the sciences, he would not be prepared to stand by every word he has written in his voluminous, and especially his earlier, writings. But, without irony, we thank him for formulating so unequivocally the diametric opposite of our own convictions.

6. Though of course most sound analysts and non-directive therapists will carefully refrain from telling him to do this, or anything else.

7. See Etienne Gilson, *Christian Philosophy in the Middle Ages* (1955), p. 398; M.-D. Chenu, O.P., *Introduction à l'étude de Saint Thomas d'Aquin* (1950), pp. 173ff.

8. Except for Jung, who uses the word *anima* in a specialized sense to cover only one class of the phenomena ascribed to the whole psyche. But he also frequently uses the word "soul" (*Seele*) as equivalent to "psyche."

9. *Summa*, I, 75, 1.

10. Ibid., I, 76, I.

11. Ibid., I, 76, 3, 4.

12. *Reason and Unreason in Psychological Medicine*, pp. 12, 13 (E. K. Lewis, 1953).

13. Nothing is gained, or changed, by using the word *mind* instead of *psyche*. This is understood by modern psychologists as "the organized totality of *psychical* structures and processes, conscious, unconscious and endopsychic" (S. Drover, *A Dictionary of Psychology* [1952], p. 170). Traditionally it is commonly applied more particularly to purely cognitive, and especially intellectual, capacities and actions.

14. *The Month* (October 1956), p. 207.

15. As we have put it elsewhere: "For him [Aquinas] it is almost axiomatic that the different human sciences and disciplines are to be distinguished, not necessarily by different subject-matter or fields of inquiry ('material objects" as the schoolmen called them), but by the different ways (*rationes cognoscibiles*) in which the subject can be rendered knowable to the human mind…. Nor will a Thomist theologian be unfamiliar with the idea that the selfsame "soul" or "psyche" which is his professional concern may also be the subject of empirical observation and scientific inquiry. Aquinas himself conducted just such an inquiry, commenting upon and developing Aristotle's *De Anima*. This inquiry was based on observation of fact no less than is that of more modern psychologies. But its methods and treatment of observed facts differed considerably. Where modern scientific method proceeds by way of generalization, postulate, hypothesis, law, prediction or…the correlation of phenomena in terms of function, the psychology of Aristotle and Aquinas proceeded mainly by way of inference…." (*God and The Unconscious*, pp. 68, 69).

16. With the *Oxford Dictionary*, we understand a "concept" to be an "idea of a class of objects," while a "conception" may also include judgments, statements or propositions.

17. See D. H. Lawrence's essay on Benjamin Franklin: "man has a soul, though you can't locate it either in his purse or his pocket book or his heart or his stomach or his head. The *wholeness* of a man is his soul. Not merely that nice comfortable bit which Benjamin marks out...

     "It's a queer thing is a man's soul. It is the whole of him. Which means that it is the unknown him, as well as the known...."

     "The soul of man is a dark forest. The Hercynian wood that scared the Romans so, and out of which came the white-skinned hordes of the next civilization...."

     "Who knows what will come out of the soul of man? The soul of man is a dark vast forest, with wild life in it. Think of Benjamin fencing it off!"

     Studies in Classical American Literature, quoted in *Selected Essays* (Penguin Books, 1950), pp. 252f.

18. "Psychological Medicine and Catholic Thought," *The Month* (October 1956), pp. 207f.

19. Aristotle's full definition of the soul or psyche, taken over by Aquinas, is "the form (or psyche) of a physical, organic body which is able to have life" (*De Anima*, 412a, 21, 29). In *God and the Unconscious*, pp. 90ff., we have tried to explain how and why he defined it in these terms. The same idea is, quite independently, excellently stated by C. G. Jung: "The body is a system of material units adapted to the end of life and co-ordinated within itself...a purposeful arrangement of matter, making possible a living being... The body cannot be understood merely as a heaping together of dead matter, but must be taken as a material system prepared for life, and making life possible; though with the condition that, notwithstanding the utmost readiness, the system could not live without the addition of the "living being." For, quite apart from the possible significance of the "living being," there is lacking to the body by itself something necessary to its life, namely the psychic factor. This we know immediately from our own experience, and mediately from experience with our fellow men; further, through scientific findings in our study of the higher vertebrates and in no way contradicted, at least so far as our evidence goes, in regard to lower animals and plants." (*Contributions to Analytical Psychology*, p. 79.)

20. Especially in his *De Unitate Intellectus*.

21. This word is preferable to the highly ambiguous word "survival" which has no place in orthodox Christian theology.

22. The Councils of Vienne (1311–1312) and of the Lateran (1513), Denzinger–Bannwart, *Enchiridion Symbolorum*, 481, 738.

23. "Vous devez, vous, les psychologues et les thérapeutes, tenir compte de ce fait: l'existence de chaque faculté ou fonction psychique se justifie par la fin du tout. Ce qui constitue l'homme, c'est principalement l'âme, forme substantielle de sa nature. C'est d'elle que découle en dernier lieu toute la vie humaine; en elle, s'enracinent tous les dynamismes psychiques avec leur structure propre et leur loi organique; c'est elle que la nature charge de gouverner toutes les énergies, pour autant que celles-ci n'aient pas encore acquis leur dernière détermination. De ce donne ontologique et psychique, il s'ensuit que ce serait s'écarter du réel que de vouloir, en théorie ou en pratique, confier le rôle déterminant du tout à un facteur particulier, par exemple à l'un des dynamismes psychiques élémentaires, et installer ainsi au gouvernail une puissance secondaire.... On a cru devoir accentuer l'opposition entre métaphysique et psychologie. Bien à tort! Le psychique lui-même appartient au domaine de l'ontologique et du métaphysique" (*L'Osservatore Romano* (Giovedi 16 Aprile, 1953), p. 1).

24. G. Abbott-Smith, D.D., *A Manual Greek Lexicon of the New Testament* (1923), pp. 488, 489.

25. G. W. A. Lampe, "The Healing Church in the New Testament," *The St. Raphael Quarterly* (November 1957), p. 460.

26. It is interesting to note that in early and Homeric Greek *psyche* seems to have covered unconscious life only, consciousness being ascribed to *thymos* (see R. B. Onians, *The Origins of European Thought* [Cambridge, 1951], pp. 59ff., 93ff.). But later there is a "breakdown of the original duality *psyche* and *thymos*, and their fusion in a more complex *psyche*" (ibid., p. 117), and psyche becomes especially—though never exclusively—the seat of waking consciousness. For the development of the parallel Hebrew word *nephesh*, see ibid.,.pp. 480ff. and F. Delitzsch, *System der biblischen Psychologie* (Leipzig, 1861).

27. E. Gilson, *Christian Philosophy in the Middle Ages*, p. 26.

28. *Adversus Haereses*, 5, 6.1; 5.7.1.

29. *De Anima*, PL 2:650.

30. J. Bainvel, *Dictionnaire de théologie catholique*, I, col. 999.

31. *De Testimonio Animae, passim*. See *God and the Unconscious*, pp. 38, 39.

32. As Cambridge Platonists were much later to call it.

33. *De hominis opificio* (A.D. 379), viii (145c), xiii (168b).

34. F. Coplestone, S.J. (*A History of Philosophy*, II, 78) claims that "Augustine is quite clear about the fact that man does consist of soul and body, as when he says that 'a soul in possession of a body does not constitute two persons but one man'" (*In Ioann.* 19, 5, 15). But do not these words say that a man is *not* body and soul, but a soul possessing a body? Aquinas also (*Summa*, I, 75, 4, *sed contra*) actually invokes St. Augustine (*De Civitate Dei*, XIX, 3) in support of his own view that man is soul and body and not soul only. But it seems that Augustine in this passage only describes this view (among others) and in no way "commends" it, as Aquinas says he does.

35. *De moribus eccl.*, I, 27.

36. *Enarratio in Ps.* 137, 4.

37. *Enarratio in Ps.* 3, 3, and *in Ps.* 145, 5.

38. Decima Douie, "Pecham's Tractatus de Anima," *Dominican Studies* (January 1950), p. 89.

39. The preamble to the decree of definition makes it clear that theological issues, especially regarding the Incarnation, were at stake (see J. Leclercq, *Dict. de Theologie cath.*, s.v. Vienne, col. 2975). The Council is careful not to define that the soul *is* the form of the body, or to say that it is philosophically true or false; but it defines that to *deny* it is heresy—i.e., contrary to the integrity of the faith. The Aristotelian thesis does not thereby become an article of faith, nor are other speculations about the soul forbidden so long as they do not involve such a denial.

40. Vanderveldt and Odenwald, *Psychiatry and Catholicism*, p. 92.

41. Some other proposed divisions are examined in Appendix I (pp. 237–42).

42. Michael Fordham, M.R.C.P., in *The British Journal of Medical Psychology* (1953), p. 320.

43. J. de Tonquédec, S.J., *Les maladies nerveuses ou mentales et les manifestations diaboliques* (Paris, 1938). We have been able to consult only the Spanish translation (Madrid, 1948) significantly entitled *¿Accion diabolica o enfermedad?* See also J. Lhermitte, *Vrais et faux possédés* (Paris, 1956).

44. The theory naturally leads its upholders into the most improbable positions. They are compelled to maintain that the various symptoms which Charcot and others have likened to those recorded of diabolic possession are not "truly" such, but only "analogues" which are "really" to be attributed to the various categories of mental disease (thus de Tonquédec,

Les maladies nerveuses, p. 29 and *passim*). They must and do hold that many or most of the cases of "possession" recorded in history were really "only" psychopathological cases, and that their attribution to the devil was ignorant superstition, now happily outmoded by modern science. But they must draw the line at the inspired Scriptures, especially the utterances of Jesus himself, and assert that the possessions by evil spirits recorded in the Gospels were "truly" such, and therefore not mental illnesses—however much the recorded symptoms resemble those of epilepsy (e.g., in Mark 9:17) and other recognized syndromes. The confusion which must arise between therapist and patients when (as is frequent) the latter are firmly convinced that they are oppressed by demons, can only be imagined.

45. See "Devils and Complexes" in our *God and the Unconscious*, pp. 175–189.

46. *The Divine Institutes*, ii, 15 (written between A.D. 304 and 315).

47. *De Principiis*, III, iii, 3 (begun A.D. 220). Here we have perhaps one of the earliest attempts to distinguish psychosis from neurosis!

48. Psychotherapists who are ready to take psychological images and phenomena at their face value, and who may also have some understanding of what is understood by "devils" in traditional theology, do not always find this so easy—whatever their own theological or philosophical prejudices. As Jung has said: "it is incredible how people can allow themselves to be bewitched by words. They always imagine that a name can actually create a thing; as if, for instance, we had dealt the devil a serious blow by calling him a neurosis." (*Wirklichkeit der Seele* [1934], p. 52.) Theologians, one might have thought, have less excuse than most for encouraging this magical thinking and drawing such secularist conclusions.

49. See our chapter on "Revelation and the Unconscious" in *God and the Unconscious*, pp. 107ff. Reviewing this in *Theological Studies* (September 1953), pp. 499ff. (Woodstock, MD), Dom Gregory Stevens, O.S.B., complains that "it is not enough to distinguish natural from supernatural prophecy only on the basis of purpose," without telling us how else it is to be distinguished. We did not however say "only" but "primarily" (p. 130). We also pointed out that they differ in their content, inasmuch as "the supernatural prophet is concerned with the ultimate designs of the Author of men and stars," though we also insisted that this content (and surely this is hardly disputable) is itself determined by the purpose for which man is destined. He also complains that, in our presentation of

St. Thomas's conception of revelation, we give a "preponderating role to the imagination" (we did not; we said St. Thomas gives it a preponderating role "in determining human behaviour"—*de facto*, of course, not *de jure*) and say "nothing about the role of intellect and will" or the *vis cogitativa*. We are still not too clear where will comes in (we were talking of revelation itself, not the faith of the prophet in it, and we pointed out that, according to both the Bible and St. Thomas, revelation often takes place contrary to the recipient's volition). But we were at some pains to explain that "what is *essential*, and indeed *fundamental* is the *primary* importance of the *judgment*" in St. Thomas's theory of revelation (p. 128). It is difficult to know how we could say "nothing" with more of the "verbiage" and less of the "seeming confusion" of which Dom Stevens more justly complains.

50. According to the theologian there are, of course, also other "supernatural effects" which by definition escape empirical observation altogether—e.g., creation, justification, transubstantiation. There are others which are not directly observable, but can (given certain premisses) be "conjectured" from their effects or signs which can be observed—e.g., the presence of grace or charity in a soul. On the other hand, a "miracle" in the strictest sense is an observable event which can be shown to transcend the powers of any finite cause, though this does not exclude (but usually includes) the instrumentality of such causes, which may or may not be empirically observable. Empirical psychology is concerned to observe, and to classify and correlate its observations, not to assign them to their ultimate causes. To the extent that it assigns them to the "unconscious" it is precisely assigning them to the empirically unobservable. But such is the character of these observations that Jung relates, "I fancied I was working along the best scientific lines, establishing facts, observing, classifying, describing causal and functional relations, only to discover in the end that I had involved myself in a net of reflections which extend far beyond natural science and ramify into the fields of philosophy, theology, comparative religion and the humane sciences in general. This transgression, as inevitable as it was suspect, has caused me no little worry." "The Spirit of Psychology," *Spirit and Nature*, ed. J. Campbell (1955), p. 426.

51. *God and the Unconscious*, p. 145; see also Appendices I and II.

CHAPTER TWO

1. *Modern Man in Search of a Soul*, p. 264.
2. *CW*, XVI, pp. 76ff.
3. *God and the Unconscious*, pp. 15ff.
4. *CW*, XVI, p. 115.
5. *Psychoanalyse und Synthese der Existenz* (Wien, 1952), pp. 158ff.
6. Kenneth Walker, *The Healing Arts and Their Future* (1953), p. 69.
7. See Chapter III, note 40.
8. J. P. Sartre, *L'existentialisme est une humanisme* (Paris, 1946), p. 22.
9. Viktor Frankl, *Der unbedingte Mensch* (Wien, 1949).
10. Viktor Frankl, *Der Unbewusste Gott* (Wien, 1948).
11. A noteworthy example is von Siebenthal's distinction between pathological, existential and moral guilt and his study of their interrelation with one another and with the recognized syndromes. His phenomenology of Man as *viator* between life and death also provides an invaluable diagnostic norm. See his *Schuldgefühl und Schuld bei psychiatrischen Erkrankungen* (Zürich, 1956).
12. "Unbiassedness," see *Psychological Types* (1938), p. 17.

CHAPTER THREE

1. E. B. Strauss in *The Month* (May 1956), p. 308.
2. *CW*, XVI, p. 37.
3. Ibid., p. 9.
4. Cf. E. B. Strauss, "Causality in Psychological Medicine," in *Reason and Unreason in Psychological Medicine* (1953).
5. Cf. C. G. Jung, "Synchronicity, an acausal connecting principle," in *The Interpretation of Nature and the Psyche* (1955).
6. Especially Reik and Rank.
7. See Appendix III.
8. By "religious" phenomena and factors, we here understand those which, historically and empirically, are associated exclusively or principally with religion or the "sacred." This is without prejudice to the belief that all human activities can and should be religious (see Chapter I, note 4, and

Chapter XI, *passim*), or to Eliade's contention that Christianity in principle abolishes the old distinction between the sacred and the profane (see
his *The Myth of the Eternal Return*).

9. Raymond Hostie, S.J., *Religion and the Psychology of Jung* (1957).

10. *Studies in Analytical Psychology* (1948), pp. 148ff.

11. Quoted from Jung, "Zur Psychologie der Trinitätsidee" in *Eranos Jahr-buch* (1940–1941), p. 50.

12. Quoted from Jung, *Psychology and Religion* (Yale, 1938), p. 3.

13. Cf. C. Flugel, *Man, Morals and Society* (1945), pp. 265ff.

14. Cf. Erich Schaeder, "Statements in Physics," in *Blackfriars* (June 1956), pp. 244ff.

15. C. G. Jung, *Psychology and Alchemy*, p. 14.

16. G. Adler, "The Psychological Approach to Religion," p. 162.

17. In his Foreword to my *God and the Unconscious*, p. xvii.

18. "Jungian literature is like a vast quaking bog. At every painful step the reader sinks to the hip in jargon and generalizations, with never a patch of firm intellectual ground to rest on, and only rarely, in that endless expanse of jelly, the blessed relief of a hard, concrete, particular fact. And yet, in spite of everything, the Jungian system is probably a better description of psychological reality than is the Freudian...." Aldous Huxley, *Adonis and the Alphabet*, p. 172. The judgment is surely too sweeping. When, as throughout Volume XVI of the *Collected Works*, Jung is writing of the *practice* of psychotherapy, his writing is a model of lucidity.

19. From a letter published in *God and the Unconscious*, p. 72.

20. Hostie, *Religion and the Psychology of Jung*, p. 215 (retranslated from the French, p. 196).

21. Foreword to *God and the Unconscious*, p. xvii.

22. It should not be any longer necessary to say that such an assertion *is* of a philosophical, indeed an *a priori*, character and not itself an empirically verifiable fact. Empirical observation and correlation can never prove the non-existence of any other method of knowing—any more than see-ing can prove the non-existence of hearing or smelling. It is logically impossible to prove a negative proposition from any number of affir-mative premises. But the empirical psychologist can hardly fail to notice the psychological fact that many men *believe* that they "know" in other ways—e.g., by deduction or strict inference from events to causes which are not empirically verifiable.

23. These points have been more fully developed, and with copious documentation from Jung's writings, by Hostie, *Religion and the Psychology of Jung*, pp. 141–161.

24. It may legitimately be objected that psychotherapy does not in fact adjust the patient to the "real" parent: the "real" parent is usually unknown to the therapist, and often to the patient also. The most that therapy can achieve is the replacement of one image by another which is more conscious and "realistic": the "real" parent (like God!) is still unknown except in some image. This is true, but does not affect our contention. If psychology is to confine itself to the manifestations of the irrational God-imago, and exclude all rational and conscious approaches to God, there can be no parallel replacement of images, and no interaction of consciousness and of the unconscious in religious matters such as would permit religious development and growth. Parental adjustment, and maturation of relationship to the parents, presupposes at least the rational assumption that "real parents" exist or have existed.

25. Hostie, *Religion and the Psychology of Jung*, p. 134.

26. It has however been noted that Jungians tend to ignore the "sense of creatureliness," which Otto stressed as characteristic of religion.

27. *Religion and the Cure of Souls in Jung's Psychology*, p. 100.

28. *Psychology and Religion*, p. 98.

29. *Symbols of Transformation* (1952). (*CW*, V. p. 72.)

30. They do not of course maintain that such absence is of itself meritorious or "religious"; it *can* be quite irreligious, pathological and even blameworthy. We wish only to point out that the "religious" is undoubtedly separable from "numinous experience."

31. Patanjali's *Yoga Aphorisms*, I, 2. *Vrillis* "comprehend all the manifold states of consciousness of our phenomenal existence," S. Dasgupta, *Yoga as Philosophy and Religion* (1924), p. 192.

32. *The Ascent of Mount Carmel, passim.*

33. *Summa*, II-II, 56, 2, 3, 7.

34. See especially Jung's "Principles of Practical Psychotherapy" (1935), in *CW*, XVI, pp. 4ff. We shall point out later that Jung has *also*, of course, drawn particular attention to these similarities, not only of psychic processes, but also of psychic contents. Psychotherapy however, though it uses the generalizations of science, is an *art* whose primary concern is with the concrete particular.

35. The analogical character of the name "God," and the absolutely non-identical but related senses which it has in human speech, has long been recognized by semanticists, logicians and theologians. See Aquinas, *Summa*, I, 13, 10; *Utrum hoc nomen, Deus, univoce dicatur de Deo per naturam, et per participationem, et secundum opinionem.*

36. See especially *God and Philosophy* by Etienne Gilson (Yale University Press, 1941); *The God of Reason*, by J. K. Heydon (Sheed & Ward, 1939), and our own "Prelude to the Five Ways" in *God the Unknown* (Harvill Press, 1956), pp. 35–61.

37. See *God the Unknown*, pp. 16–34.

38. Such statements seem to do this, as a matter of fact, very seldom outside of the Bible and the philosophers. The Gods of the Greeks, for instance, are not omnipotent but restricted by Fate and by one another; they are not omniscient but often both deceived and deceiving; and although they are immortal, they are very far from being eternal in the sense of being immutable and *totum simul*—which is the sense in which eternity is ascribed to their God by Jewish and Christian thinkers. More generally, Raffaele Pettazzoni in his monumental work, *The All-Knowing God* (Methuen, 1956), has shown conclusively that "omniscience, far from being an attribute of every God, is a power belonging only to certain particular deities, who are in the first place deities of light."

39. The point is perhaps more self-evident if put the other way round: It makes a very great difference indeed whether it is Jahwe, Allah, Zeus, Shiva or Huizilopochtli—or an "autonomous complex"—which a man calls his God.

40. In fairness it must however be explained that Jung himself does not so regard it. It is clearly not his *intention* to produce monologues of a theo-logical, philosophical or historical character, still less to make *ex cathedra* pronouncements which require his patients' or readers' assent. He sees these utterances simply as his own, confessedly one-sided, contribution to that *dialogue* with the patient (and presumably the reader) in the field of *Weltanschauung* to which the competence of the physician restricts him, but which is both unavoidable and necessary for the majority of patients (see *CW*, XVI, pp. 3ff., 18, 78, 117, also XII, pp. 27, 28). Jung must be believed when he tells us that these views and opinions, although not strictly empirical observations, have nevertheless arisen from the practical needs of therapy. It is not however surprising that the event often defeats

his intentions, and that the dialogue tends to become a monologue. For, as he himself has pointed out, the patient frequently lacks any "firm ground" from which to answer back, and the resulting vacuum immeasurably intensifies the positive transference and the physician's burden outside his professional sphere of competence (see *CW*, XVI, pp. 99f., XII, pp. 4ff.). It is also questionable how far theological or philosophical dialogue can fruitfully be carried on without theological and philosophical equipment on both sides. It is, in any case, no small task for the reader to sort out the empirical observations and the legitimate general laws and hypotheses from these contributions to "dialectical procedure"; and it is inevitable that all alike are commonly assumed to be part and parcel of "Jungian Psychology."

41. *Answer to Job*, p. xviii.

42. *Modern Man in Search of a Soul*, p. 260.

43. *Psychology and Alchemy*, p. 28.

44. For example, *CW*, XVI, p. 122; *Aion* (1951), pp. 60, 61.

45. Indeed this problem of communication has been the principal preoccupation of Protestant theology during the past half-century. The discussions which have successively centred around the concepts of "restatement," the "*Anknüpfungspunkt*" (the point of contact between the Gospel and the "natural man"), "*Kerygma*," "Demythologization," are all evidently stimulated by this sense of failure in "putting across" the Gospel. Catholics, for whom the interrelation of grace and nature has long been settled by dogma and theology, are not confronted by the same *theoretic* problems; and they should welcome the return to a more balanced and traditional solution which they find in such Protestant writers as Paul Tillich. With their own flocks, who share not only a common faith, but a common education and language, Catholic divines and pastors do not experience the same practical problems. But they too are usually acutely aware of the deep chasm of incomprehension which separates them from others.

46. *CW*, XII, p. 27.

47. Ibid., pp. 6ff.; XVI, pp. 99ff.

48. From a letter quoted in *God and the Unconscious*, p. 72.

49. *CW*, XVI, p. 100.

50. Ibid., p. 16.

CHAPTER FOUR

1. Cf. *CW*, XVI, p. 117: "One cannot treat a Mohammedan on the basis of Christian beliefs, nor a Parsi with Jewish orthodoxy, nor a Christian with the pagan philosophy of the ancient world, without introducing dangerous foreign bodies into his psychic organism. This sort of thing is constantly practised, and not always with bad results; but, for all that, it is an experiment whose legitimacy seems to me exceedingly doubtful. I think a conservative treatment is more advisable. One should, if possible, not destroy any values that have not proved themselves definitely injurious. To replace a Christian view of the world by a materialistic one is, to my way of thinking, just as wrong as the attempt to argue with a convinced materialist. That is the task of the missionary, not of the doctor."

2. For these it may indeed be a vital necessity, required by that very unity of the personality on which Dr. Igor Caruso has rightly laid great stress, and which is threatened with grave disturbance and dissociation without such correlation. Dr. Caruso seems to overlook this when he accuses the efforts of Dr. G. P. Zacharias and myself in this direction of a pointless "syncretism" in his *Bios, Psyche, Person* (Freiburg, 1957), p. 392.

3. *CW*, XVI, p. 79.

4. Nor can he escape from the task of correlation by saying, with R. Hostie: "The religious function is rooted in man, but revealed truths have their source in God; and whenever these two realities come together any confusion of them is fatal." For any conceivable "religious function" in man also has its source in God, and (even were there no evidence of similarity between the contents of the archetypes and of revelation) any conceivable "revealed truths" must have some positive correlation with this function, and not be in irreconcilable conflict with it. See below, Chapter V, note 59.

5. Seminar, given at Basle, October 1934, quoted in *Psychological Reflections*, ed. J. Jacobi, p. 320. We have been unable to consult the original, but we may surmise that it has *Christenheit* (Christendom) rather than *Christentum* (Christianity) in the opening sentences.

6. *Psychological Types* (1938), p. 230. This, like similar statements by Jung, is no less true for being one-sided. A complete picture would also stress that, not only does the past condition the present, but the present conditions

our inheritance of the past. An "intellectual change of opinion" itself has deep roots which spread widely and grow deeper, and while it may not influence the unconscious (it certainly does not get rid of it) changed conscious altitudes will greatly modify its manifestations. The process is not unidirectional, and Jung deplores an atavistic return to the past which would ignore the later developments and demands of consciousness. He has repeatedly emphasized the reciprocity of influence between consciousness and the unconscious, and that modern psychology itself, his own included, is the outcome of a changed mentality which itself has unconscious roots. (See especially his "The Spiritual Problem of Modern Man" in *Modern Man in Search of a Soul*, pp. 226ff. and his Foreword to our *God and the Unconscious*.)

7. *CW*, V, p. 20.

8. See "The Theologian's Task" in my *God the Unknown*, pp. 3–15.

9. Cf. V. White, O.P., *Holy Teaching: The Conception of Theology in St. Thomas Aquinas* (Aquinas Paper, No. 33, 1958).

10. *Psychology and Religion*, pp. 56, 57.

11. Provided, of course, that "the unconscious" be understood in the unlimited sense of the Jungians, and not in the restricted sense of early psychoanalysis. See *God and the Unconscious*, pp. 35–37.

12. *Psychology and Religion*, p. 6.

13. Ibid., p. 57.

14. Ibid., p. 63.

15. Ibid., pp. 52f.

16. R. Hobson, *The Journal of Analytical Psychology*, III, 1 (January 1958), p. 65.

17. *Book of the Foundations*, chapter viii: *The Complete Works of Saint Teresa of Jesus*, trans. and ed. E. Allison Peers (1946), Vol. III, pp. 41f.

18. *The Ascent of Mount Carmel*, Book II, especially chapter xix, "Wherein is expounded and proved how, although visions and locutions which come from God are true, we may be deceived about them," and chap. xx, "Wherein is proved how the sayings and words of God, though always true, do not always rest upon stable causes" (!)—*The Complete Works of Saint John of the Cross*, trans. and ed. E. Allison Peers (1943), Vol. I, pp. 149–158.

19. *CW*, XII, p. 34.

20. Ibid., p. 18.

21. This basic hypothesis of depth-psychology accords with the classical, Aristotelian and Thomistic view that all our intellectual understanding is dependent upon phantasms which the active power of the mind (*intellectus agens*) "illuminates" and renders intelligible. It is a corollary of this view that our understanding is restricted to this field of phantasms, and largely conditioned by the "pictures" presented to it. Although the medieval schoolmen had little occasion to draw this corollary, or to face its immense implications for philosophy and human communication generally, it has recently received from Thomists some of the attention it demands (cf. F. D. Wilhelmsen, "The Philosopher and the Myth," *The Modern Schoolman* [November 1954]). It should be noted that this Aristotelian view of the dependence of thought on sensory imagery for its *acquisition* does not contrast the view that thought itself (especially apprehension, judgment and ratiocination) is itself imageless. Professor George Humphrey (*Thinking* [1951], p. 31) is surely mistaken in supposing that the important findings of the Würzburg School about "imageless thought" contradict this "Aristotelian dogma." Quite certainly Aristotle himself held that the operations of *Nous* were themselves *chorista* (separate) from all organic functions and imagery, even while they presupposed them and are, in this life, impossible without them. (Cf. *De Anima*, 429a, 10ff.)

CHAPTER FIVE

1. We use the word "experience" in the broadest sense as it is defined by the *Oxford English Dictionary*. "The fact of being consciously the subject of a state or condition, or of being consciously affected by an event. Also an instance of this; a state or condition viewed subjectively; an event by which one is affected." The word has unfortunately gathered different and opposing emotional overtones for psychologists on the one hand and for theologians on the other. The empirical psychologist, as his name implies, regards experience—his own and others'—as a primary concern, the most secure *terra firma* for his investigations. To the extent that religion interests him at all, religious *experience* tends to occupy the foreground. If his psychology is introvertedly orientated, *inner* experience will attract him particularly, and he may be tempted (as we have

seen in Chapter III) almost to deify it and to disregard other religious facts. On the other hand, the emphasis on emotional experience among some sects, and the claims made for inner religious experience by the Modernists, have tended to make the very word suspect to many theologians. The Modernists exalted the "religious sense" (concerning which they had their own unorthodox theories) at the expense of voluntary intellectual assent, and were condemned by Pope Pius X for identifying faith itself with "a blind sense of religion which erupts from the hidden places of the subconscious" (Denzinger–Bannwart, 2145, cf. 2074ff.).

2.   So far as we are aware, no such *phenomenological* description has yet been attempted. Jean Mouroux's *The Christian Experience: An Introduction to a Theology* is an exceptionally valuable work, and not least for its preliminary examination of "experience" itself. But it is, in great measure, historical, and describes what Christian experience has been or should be, rather than what factual investigation might show the distinctive experience of Christians today actually to be. We are aware that our own allusions to the subject in this chapter suffer from the same defect: it is a sad fact that, for instance, the baptismal ritual which we describe is nowadays seldom actually experienced by anybody, least of all by the infant candidate. There is indeed a wide gap between this type of experience and that reflected in the "popular" religious press and devotional literature. But this does not render Mouroux's description, nor our own briefer allusions, altogether valueless, even for the practical psychologist. For they should indicate the kind of experiences which are *authorized* and *available* within the Church. It is, of course, a primary aim of the contemporary liturgical movement that they should again become generally and actually experienced.

3.   See "Revelation and the Unconscious" in *God and the Unconscious*, pp. 107ff.

4.   So also, as Dr. Austin Farrer says, "The mere physical appearance of that death, to one who stood by then, would by no means express what the Christian thinks it, in itself, to be; it took many years for the Cross to gather round itself the force of a symbol in its own right.... There is a current and exceedingly stupid doctrine that symbol evokes emotion, and exact prose states reality. Nothing could be further from the truth; exact prose abstracts from reality, symbol presents it. And for that very reason, symbols have some of the many-sidedness of wild nature" (*A*

Rebirth of Images, p. 20). This is true, but it is also true that the unemotional prose of dogma, just because it abstracts from the concrete, which can "mean" anything or nothing, expressly relates it to a reality which transcends it.

5. This is the rendering of "Fides quid tibi praestat?" in the new (1956) *Ordo Administrandi Sacramenta* for English Catholics. It is a considerable improvement on "What doth faith bring thee to?" in previous editions—as curious a survival of "pie-in-the-sky" Christianity as it is a howler in translation.

6. 1 Corinthians 13:13.

7. *Summa,* I-II, 52, 4.

8. Ibid., aa. 1 and 2.

9. Hebrews 11:1 (RSV).

10. *Summa,* II-II, 1, aa. 3 and 4.

11. C. G. Jung, *The Secret of the Golden Flower,* p. 92.

12. Cf. J. Jacobi, *The Psychology of C. G. Jung* (1942), pp. 91, 134.

13. It is of course true that these archetypal experiences, being prescribed and guided, differ to that extent from the spontaneous emergence of such experiences in psychological analysis, dreams and active imagination. But this is only to say that they serve a pedagogic and initiatory, rather than a therapeutic, purpose. It seems probable that it is precisely the absence of such archetypal initiations in modern society, and the consequent divorce of the ego from its natural and archetypal roots, that calls forth their activation in psychotherapy. But it would clearly be a mistake to suppose that the prescription and guidance imply a superimposition from outside which does violence to the psyche of the recipient. Depth-psychology itself shows that what is here prescribed conforms to the natural structure and dynamics of the psyche, and it must be from the same basic structure of the psyche that the prescriptions themselves take their origin. There can be no question of "indoctrination" in the sense of the injection of a body foreign to the psyche itself.

14. 1 Corinthians 15:44ff.

15. To this witnesses the frequency with which, in various languages, the word for "breath" (as the sign of life) becomes the word for "life" or "soul"—cf. R. B. Onians, *The Origins of European Thought* (1951), pp. 168ff., 488ff.; Walter Wili, "The History of the Spirit in Antiquity," in *Spirit and Nature: Papers from the Eranos Yearbooks* (1955), pp. 83ff.

16. That is, "Depart from him, unclean spirit, and make room for the holy Spirit, the Comforter."

17. Countless references to the symbolism of the cross, and other "foursome" images will be found in the indexes to *CW*. See above, pp. 97ff.

18. See R. B. Onians, *The Origins of European Thought*, pp. 497f.

19. "The Symbolic Significance of Salt," its antiquity and universality, has been studied by Ernest Jones, *Essays in Applied Psycho-Analysis* (1922), pp. 112–203. Jung has remarked that, archetypally, "mind and salt are close cousins—*cum grano salis*—it is *sal sapientiae*" (*CW*, XII, p. 244). Aquinas derives *sapientia* (wisdom) from *sapere*, to taste, and describes it as knowledge by a direct "savouring" (*Summa*, I, 43, 5 ad 2). We may here mention that the psychological importance of these pro-baptismal ceremonies was first brought to our notice by a young woman who came to us with "religious doubts" accompanied by severe hysterical symptoms. Before her first interview she had dreamed that a voice had told her that she needed "lots of salt." She had been a convert from the Church of England, and so, on becoming a Catholic, had been baptized only conditionally and had missed these preliminary ceremonies. She had "read herself into" the Catholic Church, and her conversion had been one almost wholly of purely intellectual conviction. Discussion of these ceremonies brought some amelioration.

20. See our *God and the Unconscious*, p. 189.

21. See J. N. D. Kelly, *Early Christian Creeds* (1950), p. 40.

22. Cf. Erich Neumann, *The Origins and History of Consciousness* (1954): "The mythological stages in the evolution of consciousness begin with the stage when the ego is contained in the unconscious, and lead up to a situation in which the ego not only becomes aware of its own position and defends it heroically, but also becomes capable of broadening and relativizing its experiences through the changes effected by its own activity" (p. 5). "The original question asks about the origin of that which moves all life. To this the creation myths give one answer: they say that creation is something not altogether expressible in the symbols of sexuality, and they proceed to formulate the unformulable in an image. The creative word, creative breath—that is creative spirit.... Mankind asks about the origin of life, and immediately life and soul fuse into one, as living psyche, power, spirit, motion, breath, and the life-giving manna. The one who stands at the beginning is the creative

force contained in the uroboric unity of the World Parents...." (p. 20). The uroboros is, for Neumann, the principal symbol of this pre-sexual, preconscious condition of totally undeveloped life in which "the ego is contained m the unconscious"—i.e., not yet existing as a conscious "I" at all.

23. M. Eliade, *The Myth of the Eternal Return* (1955) pp. 109, 110. The point is more fully established in his *Images et Symboles* (1952), especially in ch. V.

24. W. A. Whitehouse, in *A Theological Word Book of the Bible* (1953), p. 75.

25. We shall treat of this in the next chapter.

26. Whitehouse, *A Theological Word Book of the Bible*, p. 75.

27. This is no esoteric doctrine, but is familiar to Catholics from their regular "acts of faith" (e.g., "O my God I believe in thee...*because* thou hast spoken and thy word is true") and their elementary catechisms (e.g., "Faith is a supernatural gift of God, which enables us to believe without doubting whatever God has revealed...*because* God is the very truth who can neither deceive nor be deceived"). Faith, as we understand it, is wholly conditioned by its object, and because this object lies outside the field of human psychology, the language of psychology can never be adequate to describe it. In this sense we must agree with Lovell Cocks when he writes: "Our closer and fuller definition of faith will not be extracted by psychological or epistemological analysis out of the "hearing," but will be a theological statement in terms of "the Word" which faith hears and obeys. Though we are dealing throughout with a human experience, neither psychology nor epistemology can give us a real understanding of it.... Psychology and epistemology are concerned only with human capacities and possibilities. But when we say that faith is the hearing of the Word of God we deny that this is a human possibility even while we affirm that it is a human experience" (*By Faith Alone* [1943], p. 74). Psychology may observe faith to the extent that it is a human activity and a human response, and it may observe, as does Jung, that events occur in the psyche "as if they were a grace" or "a miracle," and the statements which are made about them. It may say that they originate "outside the ego" or "in the unconscious" (i.e., *not* in the conscious ego-complex). It can say nothing whatever about the ground of faith, which makes faith to be faith; though the psychologist can, and we think sometimes should, listen to what other disciplines such as theology have to say about it. For,

whether true or false, these statements are *also* psychological facts which may be of great importance for the people with whom he has to do, as has been said in Chapter III.

28. Whitehouse, *A Theological Word Book of the Bible*, p. 75.

29. A. R. Whately, *The Focus of Belief*, p. 12, criticizing the Barthian (and original Lutheran) account of faith.

30. See Louis Bouyer, *The Spirit and Forms of Protestantism* (1956).

31. In *Dynamics of Faith* (1957), *passim*.

32. See *Dictionnaire de théologie catholique* (1947), VI, col. 56ff.

33. Paul Tillich, *Dynamics of Faith*, p. 10.

34. J. N. D. Kelly, *Early Christian Creeds*, p. 8. The whole of this first chapter on "Credal Elements in the New Testament" should be read as a counterblast to the liberal view that creeds and dogmas are ecclesiastical accretions and distortions of the Gospels.

35. *Summa*, II-II, 2, 2.

36. A "hierophany in its widest sense is anything which manifests the sacred." M. Eliade, *Patterns in Comparative Religion* (1958), p. xii and *passim*. See also Eliade's *Mythes, Rêves et Mystères* (1957), pp. 165ff., and *Das Heilige und das Profane*, pp. 8, etc.

37. *Summa*, II-II, 1, 2.

38. See *Summa*, II-II, 1, 6; also our "St. Thomas's Conception of Revelation," *Dominican Studies* (1948), No. 1, pp. 3ff.

39. See *Summa*, II-II, 1, a. 10; cf. *God and the Unconscious*, pp. 108ff.

40. The late Archbishop William Temple and other divines have opposed "revelation in events" to "revelation in propositions." But, in fact, in the Bible, the events include propositions, and these propositions are themselves events. Moreover, even when the events are not propositions, they are *enuntiabilia*, i.e., events about which statements can be, and, implicitly or explicitly, are made. Cf. "St. Thomas's Conception of Revelation," *Dominican Studies* (1948), No. 1, pp. 3ff.

41. This is Jung's definition of the function of intuition.

42, Matthew 3:17; 17:5; and parallel accounts of the Baptism and Transfiguration of Christ in Mark and Luke.

43. The General Council of Nicaea (A.D. 325) defined as dogma that the Son is *Homoousios* (consubstantial, of the same kind or nature) with the Father; and rejected the Arian doctrine that he is only *homooisios* (of similar but inferior kind or nature). The General Council of Chalcedon (A.D.

451) defined that the incarnate Son, Jesus Christ, is of two unmixed natures, divine and human, in one Person or Hypostasis.

44. See above, pp. 45f.

45. *CW*, XI, p. 61.

46. Ibid., p. 323.

47. *CW*, XII, p. 205 and *passim*.

48. Dr. Phil. Marie-Louise von Franz, "Die Passio Perpetuae: Versuch einer psychologischen Deutung," included in G. G. Jung's *Aion* (1951), pp. 389ff.

49. See Austin Farrer, *A Rebirth of Images*, pp. 13–18.

50. This has, of course, always been implicitly assumed in the Church, but was not explicitly stated until the contrary views of Liberalists and Modernists became current. See *Dictionnaire de théologie catholique*, IV, 1579ff.

51. Vatican Council (1870), *Constitutio de Fide Catholica*, cap. iv. ("Divina enim mysteria suapte natura intellectum creatum sic excedunt, ut etiam revelatione tradita et fide suscepta ipsius tamen fidei velamine contecta et quadam quasi caligine obvoluta maneant, quamdie in hac mortali vita 'peregrinamur a Domino: per fidem ambulamus et non per speciem' (2 Corinthians 5:6)." Quoted, Denzinger–Bannwart, *Enchiridion Symbolorum*, 1796).

52. *Summa*, I, 13, 10 ad 5, and I, 12, 13 ad 1. Cf. our *God the Unknown*, pp. 16–25.

53. Or, even no thinking at all, but rather a thoughtless acceptance of conventional ideas. Orthodoxy derives from *orthos*, "straight or right"; and *doxa* from *dokeo*, "to think, suppose" (in intransitive form, "to seem or appear"). "Dogma" derives from the same root, and from meaning "that which one thinks true" came to mean "a resolution, or decree." (See Liddell and Scott's *Greek Lexicon*). In the fourth and fifth centuries its use came to be restricted, among Christian writers, to mean truths of faith, authorized by the Church, as containing what God had revealed. *Articuli fidei* (items of the faith) is practically equivalent to *dogmas*, but may be further restricted to cover only those that are explicitly contained in the creeds. (See *Dict. de theol. cath.*, IV, 1574f.)

54. The Greek *hairesis* derives from *haireo*, "to grasp or seize" through *haireomai*, "to take for or to oneself" and therefore "to choose" what one can grasp. (Liddell and Scott, *Greek Lexicon*.) It was first used in the Church of

the gnostics, who chose only what they could grasp by their *gnosis* (see *God and the Unconscious*, pp. 196ff.). Later it came to be used of any "picking and choosing" in the content of the Christian faith, whether of one element at the expense of another (e.g., of the divinity of Christ at the expense of his humanity), or to the impoverishment or distortion of the whole.

55. Thus Aquinas points out at the beginning of his *Summa* that the whole purpose of the *sacra doctrina* (holy teaching), which includes revelation, dogma, theology, preaching, is the *salus humana*. See our *Holy Teaching: St. Thomas's Conception of Theology*, Aquinas Paper No. 33 (1958).

56. "Quicunque vult salvus esse, ante omnia opus est, ut teneat catholicam fidem, quam nisi quisque integram inviolatamque servaverit, absque dubio in aeternum peribit." Quoted Denzinger–Bannwart, *Enchiridion Symbolorum*, 49, from the Roman Breviary. The so-called Athanasian Creed is certainly not the work of St. Athanasius, but may be that of St. Ambrose of Milan. It is used in the liturgies of the Roman, Eastern and Anglican churches. The unhappy translation, "Whosoever will be saved," of the Book of Common Prayer was corrected in the proposed 1928 revision to "Whosoever would be saved."

57. See Appendix IV.

58. The popular and foolish idea that it is of no importance what we believe and think, and all that matters is how we behave, is contradicted not only by the Catholic Church, but by all spiritual guides of any consequence. "Right Thinking" is the first step in the Eightfold Path of the Buddha, who is often claimed to be the least "dogmatic" of such guides. The Buddhist *Dhammapada* opens with the words: "All that we are is the result of what we have thought: it is founded on our thoughts, it is made up of our thoughts." Taking "thoughts" to cover images, phantasies, emotions—conscious and unconscious—this is also the basic hypothesis, confirmed by experience, of modern psychotherapy. Igor Caruso shows that *Lebensorthodoxie* is the basis of all mental health, and *Lebenshäresie* at the root of all mental disorder (*Psychoanalyse und Synthese der Existenz* [Wien, 1952], pp. 59–79, 146–153).

59. Even Father Hostie (*Religion and the Psychology of Jung*) lays himself open to the charge of removing dogma altogether, both in its effects and its origin, from human psychology. There is some justice in Dr. Robert Hobson's complaint: "Neither Jung nor Hostie talks about dogma, as I understand it. The one describes a possible attitude towards dogmatic

formulations, the other defends dogma by rejecting the Incarnation [*sic*] and neither seems to have studied the work that the dogma does in a Christian, or heathen, who is still alive enough to think, imagine and copulate.... The Incarnation implies that God expressly reveals Himself through bodies and minds, and the dogma must be at least 'a psychic utterance'—although not 'equivalent' to it. I cannot conceive how dogmatic truths can be made manifest except through the personal and group psychodynamics of the Apostles and subsequent General Councils of the Church. The fact that the operations of faith, hope and charity are open to psychological study makes them no less gifts of God." *Journal of Analytical Psychology*, III, 1 (1958), pp. 65, 68.

60. *CW*, XI, pp. 109–200.

61. Ibid., p. 194.

62. Ibid., pp. 252ff.

63. Cf. ibid., pp. 334f.

64. See letter quoted in *God and the Unconscious*, p. 72 (cf. *CW*, XI, p. 189: "the Trinity represents the most perfect form of the archetype in question").

65. *CW*, XI, p. 89: "I am not addressing myself to the happy possessors of faith, but to those many people for whom the light has gone out, the mystery has faded, and God is dead."

CHAPTER SIX

1. Apocalypse (Revelation) 21:16ff.

2. Ibid., 4:6fff.

3. Ezechiel 1:5ff.

4. As in the dream of the "world-clock" related by Jung in *Psychology and Religion* and *Psychology and Alchemy*.

5. Cf. *CW*, XI, p. 522.

6. Notably in *The Secret of the Golden Flower* (1935), and the essay "Heber Mandalasymbolik," *Gestaltungen des Unbewussten* (Zürich, 1950).

7. Jung, *Psychology and Alchemy*, *CW*, XI, *passim*.

8. Arnold Ehrhardt, "Vir bonus quadrato lapidi comparatur," *Harvard Theological Review*, Vol. 38, No. 3 (1945), p. 177.

9. Ibid.

10. Blake wrote to Butts on November 20, 1802:

    > *Now I a fourfold vision see*
    > *And a fourfold vision is given to me,*
    > *'Tis fourfold in my supreme delight*
    > *And threefold in soft Beulah's night.*

    J. Middleton Murry commented, "Threefold vision, which is the soft night of Beulah, the place 'where Contraries are equally true,' is the peaceful escape from the living stress of opposition between the Contraries... but fourfold vision is at once to experience the conflict of the Contraries, and in the same moment to transcend that conflict"—*William Blake* (1936), p. 191. Cf. Margaret Rudd, *Divided Image* (1953), pp. 121ff. The resemblance of Blake's Four Zoas to Jung's four functions has often been noted: see L. A. Duncan-Johnstone, *A Psychological Study of William Blake*, Guild of Pastoral Psychology Lectures, No. 40. In view of what will be said presently, it may be remarked that Blake clearly distinguished the Divine Threefold—as well as the threefold bliss of Beulah—from the Human Fourfold, and never seems to have regarded the latter as an extension of the former.

11. A. Ehrhardt, "Vir bonus quadrato lapidi comparatur," p. 182.

12. Ibid., p. 173.

13. Cf. *CW*, XI, pp. 52, 64.

14. R. B. Onians, *The Origins of European Thought* (1951), pp. 426ff.

15. Ibid., p. 440. The circular bond or band is thus also the protective wall of the *temenos* and of the *vas hermeticum*. Psychologically, it "prevents an outburst or disintegration," *CW*, XI, p. 95.

16. See Erich Neumann, *The Origins and History of Consciousness* (1954), pp. 8ff. Cf. Jung, *CW*, XII, p. 187: "The ideal of completeness is a circle or sphere, but its natural minimal division is a quaternity."

17. *CW*, XI, p. 284.

18. Romans 6:6, Ephesians 4:22, and Colossians 3:9.

19. A. Ehrhardt, "Vir bonus quadrato lapidi comparatur," p. 179.

20. A cross in a circle was the Egyptian hieroglyph for a village—see F. L. Griffith, *A Collection of Hieroglyphs* (1898), Fig. 142. Compare Eric Gill's remarks on the "shape" of Chichester as compared with the shapelessness of Brighton—*Autobiography*, pp. 73, 80. For further data on the "symbolism of the centre," see Mircea Eliade, *Images et Symboles* (Paris, 1952), pp. 33ff., and *Patterns in Comparative Religion* (1958), pp. 143ff.

21. *Psychological Types* (1938), *passim*. His most succinct account of these four functions, each contributing to complete human judgment, is found in *CW*, XI, p. 167: "In order to orient ourselves, we must have a function which ascertains that something is there (sensation); a second function which establishes *what* it is (thinking); a third function which states whether it suits us or not (feeling); and a fourth function which indicates where it came from and where it is going (intuition). When this has been done, there is nothing more to say." The two judgment-functions of thinking and feeling correspond to the *indicium per modum cognitionis* (or *studii*) and the *indicium per modum inclinationis* of Aquinas (*Summa*, I, 1, 6 ad 2, etc.).

22. A. Ehrhardt, "Vir bonus quadrato lapidi comparatur," p. 181.

23. J. Jacobi, *The Psychology of C. G. Jung* (1942), p. 124.

24. See Jung, *Aion* (Zurich, 1951), pp. 107ff., 307ff. Although, as Jung points out, the distinction corresponds to a notorious difficulty in translating the N.T. *teleiosis*, there seems to be no legitimate ground for opposing Christian "perfection" to "wholeness" or "completeness." For Aquinas, the "perfect" is what is "totaliter factum" (wholly made) and whose potentialities are fully actualized (*Summa*, I, 4, 1 ad 1). But there can be no doubt that here again Jung is "clinically correct," and that "Christian perfection" is often understood as a one-sided development which may come into serious conflict with the "natural inclination" for wholeness.

25. Cf. *CW*, XVI, pp. 129, 153ff., and Culver Barker, *Some Positive Values of Neurosis*, Guild of Pastoral Psychology Lectures, No. 50.

26. See Jung, ibid., p. 24: "Neuroses may be extremely deleterious in their psychic and social consequences, often worse than psychoses, which generally lead to the social isolation of the sufferer and thus render him innocuous." The catastrophic consequences with which neurotic repression and unbalance threaten our civilization, but also their possibilities for the dawn of a new era, are the principal theme of Jung's *Aion* (1951), *The Undiscovered Self* (1958) and *Ein moderner Mythus* (1958) on the psychological significance of "flying saucers" and space-fiction.

27. *Integration of the Personality* (1940), p. 64.

28. Published as *Psychology and Religion*; amplified version in *CW*, XI, pp. 5ff.

29. Translated, with the less exact title "A Psychological Approach to the Dogma of the Trinity," in *CW*, XI, pp. 109ff.

30. Ibid., p. 110f.
31. Ibid., p. 113.
32. Ibid., p. 115, quoting Jacobsohn, *Die dogmatische Stellung des Königs in der Theologie der alten Aegypter*, p. 58.
33. Karl Barth, *Credo*, p. 70. Cf. the Augustinian–Thomist doctrine according to which the Holy Ghost is the mutual love (*amor*) or link (*nexus*) of the Father and the Son (*Summa*, I, 37, *passim*) and also the love whereby the Father and the Son love mankind (ibid., 2 ad 3). For this reason, the Holy Ghost is also God's gift (*donum*) to man for his possession (*frui et uti*), enabling him to share in the mutual love of the divine Persons (ibid., 38, *passim*; 43, 7). Cf. St. Paul's "He who is united to the Lord becomes one spirit with him" (1 Corinthians 6:17, RSV).
34. Eduard Zeller, *A History of Greek Philosophy* (1881), I, p. 429.
35. Jung, *CW*, XI, p. 119.
36. Plato, *Timaeus*, 31b.
37. Jung, *CW*, XI, p. 127. Jung finds the problem of the "missing fourth" suggested also in the Cabiri scene in Goethe's *Faust:*

    > *Three we brought with us,*
    > *The fourth would not come.*
    > *He was the right one*
    > *Who thought for them all.*

    But, he suggests, whereas Plato's fourth, "inferior" function—who was too "unwell" to join in the Dialogue—was "feeling," Goethe's was "thinking." For the latter, "Feeling is all; Names are sound and smoke."
38. Ibid., p. 149.
39. See ibid., p. 136.
40. That is, 1 John 5:7.
41. In Matthew 28:19.
42. Jung, *CW*, XI, p. 138f.
43. Ibid., p. 189.
44. Ibid., p. 149.
45. Compare Jung, ibid., pp. 131f. with Aquinas, *Summa*, I, 27, 4, according to which the procession of the Holy Ghost cannot be called begetting or generation, but only—and metaphorically—a breathing (*spiratio*).
46. Compare Jung, ibid., p. 159, with Aquinas, *Summa*, I, 36, 1, according to which no distinctive name can be found for the Holy Ghost, but names belonging also to Father and Son (Holy, Spirit, Love, etc.) are

specially applied to stand ("*notionaliter*") for the Third Person; or he can be designated only metaphorically (breath, wind, fire, etc.).

47. Jung, ibid., pp. 148, 152f., 159f. Jung also points out "how important it was that the *homoousia* should triumph over the *homooisia* for the whole development of Western man's reflective consciousness" (ibid., p. 194). While this does not prevent his making some utterances of his own of doubtful orthodoxy, we may note the accord of his account of the development of the doctrine with the famous saying of St. Gregory Nazianzen: "The Old Testament clearly proclaimed the Father, and more obscurely the Son; the New Testament has manifested the Son and suggested the divinity of the Spirit. But now, the Spirit dwells in us, and manifests himself to us more clearly. It was not safe, before the divinity of the Father was acknowledged, to proclaim the Son openly, and, before the acknowledgement of the divinity of the Son to thrust upon us—to speak very boldly—the Holy Ghost into the bargain" (*Orat.* XXXI, 26; Migne, *PG* 36:161).

48. E. Zeller, *A History of Greek Philosophy*, p. 430, who also points out that "seven is the only number within the decade which has neither factor nor product."

49. Thus the square and the triangle are clearly distinguished from each other in Figs. 59, 60, 195 and 199 of this book (*CW*, XI).

50. *Rosarium Philosophorum*, quoted ibid., p. 122.

51. Ibid., p. 26.

52. *CW*, XI, p. 72.

53. *Psychological Types*, p. 547.

54. See the fifth-century *Expositio Eidei* promulgated by the Council of Toledo (A.D. 675) in Denzinger–Bannwart, *Enchiridion Symbolorum*, pars. 278–280; also Aquinas, *Summa*, I, 28, 1, 2, 3; 29, 4; 36, 4; 40, *passim*.

55. The relatively few examples which we find of quaternary deities such as Hermes Tetragonos (see other examples in A. Ehrhardt, "Vir bonus quadrato lapidi comparatur") may well be understood as deifications of the cosmos or of man: see Jung, "Der Geist Mercurius," in *Symbolik des Geistes* (Zürich, 1948), pp. 71ff. Jung often refers to Nicholas of Cusa as having called God the *coincidentia oppositorum* (e.g., *CW*, XI, p. 187, XVI, p. 317), and therefore, by implication, a quaternity. But in fact Nicholas did not do so. The heading of the relevant chapter X of his *De Visione*

Dei runs, "God is seen *beyond* the Coincidentia Oppositorum"; and in the text itself we read "I behold thee [God] *in the door of* the Coincidentia Oppositorum"—which is not at all the same thing. A Protestant theologian, Rudolf Affemann (*Psychologie und Bibel; eine Auseinandersetzung mit C. G. Jung* [Stuttgart, 1957]), roundly charges Jung with deifying the "world-soul," the cosmos, the "self" and the whole collective unconscious. This is an unjust over-simplification, but it must be allowed that, as we have seen in Chapter III above, Jung's methods and philosophical preconceptions permit no clear distinction between, let alone an infinite otherness of, the transcendent and the immanent, the Creator and the creature. It is nevertheless a fact that the "world soul," or totality of creation, has by some been deified: the transcendent *and* immanent Ultimate been replaced by the purely immanent penultimate.

56. There is also the Taoist formula: "Tao begets One: One begets Two; Two begets Three: Three begets all things"—*Tao Te Ching*, xlii, trans. Ch'u Ta-Kao (1942), p. 55.

57. See above, pp. 53ff.

58. The so-called Athanasian Creed, "*Quicumque vult*."

59. This is the clear teaching of Augustine, reproduced and condensed by Aquinas, *Summa*, I, 93, 6. Only the *mens* is capable of *reflection*, i.e., knowing that it knows and uniting knower and known by *voluntas et amor*. It is nevertheless allowed that perceptions of the senses and the imagination also display a certain, but less perfect, "trinitarian" process; but they fall short of that of the *mens* inasmuch as they are dependent on external forms (ibid., reply 4, based on Augustine, *De Trinitate*, XI, 2).

60. Augustine, *De Trin.*, X, 2. By *memoria*, Augustine understands not merely "memory" of past events, but "everything which is retained habitually in the *mens* without its issuing in act" (Aquinas, *De Veritate*, 10, 2)—the act being *intelligentia* itself.

61. On the impossibility of a fourth divine Person, see *Summa*, I, 30, 2.

62. *Summa*, I, 27 and 28.

63. "In God there is one reality which is neither only absolute nor only relative, but which transcendentally (*eminentissime*) but strictly (*formaliter*) includes both what is absolute and what is relative"—Cajetan, *Comment. in Summa*, I, 35, 1.

64. Cf. Eckhardt's *Gott* and *Gottheit*. There is, of course, no real distinction between *Deus* and *Deitas*, such as there is between *homo* and *humanitas*,

but *Deus signifies* God as distinct and personal, *Deitas signifies* him as infinite nature (Aquinas, *Summa*, I, 3, 3). There is no distinction (according to Catholic belief) between nature and person (or persons) in God: the three persons are distinct from one another (not from the nature) solely by relationships of origin, which relationships are themselves identical with the divine essence. The Father is the originating unoriginated; the Son the originating and originated; the Holy Spirit the originated but not originating (*Summa*, I, 28, 1–3; 29, 3; 33, 1; 39, 1). As a "human person" means "that which is distinct in human nature," so (by analogy) a "divine person" means "that which is distinct in the divine nature," although, in the latter case, the distinction is one of distinctive relationships and not of distinct existences (ibid., I, 29, 4).

65. "Simul adoratur et conglorificatur"—Nicene Creed.

66. Aldous Huxley, *The Devils of Loudun* (1952), pp. 81ff.

67. Nicholas Berdyaev, *Spirit and Reality*, pp. 49ff., and *passim*.

68. It should be noted, in view of the misunderstandings of Barth, Brunner and others, that for St. Thomas this "natural" reflection of the mind on itself—its understanding and willing of what it knows—is only an *imago analogiae* of the Holy Trinity—i.e., a mental process *analogous* to the processions of the Trinity. The *imago confirmitatis*—the actual reflecting of the divine life in creation through human mental processes—is attained only when, by God's grace, that which is known and loved is the same as that which is known and begotten in the divine Word, and "breathed" and loved in the Holy Spirit, namely God himself. See Aquinas, *De Veritate*, 10, 7, and *Summa*, I, 93, 8.

69. *Bewusstsein, Unbewusstes und Individuation* (1929), p. 268 (quoted by R. Hostie, *Religion and the Psychology of Jung*, p. 72).

70. *Psychological Types*, p. 535.

71. R. Hostie, *Religion and the Psychology of Jung*, p. 72.

72. *CW*, XI, p. 417.

73. Ibid., p. 284.

74. Ibid., p. 170.

75. A. Ehrhardt, "Vir bonus quadrato lapidi comparatur," p. 184.

76. *Summa*, III, 3, *passim*.

77. Because of the hypostatic union of the divine and human natures in the one Person of the Son, divine and human attributes can both rightly be predicated of him. (This is the *communicatio idiomatum*; see *Summa*, III,

16, 4.) The human nature of Christ is created, and therefore, although he is the Uncreated, he is also, as man, rightly called a creature—ibid., a. 10.

78.　As might well have happened had monophysitism (which denied a real and distinct human nature to Christ) prevailed. Although rejected by the Council of Chalcedon and orthodox teaching generally, it is by no means dead in popular belief and piety; see Yves Congar, O.P., *Christ, Our Lady and the Church* (1957).

79.　*Aion*, p. 99. See also *CW*, V, p. 368; XI, pp. 191, 194; XII, pp. 18, 200, 340. Dr. Gerhard Zacharias has made a stimulating study on the subject on the contrary hypothesis (recognized as legitimate by Jung) that, instead of Christ being a symbol of the Jungian "self," the latter is a symbol of Christ: see his *Psyche und Mysterium*, Studien aus den C. G. Jung Institut Zürich, Volume V (1954).

80.　*CW*, XI, pp. 172f., cf. p. 72.

81.　Ibid., pp. 168ff., cf. p. 59.

82.　Ibid., p. 156.

CHAPTER SEVEN

1.　Exodus 20:3, 4 (RSV margin).

2.　The feminine consort of a Hindu god.

3.　Cf. Mircea Eliade, *The Myth of the Eternal Return, passim*; *Patterns in Comparative Religion*, chapter XI, pp. 388ff.

4.　Exodus 12:25–27. It is now commonly held that the Passover was originally a pre-Mosaic Semitic rite of Spring. This may be indicated by its Hebrew name *pesah*, from *pāsah*, to spring or jump (cf. our English *Spring* from OE *springan*, to jump, or burst forth); though in Exodus this is made to mean the Lord's "jumping" over the Israelites' tents. Although most of the Semitic New Year ritual came to be associated with the feast of Tabernacles (see R. Patai, *Man and Temple*, 1947), the Hebrews "like the Babylonians, virtually kept a dual observance of the New Year, the *Rosh hashshanah* in Tishri at the time of the Ingathering, and the Spring Paschal rites in Nisan" (E. O. James, *Myth and Ritual in the Ancient Near East* [1958], p. 66).

5.　J. T. Meek, *Hebrew Origins* (1950), p. 217, quoted E. O. James, *Myth and Ritual in the Ancient Near East*, p. 64.

6. E. O. James, *Myth and Ritual in the Ancient Near East*, pp. 63f.

7. Ibid., p. 65, cf. Hosea (Osee) 2:16f.

8. Ibid., p. 113. See also R. Levy, *The Gate of Horn* (1948), *passim*, also M. Eliade, *Patterns*, chapter VII, "The Earth, Woman and Fertility," pp. 239ff., and his Bibliography on the Great Mother, pp. 263ff. For the psychological interpretation of this cult, see E. Neumann, *The Great Mother*, and E. Harding, *Woman's Mysteries*.

9. E. O. James, *Myth and Ritual in the Ancient Near East*, p. 63. Of Anat we are told that "she was the chief patroness of Aleyan-Baal, and when she was killed by Mot, like Islar and Isis she went in search of him... lamenting him as bitterly as Adonis grieved for Attis, and desiring him 'as does a cow her calf or a ewe her lamb'" (ibid., p. 122).

10. Ibid., p. 64.

11. 1 (3) Kings 18:17ff.

12. E. O. James, *Myth and Ritual in the Ancient Near East*, p. 61.

13. 1 (3) Kings, 19:10.

14. Jeremias 7:18.

15. Ezechiel 8:14.

16. Luke 23:27ff.

17. E. O. James, *Myth and Ritual in the Ancient Near East*, p. 128.

18. P. Vincent, *La religion des Judeaux-Araméens d'Elephantine* (1937).

19. *CW*, XI, pp. 357ff. See Appendix V.

20. Psalm 88 in Vulgate and LXX.

21. Jonas 4:2.

22. Proverbs 8:22f.

23. Proverbs 8:27, 30, 31.

24. Ecclesiasticus 24:24.

25. *CW*, XI, p. 388.

26. Isaias 66:13; cf. ibid., 46:3, 49:15, 66:9.

27. For example, G. Koepgen, *Die Gnosis des Christentums* (Salzburg, 1939), pp. 315ff.

28. Thus the *Acts of Thomas* (trans. M. R. James, *The Apocryphal New Testament* [1924], p. 388): "Come, O communion of the male; come, she that knoweth the mysteries of him that is chosen.... Come, holy dove.... Come, hidden Mother."

29. Cf. Aquinas, *Summa*, I, 33, 2 ad 1. Although here and elsewhere St. Thomas maintains that in the *Pater noster* we address the whole Trinity as

his creatures, he also of course teaches that we are, by faith and baptism, adopted children of the Father. For instance, "We are sons of God in Jesus Christ.... You are adopted sons, because you are one through faith with Christ, who is by nature the Son of God"—*In Epist. ad Galatas expositio*, 3, lect. 9.

30. See Émile Mersch, S.J., "Filii in Filio," *Nouvelle Revue Théologique* (May, August, 1938).

31. Especially, *Das Ziveigeshlechtericesen bei den Zerdralaustraliern und anderen Völkern: Lösungsversuch der ethnologischen Hauptprobleme auf Grund primitiven Denkens* (1928); *Einführung in die Vorstellungswelt primitiver Völker* (Leipzig, 1931); *Mythos und Kult der Steinzeit* (Stuttgart, 1935); *Mythos und Religionswissenschaft* (Moosberg, 1936). For this information, and much more in the following pages, we are indebted to Prof. Gebhard Frei's unpublished lectures on *Religionswissenschaft*, given at the college for missionaries at Schoneck-bei-Beckenried, Switzerland.

32. Cf. John Layard, *Stone Men of Melekula* (1942), pp. 25ff.

33. Cf. John Layard, "The Making of Man in Malekula," *Eranos Jahrbuch*, 16 (1948), pp. 210ff. According to this, initiation in Malekula is directed to "the making of Woman in man." Layard compares this with modern Hindu identification with Mother Kali, and identification with Demeter in the Eleusinian mysteries.

34. Lehmann, *Archiv für Religionswissenschaft*, 34, pp. 338ff. Other examples from ancient and modern Europe and from elsewhere in Otfried Eberz, "Das Zweigeschlechterwesen," *Hochland*, 2, Bd (1931), pp. 402ff.

35. H. Baumann, *Schöpfung und Urzeit im Mythen der afrikanischen Völker* (Berlin) 1936.

36. M. A. Czaplika, *Der Schamanismus bei den siberischen Völker* (Stuttgart, 1925).

37. K. Haebler in a study of the Aztec man-god Cintoetl, quoted by G. Frei, p. 71.

38. H. Zimmer, *Philosophies of India* (1952).

39. Plato, *The Symposium*, trans. W. Hamilton (1951), p. 61. It will be recalled that the original hermaphrodite was a quaternary mandala! "Each human being was a whole, with its back and flanks rounded to form a circle; it had four hands and an equal number of legs...." (ibid., p. 59).

40. See O. Eberz, "Das Zweigeschlechterwesen," pp. 409ff. A like interpretation of Genesis is attributed to the Christian Eusebius of Caesarea, who also alludes to the agreement of the Bible with Plato's myth.

41. O. Eberz, "Das Zweigeschlechterwesen," pp. 409ff.

42. See Arthur Avalon, *The Serpent Power*; also H. Zimmer, *Philosophies of India*, pp. 560ff.

43. See a few examples under the heading "Physical Passion" in Aldous Huxley's *Texts and Pretexts* (1935), pp. 107ff.

44. See *Tao Te Ching*, XLII: "One begets two, two begets three; three begets all things. All things are backed by the Shade (Yin) and faced by the Light (Yang)." But according to Richard Wilhelm, Yin and Yang originally had no sexual connotation; moreover the distinction did not apply in the heavenly or creative sphere, which was represented by three Yang lines only, but only in the realm of phenomena. See his introduction to *The Secret of the Golden Flower* (1935), p. 13, and to the *I Ching*, Vol. I (1950), p. xxxvi.

45. A. Bertholet, *Das Geschlecht der Gottheit* (Tübingen, 1934), p. 20f.

46. Ibid., p. 14.

47. Ibid., p. 20.

48. Freud (e.g., in *Totem and Taboo*) considered the God-imago almost exclusively as a father-figure. Jung also at first gave more attention to the father-figure in the psychological development of the individual (see his *Die Bedeutung des Vaters für das Schicksal des Einzelnen*, 1909). The mother-figure, whether personal or archetypal, and often concretized in "numinous" feminine images, first received his detailed attention in *Symbols of Transformation* (*CW*, V). There does not appear to be much *published* case-material which testifies to the emergence of the "eternal feminine" in modern psychological analyses, though it is unquestionably of frequent occurrence and of immense significance to the analysant. Several dreams of the Mother-Maiden theme, parallel to the Demeter-Kore theme of Greek myth and ritual, are however recorded and interpreted by Jung in *Essays on a Science of Mythology* by G. G. Jung and G. Kerenyi (1949), pp. 217ff. The works of E. Neumann and E. Harding, already cited, may also be consulted; also John Layard, *The Incest Taboo and the Virgin Archetype* (1945) and, for an elementary exposition, the chapters on "Parental Images" and "Dreams of Anima and Mother," in F. G. Wickes, *The Inner World of Man* (1938). There are several "Mother" and "Anima" dreams in H. G. Baynes, *Mythology of the Soul* (1940).

49. See Maya Deren, *Divine Horsemen: The Living Gods of Haiti* (1950).

50. There are countless examples throughout Frazer's *The Golden Bough*. See also, Lewis Spence, *British Fairy Origins* (1946) and *Myth and Ritual in Dance, Game and Rhyme* (1947).

51. See C. G. Jung, "Woman in Europe," *Contribution to Analytical Psychology* (1928), pp. 164ff. See also Appendix VI, below.

52. Julian of Norwich, *Revelations of Divine Love*, LIX. Cf. S.M.A., O.P., "God Is Our Mother," *Selection I* (1953), pp. 104ff.

53. Clement of Alexandria, *Paidagogus*, I, 6 (Migne, *PG* 8:301).

54. According to Aquinas, "Father" is predicated of the First Person in the strictest sense, inasmuch as the Son is of the same nature or kind. It is predicated less strictly of God in relation to creatures, since they are not of the same nature, but only "like" it in various ways and degrees (*Summa*, I, 33, 2). The idea that the concept of Fatherhood is most perfectly realized in the First Person was encouraged by the Vulgate rendering of Ephesians 3:14: "ex quo omnis paternitas (Greek, *patria*) in caelo et in terra nominatur" (ibid., ad 4).

55. J. Ruysbroeck, *The Adornment of the Spiritual Marriage*, trans. C. A. Wynschenk (1951), pp. 177ff.; cf. ibid., p. 115: "Out of the Unity of the Divine Nature the eternal Word is incessantly born of the Father." Cf. also John Tauler: "The quality which the Heavenly Father has in his incoming and outgoing [i.e., the generation of the Word], the same should every man have who will become the spiritual mother in this divine bringing forth," quoted H. A. Reinhold, *The Spear of Gold* (1947), p. 363.

56. "The Book of Supreme Truth," included in *The Adornment*, p. 240f. (translation slightly modified).

57. Quoted in Augustin Poulain, *The Graces of Interior Prayer*, trans. L. L. Y. Smith (1950), note 63 bis., p. 270.

58. A. Chollet, in *Dict. de théol. cath.*, II, col. 2529.

59. Denzinger–Bannwart, *Enchiridion Symbolorum*, par. 389; St. Bernard, *In Cant.*, 80.

60. The Russian Sophiologists have, to some extent, done so; see S. N. Bulgakov, *The Wisdom of God: A Brief Summary of Sophiology* (1937); see above, p. 148.

61. But see 1 Corinthians 11:7, and Augustine, *Super Gen. ad litt.*, III, 23.

62. See Aquinas, *Summa*, I, 4, 3, etc.

63. *Summa*, III, 3, 3.

64. *Summa*, I, 2–26.
65. "From the womb before dawn I begot thee" (Ps. 110, Vulg. 109). The fact that this rendering is almost certainly incorrect, and has been abandoned even in the new (1945) Roman Psalterium, does not alter the fact that it has been traditionally understood in this sense.
66. *Summa*, I, 33, 3; 29, 7 ad 2. Cf. Augustine, *De Trin.*, VII, 1.
67. On this, there was a difference of opinion between St. Bonaventure and St. Thomas, see *Dict. de théol. cath.*, XV, coll. 1736f., 1744. But the controversy appears to have been verbal; St. Thomas is undoubtedly correct (I, 33, 4 ad 1) in asserting that the negative terms *ingenitus* and *innascibilitas* do not, *vi verborum*, assert origin. But he is quite clear that Father and Son are one Wisdom. "The Father is wise, not by the wisdom which he begets, but by the wisdom which is his essence" (I, 39, 6 ad 2).
68. Cf. John 1:10 (RSV).
69. Epiphanius, *Panarion*, LXXIX (Migne, *PG* 41:739ff.).

CHAPTER EIGHT

1. See Smythe Palmer, *Tehōm and Tiamat* (1897), and Hastings, *Encycl. of Religion* (1908), p. 53.
2. Genesis 1:9–13, 20–28.
3. Genesis 2:7.
4. Genesis 1:28; 2:16f.; 3:9ff.
5. Hosea (Osee) 2:16; Jeremias 3:4, 8; Isaias 54:5.
6. Ezechiel 16:8ff., 60.
7. Hosea 2:15; 3:3f.
8. Amos 5:25; Jeremias 2:1ff.; 7:22.
9. Exodus 34:5f.; Deuteronomy 31:16; Jeremias 3; Ezechiel 16:23; Hosea 1–3 *passim*.
10. Isaias 66:10f.
11. Psalm 44 (Vulgate), 45 A.V., etc.
12. Apocalypse 21:2, 9; 22:17; cf. John 3:29.
13. Ephesians 5:31f. (RSV).
14. *The Shepherd* of Hermas, Vision 2, 4; cf. Vision 3, 10.
15. Hugo Rahner, *Mater Ecclesia: Lobpreis der Kirche aus dem ersten Jahrtausend christlicher Literatur* (Einsiedeln, 1944).

16. Ibid., pp. 14ff.

17. Ephesians 5:27.

18. See Rahner, *Mater Ecclesia*, pp. 43ff., quoting St. Ambrose, Gottschalk *et al.*

19. St. Ambrose, *Comm. in Luc.*, 2, 87f., quoted Rahner, ibid.

20. See Lateran Baptistery inscription and other quotations in Rahner, *Mater Ecclesia*, pp. 59ff.

21. St. Ambrose, *PL* 16:326, quoted Rahner, *Mater Ecclesia*, p. 50.

22. *Panarion* III, 2, *PG* 42:728f., quoted Rahner, *Mater Ecclesia*, p. 14.

23. "Hymn to the Church," *PG* 89:1072, quoted Rahner, *Mater Ecclesia*, p. 113.

24. *Scivias*, 2, 6. *PL* 197:507, quoted Rahner, *Mater Ecclesia*, p. 55.

25. See Rahner, *Mater Ecclesia*, pp. 22ff., 101.

26. *Glaphyra in Genesim*, *PG* 69:224f., quoted Rahner, *Mater Ecclesia*, p. 99f.

27. Thus the Syrian Cyrillonas, quoted Rahner, *Mater Ecclesia*, pp. 78ff.

28. Apocalypse 22:17.

29. Quoted, from a sermon at consecration of a Church, by Rahner, *Mater Ecclesia*, p. 70. Cf. *Shepherd* of Hermas, Vision 2, 4: "She was created the first of all things, and for her sake was the world established."

30. Eclog., Homily 9, *PG* 63:627, etc., quoted Rahner, *Mater Ecclesia*, pp. 109ff.

31. See Rahner, *Mater Ecclesia*, pp. 32ff.

32. 1 Thessalonians 4:17.

33. *Comm. in Luc.*, 2, 87f.

34. Chrysostom, Eclog., Homily 9, *PG* 63:627.

35. Rahner, *Mater Ecclesia*, p. 14.

36. *The Demonstration of the Apostolic Preaching*, trans. J. Armitage Robinson (1920), chapter 36. Tertullian also compares Mary to "that virgin earth, not yet watered by the rains" (*PL* 2:655). Cf. St. Augustine, "Truth has sprung up from the earth since Christ is born of a virgin" (*PL* 38:1006).

38. *PL* 16:326.

39. Carmen XXV, quoted Rahner, *Mater Ecclesia*, p. 46.

40. *Panarion* III, quoted Rahner, *Mater Ecclesia*, p. 14. By the twelfth century, a disciple of St. Bernard, Isaac of Stella, is even more explicit, claiming a *communicatio idiomatum* of Mary and Ecclesia: "As the Head and Members are one Son and many sons, so Mary and the Church are one Mother and two Mothers, one Virgin and two Virgins.... In the divinely

inspired Scriptures, what is said of the Virgin Mother Church is true of the Virgin Mother Mary in particular, and what is said of the Virgin Mother Mary is true of the Virgin Mother Church in general, so what is said of the one may ordinarily be said of the other." (Sermon 51, *PL* 194:1863, quoted by Claude Chevasse, *The Bride of Christ* [1940], p. 166.) That is, the story of man's healing or salvation by God.

41. Cf. the vesper hymn for the feast of dedication:

> *Urbs Jerusalem beata...*
> *Nova veniens a caelo,*
> *nuptiali thalamo*
> *praeparata, ut sponsala,*
> *copuletur Domino....*

42. *She is his new creation*
    By water and the Word;
    From heaven he came and sought her
    To be his holy Bride;
    With his own blood he bought her,
    And for her life he died.

43. For examples, see C. Chevasse, *The Bride of Christ*, and E. A. Reinhold, "The Bride," in *The Spear of Gold* (1947), pp. 259ff.

44. See the Form for the Consecration of Virgins in the *Roman Pontifical*, quoted by Reinhold, *The Spear of Gold*, pp. 270ff.

45. This is particularly notable among the German Dominican mystics, Tauler, Eckhardt and Suso.

46. On the need for mental images, and the need also for renouncing them, see especially his *Ascent of Mount Carmel*, II, chapter 17; on the use and abuse of external sacred images, ibid., III, 35, 36. For all his strong emphasis on the dangers of images, few Christian writers have employed a richer or more sensuous imagery than St. John of the Cross in his poems.

47. We are indebted to Fr. Sebastian Bullough, O.P., for this rendering of,

> *Sie ist mir lieb, die werte Magd,*
> *Ich kann sie nicht vergessen;*
> *Lob, Ehr und Zucht man von ihr sagt:*
> *Sie hat mein Herz bessessen.*

—"Ein Lied von der heiligen Kirchen/aus dem xii. capitel Apocalypsis" (1532?); Martin Luther, *Sämtliche deutsche geistliche Lieder*, ed. F. Klippgen (Halle, 1912), p. 54.

48. *CW*, XI, p. 48f.
49. Ibid., p. 47.
50. Ibid., p. 161.
51. Ibid., p. 465.
52. Ibid., p. 171. In fact, however, the accepted doctrine of the Assumption positively excludes any such development. As we have put it elsewhere (V. White, "The Scandal of the Assumption," *Selection I* (1953), pp. 99f.):

> (1) At the Incarnation, the three divine Persons "assume" (i.e., "take to themselves') a created human *nature* (not a human person) into hypostatic union with the Person of the Son: Jesus Christ is one single Person, the Son of God, with two natures, divine and human: God and Man in one single Being (*habet unum esse*). At the Assumption of our Lady, the three divine Persons "assume" a human *person* into the glory of the Godhead: her human personality, being and nature, remain intact in their pure creatureliness...she eternally remains purely human, and infinitely distinct from the eternal Godhead.

> (2) The mysteries of Christ (the Incarnation, Atonement, Resurrection, Ascension, etc.) are the mysteries of the *Redeemer*, although also prototypes (*causae exemplares*) of the processes in which we must share for our redemption. The mysteries of Mary (immaculate conception, progressive sanctification, Christ-begetting, assumption) are exclusively those of the *redeemed*: the first and supreme specimens of the effects of God's saving work through Christ. It is "in view of the merits of Christ" that the Church has defined her to be conceived immaculate, and in virtue of the same merits and through the sole power of God that she is assumed into heaven. (Mary is "assumed" by God: Jesus "ascends" in his own power.)

> (3) The doctrine of the Assumption, so far from encouraging, should therefore act as a safeguard against "mariolatry," any derogation of the all-sufficiency of Christ's merits and mediatorship, and any dilution of the *Soli Deo Gloria* (Glory to God only) principle. Her glory is *entirely* God's, and none is her own independently of him.... Her Assumption, body and soul, into the glory of the one God ensures that in no sense she becomes a Goddess, if this means (as it seems it must) some superhuman being and power, independent of God Almighty. Yet her exaltation by the one God, and her sharing in his glory, may well mean that she is raised above anything ever claimed for any goddess, and entitles her to worthier attributes than were ever claimed for a goddess.

(4) Nevertheless there is a true and important sense in which the Assumption of our Lady may be called her apotheosis, divinization, even her deification; though such words must be used only with understanding and caution. Most early Fathers of the Church, and many spiritual writers, use the words *theosis* or *deificatio* for the final sanctification or glorification of *all* the predestined; sometimes they even call them God or Gods, e.g., in commenting on the psalm-verse (quoted by Jesus), *Ego dixi, dii estis* (I said, ye are gods: Ps. 81:6; John 10:34). St. Thomas follows this usage (*Summa*, III, I, 2) and he justifies and explains it in his careful analysis of the various analogous (i.e., essentially different but related) meanings of the noun "God" (*Summa*, I, 13, 8, 10). Thus understood the Assumption is in a supreme degree a "deification" effected, not of course by the Pope or the Church who only proclaim it, but by the one God himself.

Too often, however, some Jungians give the impression of understanding the Assumption as a positive disembodiment rather than as an Assumption of the *body*, as well as the soul, of Mary. This causes some understandable irritation among Christian Jungians themselves: "To a Christian, analytical psychology has many defects.... Jung's psychological treatment of the dogma of the Assumption of the Blessed Virgin is interesting but, as a believer in the Incarnation, I often feel that, in the writings of some Jungians, there is a lot too much assumption of the body into heaven. We are seldom allowed to let a penis or a breast remain as a concrete living symbol. It quickly becomes not really flesh but a sign leading to an aerial sphere where we float around amongst wraith-like animas and esoteric mandalas, searching fruitlessly for a solid bed on which to consummate the *hieros gamos*" (Robert Hobson, *Journal of Analytical Psychology*, III [January 1958], p. 69).

53. Ibid., p. 399.
54. Luke 1:49.
55. *CW*, XI, p. 399.
56. *Essays on a Science of Mythology*, p. 239.
57. Cf. Jung, "Woman in Europe," *Contributions to Analytical Psychology*.
58. *CW*, VII, p. 52.
59. Cf. Luke 1:28, 48.
60. Aristotle, *De Memoria et Rem.*, 450b, 12ff.
61. *Summa*, III, 25, 3.
62. Ibid.

63, Ibid., a. 5.

64. *Dict. de theol. cath.*, VII, 825ff.

65. This dictum of St. Basil became axiomatic in both East and West; but while in the East it was taken to mean that the images (ikons) as things were to be reverenced because of the prototype, and this included even the making of them, the West generally drew the opposite conclusion— the image as a thing was nothing, the prototype alone was venerable. See ibid., *passim.*

66. Denzinger–Bannwart, *Enchiridion Symbolorum*, 302–304.

67. See V. White, "The Platonic Tradition in St. Thomas Aquinas," *God the Unknown*, pp. 62ff.

68. Session XXV. See *Dict. de theol. cath.*, IX, 24, 54.

69. This term, though clumsy, seems preferable in this context to the term "projection."

70. S. N. Bulgakov, *The Wisdom of God: A Brief Summary of Sophiology* (1937), p. 179.

71. Ibid., p. 180. Cf. Jean Guitton, *The Blessed Virgin* (1952), pp. 150f.: "The relationship between the Virgin and the Spirit, empirically so close, has not engaged the attention of [Western] theologians and mystics. The Virgin, in popular devotion, is an effective equivalent to the Holy Spirit—the Unknown. Here, Russian theology seems to be ahead of ours, insisting on the fact that the Incarnation, the common achievement of the Three, implies that as early as the Annunciation the Holy Spirit descended upon Mary. Hence it applies to her that beautiful title *Pneumatophoros*, she who bears the Spirit." Guitton's book, which came to our notice only after this chapter was written, is exceptional for its original and thoughtful approach to the subject, and as the work of a layman acutely aware of the spirit of our times.

72. Ibid. p. 184.

CHAPTER NINE

1. See *Summa*, I-II, 23 and 24; 56, 4; 61, 4 and 5; 68, 4.

2. Matthew 1:3, 5, 6.

3. See J. Jacobi, *The Psychology of C. G. Jung* (1942), pp. 102ff., and the diagram on p. 122.

4. See "The Dual Mother," chapter VII of Jung's *Symbols of Transformation*, *CW*, V, pp. 306ff., which contains abundant mythological and dream material on the subject.

5. Erich Neumann, *The Origins and History of Consciousness*, pp. 154f., 158. The whole of this chapter, "The Slaying of the Mother," should be read in this context.

6. See the chapter on "The Perils of the Soul," in J. G. Frazer, *The Golden Bough* (chapter XVIII in abridged edition). Cf. *CW*, XVI, pp. 180, 266; VII, pp. 148f.

7. Genesis 2:24; Matthew 19:5; Mark 10:7; Ephesians 5:31.

8. Luke 2:49.

9. John 19:27.

10. Luke 2:51f.

11. *CW*, XI, p. 76.

12. Ibid., p. 197f.

13. Romans 7:17, 19, 20, 21.

14. It could, we suggest, be misleading in many instances to identify the "shadow" only with the "animal part of ourselves" (cf. Frieda Fordham, *An Introduction to Jung's Psychology* [1953], p. 59). The contents which are accounted "evil" and "shadow" will differ greatly according as to what the individual accounts "good" and "light," and, as Jung has frequently pointed out, according to what, in each case, are the individual's "superior" and "inferior" functions.

15. Walter Hilton, *The Scale of Perfection*, ed. Evelyn Underhill (1923), pp. 125ff. Cf. V. White, *Walter Hilton: An English Spiritual Guide*, Guild of Pastoral Psychology Lecture, 31, pp. 13ff.

16. W. Hilton, *The Scale of Perfection*, p. 269.

17. Notably in his introduction to *Psychology and Alchemy*, in his *Aion*, *Answer to Job*, *The Undiscovered Self* and *Ein moderner Mythus*. The ideas summarized in the following paragraphs will be found scattered throughout these works, and we have thought it unnecessary to give precise references except when making actual quotations.

18. This is the principal theme of Jung's *Answer to Job*.

19. V. White, "Guilt: Theological and Psychological," *Christian Essays in Psychiatry* (1956), pp. 155ff.

20. 1 John 1:5.

21. 1 Peter 2:22.

22. This is the unfortunate Authorized Version of Matthew 16:23. The Douai version has "Go behind me," which is nearer the Greek, *hypage opiso mou*. So far from dismissing Peter–Satan—the shadow—Christ orders him to follow behind him on his way to suffering, instead of being a *skandalon*, a stumbling-block in front of him.
23. Ephesians 5:3.
24. *Aion*, p. 64.
25. From G. K. Chesterton's hymn, "O God of earth and altar."
26. The psychological significance of UFOs (flying saucers) and space-fiction is the subject of Jung's *Ein Moderner Mythus* (1958).
27. 1 John 2:18.
28. Apocalypse 20:7.
29. 2 Thessalonians 2:3.
30. *CW*, XI, p. 419.
31. Isaias 45:7.
32. This idea is found in the pseudo-Clementine homilies; cf. *Aion*, pp. 71ff.
33. *CW*, XI, pp. 449ff. The reference is to the "eternal gospel" of Apocalypse 6f., which is to "Fear the Lord and give him honour, because the hour of judgment is come." However, the Greek *phobethete* may as often be rendered "hold in reverential awe" as "be terrified of," and the context seems to demand the former rendering in this passage.
34. For example, Exodus 33:23: "Thou shalt see my back parts, but my face thou canst not see."
35. *Summa*, I, 6, *passim*; 13, 5, 6. Cf. V. White, "Talk about God," *God the Unknown*, pp. 26ff.
36. *Summa*, I, 49, 1, 2.
37. Jung's *Answer to Job* is introduced by the text, *Doleo super te frater mi*—"I am distressed for thee, my brother"—1 Kings (2 Samuel) 1:26.
38. Mark 3:17. Cf. Luke 9:54.
39. Cf. 1 John 1:8, 10 with 5:18 (RSV).
40. John 16:8.
41. Acts 15:10.
42. Cf. *Summa*, III, 106–109, *passim*.
43. Greek philosophers, significantly enough, paid little attention to evil. Plato cheerfully discussed at length the "Idea of the Good" and Aristotle the virtuous or "good life," with little or no reference to badness or evil—contrary to what Jung considers logically or psychologically possible.

They *assumed*, rather than explicitly stated, that badness is the absence of what they consider to be good. They made, however, much use of the concept of privation (*sterēsis*), especially in their conception of matter; and Aristotle was well aware of the difference between the opposition of two contraries and that of a positive and its privation. (See V. White, "Kinds of Opposites," *Studien zur Analytischen Psychologie C. G. Jung* [Zürich, 1955], I, pp. 141ff.)

It was not until after the coming of Christianity that we find any attempt to define evil in general, but it is not first among Christians, but rather among the Neoplatonists that we find it. Plotinus shows that it is not an essence or substance (*ousia*) but a privation (*sterēsis*) of being. It is not, however, "nothing" (*oukon*) but a not-something (*to mē on*) (see W. R. Inge, *The Philosophy of Plotinus*, I, pp. 129ff.). "Nothing" is altogether unreal; privation is the absence of something real from something real, and is real on account of the reality of its subject—a point which Jung consistently misses. Being a privation, *malum* in the abstract does not exist; but *mala*—evil or deprived things—undoubtedly do; and if their subjects are active then they will be active too.

In the West it is undoubtedly to St. Augustine that we owe the general recognition that evil is *privatio boni*. From his *Confessions* we learn that the discovery and realization of this was for him no academic enterprise, still less an apologetic device to buttress up a Christian orthodoxy which he had already embraced (he had not), but a hard-won and vital personal experience—an enlightenment which changed his whole life. He relates how he had become enmeshed in Manichaeanism and tells of the mental and moral confusion it had brought him, precisely on account of its assertion of the substantiality of evil on a par with that of good. "Evil I saw not only as substance but even as life; and yet, poor wretch, I held it was not from You, my God, from whom all things are.... For I did not as yet know, I had not been taught, that evil is not in itself a substance.... It seemed that I was coming to the truth when I was in fact going away from it. I did not know that evil has no essence of its own, but is an absence of what is good" (*Confessions* IV, 15; III, 7 [trans. F. J. Sheed]).

What for St. Augustine was a vital personal discovery became for the Schoolmen a subject of close, dispassionate logical analysis of which the most concise example is *Summa*, I, 48 and 49.

44. See V. White, "Kinds of Opposites," pp. 146ff.

45. *Summa*, I, 49, 1.
46. *CW*, XI, p. 383.
47. *Aion*, p. 85. Jung maintains that the assertion that evil is *privatio boni* begs the question on the assumption that it is deduced from the "premiss" that God is *Summum Bonum*. We know of no author who has made such a deduction though the assertion logically compels us to deny evil of God and the impossibility of *Summum Malum* (*Summa*, I, 49, 3) and of evil existing independently of a "good" subject (ibid., 48, 3, 4). The assertion is not, in fact, a conclusion from any premiss, but a simple definition based on an analysis of experience—a generalization of what men mean when they use the words "evil" or "bad." Notwithstanding his theory, Jung himself appears often in practice to accept the privative conception of evil correctly understood. Hostie (*Religion and the Psychology of Jung*, p. 197) remarks: "Jung himself has frequently stressed the fact that the mark of psychotherapy 'is not the imaginary entity known as neurosis but the distorted totality of the human being.' Does not this clearly mean that psychic evil is a lack of something, in fact a privation of some good that should be there?" And in one passage in *Aion*, Jung describes "good" without reference to evil, as "was von einem gewissen Standpunkt aus als passend, annehmbar oder wertvoll erscheint; böse ist das entsprechende Gegenteil" ("Good is that which from a particular standpoint appears to be suitable, acceptable or valuable; evil is the corresponding opposite," *Aion*, p. 86). But what can be the "entsprechende Gegenteil" if not the "*un*passend" (*un*suitable), the "*un*annehmbar" (*un*acceptable) or the wert*los* (value*less*)? This in fact corresponds exactly to the Aristotelian-Thomist and common-sense view, according to which the good is the object of *orexis* or appetite (whether rational or sensitive), and evil the absence or privation from an object of that good.
48. Foreword to R. J. Z. Werblowsky, *Lucifer and Prometheus*, *CW*, VII, p. 313.
49. *Aion*, p. 87.
50. Foreword to V. White, *God and the Unconscious*, *CW*, VII, p. 304.
51. Jacques Maritain, *St. Thomas and the Problem of Evil* (Milwaukee, 1942), pp. 2ff.
52. Robert Hobson, *The Journal of Analytical Psychology*, III, 1 (January 1958), p. 67. The *Concise Oxford Dictionary* recognizes that "evil" is both an adjective and a noun, but that as a noun it means "an evil thing."

Aquinas recognized the ambiguity in the Latin *malum* since it is both a concrete and an abstract noun ("bad thing" and "badness"): "In one sense *malum* can be understood as the subject of badness (*mali*), and this is something real; in another sense it can be understood as badness itself" (*ipsum malum*) and this is not something real (*aliquid*) but is the privation of some particular good (*De Malo* I, 1)." The Greek *to kakon* can also be understood in both these senses. Jung, in translating Greek and Latin Fathers, renders both *malum* and *to kakon* as *das Böse*, and, apparently using it as a concrete noun, easily makes nonsense of their statements. The English "badness" or the German "*Schlechtigkeit*" would have rendered their undoubted meaning less ambiguously, and possibly spared us the whole polemic!

53. *Summa*, I-II, 36, 1.

54. G. P. Zacharias, *Psyche und Mysterium* (Zurich, 1954), pp. 75.

55. See Aquinas, *Summa*, I, 48, 5 and *De Malo*, I, 4. The definition of *malum culpae* as "malum quod agimus" (the evil we do) and of *malum poenae* as "malum quod patimur" (the evil we undergo) goes back to St. Augustine. These terms, though less familiar, seem preferable to those of "moral evil" and "physical evil." By no means all the evil we undergo or suffer is physical, and we can do evil physically.

56. See J. Maritain, *St. Thomas and the Problem of Evil*, pp. 20ff.

57. See *Summa*, I-II, 109, 8, and above, pp. 199ff. It is Pelagian heresy to assert that fallen man is able to avoid every sin, that he retains his "naturalis possibilitas," or that his freedom of will is not diminished. (Denzinger–Bannwart, *Enchiridion Symbolorum*, 105, 107, 108, 130, 133, 181, etc.). It is also, for Catholics, a matter of faith that, even after baptism and with sanctifying grace, he is unable to avoid *every* sin, even venial, except by a special privilege, generally believed to be peculiar to the Blessed Virgin (ibid., 471, 833). According to Aquinas, no single sin is in itself inevitable. We can avoid *each* sin, but on account of the disorder and consequent insubordination of our psychological functions, and the inability of our weakened intelligence and will to cope with them all, we cannot avoid *every* sin (*Summa*, ibid., and 74, 3 ad 2). The statement of Pope Pius XII to the Fifth International Congress of Psychotherapy (*Osservatore Romano*, April 16, 1953) that "original sin does not take away from man the possibility and the obligation of conducting himself by his soul" (*le péché originel ne lui enlève pas la possibilité et l'obligation de*

se conduire lui-même par l'âme) is doubtless to be understood in the light of this traditional doctrine. Original sin does not take away from man *every* possibility—nor indeed *any* obligation—to govern his life by his free and conscious will.

58. *Summa*, I-II, 72, 5; 74, 4, 8, 9, 10.

59. Ibid., I, 48, 6

60. Ibid., I-II, 1, 1.

61. Ibid., I-II, 44, *passim.* Cf. V. White "Guilt: Theological and Psychological," in *Christian Essays in Psychiatry* (1956), pp. 165f.

62. Romans 7:19. The fact that a neurotic, more or less unconsciously, is commonly found to have a certain "need to be ill" on account of the advantages which his illness brings him, and the defences with which his neurosis provides him, does not contradict the fact that the neurotic structure and its symptoms are unwilled by his conscious ego.

63. See especially, Michael Fordham, "The Origins of the Ego in Childhood," *New Developments in Analytical Psychology* (1957).

64. See above, p. 155.

65. Matthew 5:39.

66. James 4:7; 1 Peter 5:9.

67. *CW*, XI, p. 75.

68. Genesis 1:31.

69. John 3:16.

70. Galatians 5:17.

71. *Summa*, I, 63, 2, 3, 4, 7. Cf. V. White, *God and the Unconscious*, p. 183f.

72. *Aion*, p. 100.

73. 1 John 4:2f.

74. See above, pp. 83ff.

75. See above, p. 116.

76. *CW, XI*, p. 75f., VII, 57ff.

77. Louis Beirnaert, S.J. "The Mythical Dimension in Christian Baptism," *Selection I* (1953), pp. 61f.

78. From the form for the blessing of the Easter candle in the Latin rite.

79. Romans 6:1f.

80. The full and free choice of good demands the full recognition of its opposite, of what Jung calls the "counter-will," otherwise there is no true "decision." Our natural desires and inclinations are, so far as they go, also good, and it is the will of God that we should have them and

experience them, even when surrender to them would run counter to his expressed will. Discussing Christ's agony in Gethsemane ("Not what I will, but what thou willest"), Aquinas points out that Christ did not repress his natural revulsion to pain and death, but gave full play to all his psychological powers (*permittebat omnibus viribus animae agere quae propria*). In this sense ("not what I will"), he willed what God did not will, though he did not allow this "natural will" to inhibit the divine will that he should suffer and die. There was no real conflict or contrariety of wills: "for it pleased Christ, in accordance with the divine will and the will of his own reason, that his natural will and his sense-appetites should function in accordance with their own natures": there was suppression, but not repression—the "counter-will" was accepted and experienced as itself divinely ordained and an expression of the will of God (*Summa*, III, 18, 5, 6).

81. See Appendix VIII.

CHAPTER TEN

1. *The Month* (October 1956), p. 207.
2. Kenneth Walker, *The Healing Arts* (1953), p. 15.
3. Ibid., p. 11. This definition is in the Preamble to the Constitution of the World Health Organization.
4. Ibid., pp. 11f.
5. Ibid., p. 12.
6. Ibid., p. 17.
7. *Metaph.*, 986a.
8. See Pedro Entralgo, *Mind and Body* (1955), p. 41.
9. Ibid., p. 42f.
10. Ibid., p. 41.
11. *Summa*, I-II, 82, 1.
12. P. Entralgo, ibid., p. 43.
13. Paul Halmos, *Towards a Measure of Man* (1957), p. 44.
14. Ibid.
15. *Penguin Dictionary of Biology* (1951), p. 138.
16. W. von Siebenthal, *Schuldgefühl und Schuld bei psychiatrischen Erkrankungen* (1956), p. 143.

17. Antiphon still sung at Compline (the late night service) during Lent in the Dominican rite.

18. V. von Weizsäcker, *Der kranke Mensch: eine Einführung in die medizinische Anthropologie* (Stuttgart, 1951), p. 341.

19. Ibid., p. 357f.

20. Ibid., p. 362.

21. Ibid., p. 339. This standpoint is confirmed by those zoologists and biologists who have drawn attention to the quantitative and qualitative peculiarities which attend the ageing processes of human beings as compared with those of other mammals, including the anthropoids. See Adolf Portmann, *Zoologie und das neue Bild des Menschen* (Hamburg, 1956), pp. 100–105.

22. Von Siebenthal, *Schuldgefühl und Schuld*, p. 142.

23. *CW*, XVI, p. 70.

24. This is not to say that *any* concept of normality is invalid. We may agree with Paul Halmos (*Towards a Measure of Man*, pp. 45ff.) that there are recognizable "frontiers of adjustment," both psychological and social, outside of which it is legitimate to speak of "abnormality" and "abnormal psychology." But the territory they enclose is very wide, and, in the absence of some definite "disease-entity," the frontiers themselves are very hard to define with precision.

25. Jung, while allowing for the possibility of toxic concomitants in schizophrenia (whether as cause or effect is still obscure), strongly favours the latter view. See especially his paper read to the Psychiatric Section of the Royal Society of Medicine, "On the Psychogenesis of Schizophrenia (quoted H. G. Baynes, *Mythology of the Soul* [1940], pp. 37ff.) and "Die Schizophrenie," *Schweizer Archiv für Neurologie und Psychiatrie*, Bd. 81 (1958), pp. 163ff. This is an extension of Janet's view of an *abaissement du niveau mental* and *faiblesse de la volonté* as a key principle to explain the symptoms of hysteria. Kretschmer also holds that "We should no longer look on certain types of personality as psychopathic abortive forms of certain psychoses; but, *vice versa*, certain psychoses will figure as caricatures of certain normal types of personality" (see Baynes, *Mythology of the Soul*, p. 46). John Custance's account and interpretation of his own manic-depressive experiences (in his *Wisdom, Folly and Madness*) strikingly confirm this view.

26. Quoted P. Halmos, *Towards a Measure of Man*, p. 45.

27. E. Fromm, *Psychoanalysis and Religion* (1950), p. 83.

28. W. von Siebenthal, *Schuldgefühl und Schuld*, p. 138.

29. Ibid. This account of Freud's predominantly individualistic subjective and introverted, and Adler's predominantly social, objective and extroverted, conceptions of mental *health* confirms rather than contradicts Jung's contrary account of their respective views of mental *illness* (see *CW*, VII, p. 41ff.). Recognizing that both Freud and Adler spoke true, but neither the whole truth, about mental health and sickness, Jung finds the difference between them to lie in a "contrast between the two types of mentality." It was just these observations that led Jung first to classify two basic and contrary psychological attitudes (extrovert and introvert) and, later, different psychological types among different individuals, and corresponding psychological functions even within the individual. The practical upshot of this was his recognition that, in psychology also, one man's meat is another man's poison, and that each has his own way of being ill—and also of being well. Cf. *CW*, XVI, pp. 70.f.

30. *CW*, VII, p. 230.

31. See above, p. 41.

32. *CW*, XVI, pp. 86f.; cf. V, p. 40.

33. Ibid., p. 26.

34. Ibid., p. 40f.

35. Ibid., pp. 78, 81.

36. Ibid., p. 10.

37. See ibid., p. 39.

38. *Psychological Types* (1938), p. 261.

39. *CW*, XVI, p. 10.

40. *Psychological Types*, p. 563.

41. Ibid., p. 624.

42. "Since the individual is not a single, separate being but, by his very existence, also presupposes a collective relationship, the process of individuation must clearly lead to a more intensive and universal solidarity, not a mere *isolation*." Jung, ibid., p. 562.

43. Ibid., p. 561.

44. *CW*, VII, p. 108.

45. Ibid.

46. Cf. Joseph Campbell, *The Hero with a Thousand Faces* (1956). This remarkable book sets out to disengage a "monomyth" from all myths

which tell of a Hero: "to bring together a host of myths and folk tales from every corner of the world, and to let the symbols speak for themselves. The parallels will be immediately apparent: and these will develop a vast and amazingly constant statement of the basic truths by which man has lived...."

47. See especially Jane Harrison's *Ancient Art and Ritual* and Jessie Weston's *From Ritual to Romance*.

48. Note especially their familiar features of the *rite d'entrée*, the combat, the extinction and re-kindling of light, the lamentation, the folly, and notably the central feature of the death of the old and the resurrection of the divine King.

49. See M. L. von Franz, *Archetypal Patterns in Fairy Tale*, and Lewis Spence, *British Fairy Origins*; also his *Myth and Ritual in Dance, Game and Rhyme*.

50. See C. G. Jung, *Psychology and Alchemy* (*CW*, XII), *passim*.

51. See V. White, "The Way of the Cross," *Life of the Spirit*, VII, 72 (April 1952), pp. 409ff.

52. *CW*, VII, p. 224.

53. It is well known how Freud also came to recognize in the psyche a principle of *Thanatos* (death) alongside that of *Eros*, and how it revolutionized his earlier theory. The term *Thanatos*, used in this connection, originated with Stekel in 1909, and in his published work Freud never used it, preferring the term "death-instinct." The hypothesis of an *instinct* for death is indeed highly dubious, and has been subjected to much criticism on biological and other grounds. But Freud never seems to have understood that *Eros* and *Thanatos* were not irreducibly opposed to one another, but that the very aim and completion of *Eros* (as we know it in this life) is *Thanatos*, and that *Thanatos* is the precondition of new *Eros*. We are told that Freud "found considerable resistance" to his *Thanatos* among his disciples and colleagues, and that it has practically vanished among them today except "in a purely clinical sense which is remote from Freud's original theory." (Ernest Jones, *Sigmund Freud, Life and Work*, vol. 3 [1957], pp. 292ff.). However, "the neo-Freudians, notably the Kleinian school, state explicitly that all anxiety is connected with the fear of loss and ultimately with a fear of one's own extinction." (Mary Williams, "The Fear of Death," *Journal of Analytical Psychology*, III, 2 [July 1958], p. 158. The whole of this valuable article should be consulted.)

54. Michael Fordham, "Individuation and Ego Development," *Journal of Analytical Psychology*, III, 2 (July 1958), p. 117. See also Jolande Jacobi, "The Process of Individuation," ibid., pp. 95ff.

55. Ibid.

56. See above, note 25.

57. W. von Siebenthal, *Schuldgefühl und Schuld*, pp. 162ff.: "Human existence as a process is only possible because of hope. *Homo viator*, man *in statu viatoris*, is irresistibly *homo sperans.*" On the emotion of hope as a condition for action and life, see Aquinas, *Summa*, I-II, 40, 8.

58. As the object of the natural emotion of hope is the hard-to-attain humanly possible, so the object of the theological virtue of hope is God himself, whom it is humanly impossible for us to attain, but possible by God's power and help. *Summa*, I-II, 17, 1.

59. See W. von Siebenthal, *Schuldgefühl und Schuld*, and Mary Williams, "The Fear of Death," *passim*.

60. C. G. Jung, *Ein Moderner Mythus*, p. 61.

61. From the evening prayers of Bishop Challoner's *Garden of the Soul*, for long the most popular book of devotions among English-speaking Catholics.

62. *Book of Common Prayer*, "The Order for the Visitation of the Sick." These exhortations have disappeared from the "Deposited" Prayer Book of 1928.

63. G. W. A. Lampe, "The Healing Church in the New Testament," *The St. Raphael Quarterly* (November 1957), pp. 463ff.

64. The evidence is collected in *Christian Healing* by Evelyn Frost (1940), to which the contents of this paragraph are indebted.

65. 1 Corinthians 15:55; Philippians 1:21.

66. E. Frost, *Christian Healing*, p. 29.

67. *Summa*, I, 97, 1, 2.

68. *Summa*, I-II, 109, 2.

69. *Summa*, I, 95, 1.

70. Ibid.

71. Ibid., I, 96, 4.

72. Ibid., 1, 2.

73. Ibid., I-II, 82, 1, corpus and ad 1.

74. Ibid., 109, 2, 3, 4. Hence, for Aquinas, original sin brings about a corruption of the whole, though not of the individual parts: "The goodness of nature is corrupted, in so far as human nature is disorganized because

a man's will is not subject to God. For when this subjection is taken away, the result is that the whole nature of sinful man remains disordered" (ibid., a. 7). Having lost his centre in God, man's own egotism, his "bonum privatum," takes its place, and makes it impossible for him—without grace—to prefer God to himself (ibid., a. 3). This is not far from Luther's "total corruption" as J. S. Whale (*The Protestant Tradition*, p. 36) interprets it: "Just because self-love pervades the whole man (*homo* being *totus homo*), all his activities are tainted thereby, even at the highest religious level. There is no unspoiled divine nucleus at the deep centre of a man's individuality—a saving bridgehead, as it were, reaching out beyond individuality to the Infinite; the individuality itself is corrupted. 'Total' corruption means just that."

75. Ibid., 82, 4 ad 1: "Once the bond of original equity, in which all the powers of the soul were contained in an orderly fashion, has been broken, each power tends to go its own way, and all the more violently the stronger it is. It happens that some of these powers are stronger in one person than in another, on account of physical factors. So the fact that one person has stronger sexual passions than another does not arise from original sin, since in everybody the bond of original equity is broken equally, and in everybody equally the lower powers of the soul are left to themselves. But it comes about from the different dispositions of their components."

76. Conc. Trid. Sess. V. Denzinger–Bannwart, 792.

77. According to Catholic doctrine, we are, of course, already sanctified, i.e., made holy, by the single *event* of God's justification, of which baptism is the efficacious sign. It is therefore legitimate to call that event "sanctification." But it is more usual to employ the word for the subsequent life or process which that event initiates. J. S. Whale (*The Protestant Tradition*, p. 65f.) misrepresents the position when he writes that according to Catholic belief "Justification is thus confused with sanctification (which is perhaps the most serious Roman heresy)"; and he confuses the issue further by supposing that for Catholics, "So far from being a finished act...the sinner's *justification* is still a *process* which ends only in death." On the contrary, justification is a finished act, an event resulting from the "abiding attitude of the Father towards the contrite prodigal from the beginning." And although he is thereby made initially "holy," sanctification is understood as the process which is not finished this side of heaven. Cf. Aquinas, *Summa*, I-II, 113, 8 and *passim*.

78. It is perhaps unfortunate that the word "saint" has come to be used almost exclusively of those who have undergone the severe tests of the process of canonization. This very process ensures, with its demands for miracles and "heroic virtue," that they are highly exceptional members of the Church, and by no means typical of the process of sanctification among the faithful at large.

79. *CW*, XI, p. 105.

80. *Summa*, I-II, 113, 5.

CHAPTER ELEVEN

1. See V. White, "Guilt: Theological and Psychological," in *Christian Essays in Psychiatry*, pp. 155ff.

2. See above, p. 199f.

3. H. Guntrip, *Mental Pain and the Cure of Souls* (1956), p. 189.

4. See Appendix V, pp. 256ff.

5. *Summa*, II-II, 81–100.

6. Ibid., 81, 8.

7. "Such evil deeds could religion prompt," *De Rerum Natura*, i, 101.

8. See Prologue to *Summa*, I-II.

9. *Summa*, II-II, 81, 6.

10. Cf. the chapter on "Magic and Religion," in James G. Frazer, *The Golden Bough*.

11. "Religio est quae superioris naturae, quam divinam vocant, cultum caere-moniamque affert." *Invent. Rhetor.*, II, ii, 53.

12. *Summa*, II-II, 101, 1.

13. Ibid., 103, 3. Cf. St. Augustine, *De Civitate Dei*, x, 1: "The service which is due to men, as when the Apostle enjoins servants to be subject to their masters, is one thing, and is called *douleia* in Greek; the service which belongs to the *cultus* of God, called *latreia* in Greek, is quite another."

14. Virtue (*arete*) according to Aristotle (*Nic. Ethics*, 1106a15) "not only renders its subject good, but also causes it to function well": *virtus est quae bonum facit habentem et opus eius bonum reddit.*

15. James 1:27.

16. The concluding words of Jung's *Answer to Job*, *CW*, XI, p. 470.

17. We use the term "acting-out" in a wider sense than that of psychoanalysis. But it is not altogether dissimilar inasmuch as it is the performance of an archetypal pattern, though a deliberate and voluntary one.
18. John 4:24.
19. *Summa*, II-II, 81, 7.
20. Eve Lewis, "The Development of the Religious Attitude in Children," *Christian Essays in Psychiatry* (1956), pp. 89ff.
21. Ibid., 82. 3.
22. *Summa*, I-II, 28, 3; II-II, 175, 2 ad 1.
23. Cf. the Sanskrit *yoga*, "Yoke." Originally *religio* appears to have meant a tie or bond, and later, more especially being bound to a god or a cult (cf. R. B. Onians, *The Origins of European Thought*, pp. 439ff.).
24. We may here contrast the teaching of karma yoga in the *Bhagavadgita*, according to which the transcendent Self alone is the agent in all activity, and the assumption that "I am the doer" is an illusion, with that of Aquinas. According to the latter, God is indeed the first Agent in all activity ("Deus operatur in omni operante," *Summa*, I, 105), but Divine omnipotence is shown by the very fact that it communicates the power of acting and causing to creatures (ibid.).
25. That is, the identification of the ego with an archetype.
26. Jung defines the "persona" (which should be carefully distinguished from the "person" or the "personality"!) as "a complicated system of relations between individual consciousness and society, fittingly enough a kind of mask, designed on the one hand to make a definite impression on others, and, on the other, to conceal the true nature of the individual." *CW*, VII, p. 190.
27. *De Gen. contra Manich.*, II, xviii, 28, *PL* 34:210.
28. See L. Beirnaert, "The Mythical Dimension in Christian Baptism," *Selection I* (1953), p. 64.
29. H. C. Rümke, in *The Psychology of Unbelief* (1952), pp. 47f., names the "fear of effeminacy" as one of the principal sources of resistance to religion; effeminacy being associated with passivity and weakness. Hence the widespread idea that "religion is unmanly" or an "affair for women." The fear is likely to be the more inhibiting, the less the "anima" is constellated in an acceptable feminine figure such as Mary or Ecclesia. Rümke says he has observed this inhibiting fear "more with men than with women," but there can be little doubt that a similar fear can possess

the modern young woman also. It is greatly enhanced when, unlike her altar-boy or choir-boy brother, she has been given no active ritual function in childhood, and is expected to play a purely passive role in public worship thereafter. The Catholic type of worship should indeed constellate the feared "anima" in the shape of the *Virgo potens* who willingly and courageously accepts her passive and feminine role in the Divine designs. But it gives the little girl or the young woman little to *do*: the boys and lads and men do it all and have all the fun. It is not surprising that, notwithstanding preachments about the important role of women in the Church, they get the impression that their position in organized religion is an inferior one, and that it has no room for them as equal *persons* with intelligence and initiative such as awaits them nowadays in "secular" life. Protestant types of worship, while lacking the revered "anima" figure, inculcate far less ritual differentiation between the sexes. The "common prayer" is shared more equally by males and females, and does not raise the same problem.

30. *Summa*, II-II, 183, 3.
31. Jung's work is so described by Hans Schaer. Previous to Jung the unconscious (if recognized at all) was regarded as a mere appendage of the ego—the depository for its unwanted garbage. In the Jungian "model" of the psyche, the ego (though, like the earth, our habitat) is no longer central but peripheral.
32. *CW*, XI, pp. 203ff. The essay also appears in *The Mysteries: Papers from the Eranos Yearbooks* (1955), pp. 321ff.
33. See Appendix VII.
34. Galatians 5:22.
35. Cf. Igor Caruso, *Psychoanalyse und Synthese der Existenz*, pp. 9
36. Cf. C. G. Jung, "Psychotherapists or the Clergy," *Modern Man in Search of a Soul*, pp. 255ff. Elsewhere Jung has written, "Has it not been noticed that I do not write for Church circles, but for those who stand *extra Ecclesiam*? I associate myself on purpose, and of free choice, with those who are outside the Church.... I am not speaking to the *beati possidentes* of faith, but to the many for whom 'the Light has gone out, the mystery vanished.' I am speaking to those to whom God is dead." (Quoted, V. White, *God and the Unconscious*, pp. 260, 256.)
37. Eve Lewis, "The Development of the Religious Attitude in Children," pp. 102ff.

38. H. C. Rümke, *The Psychology of Unbelief* (1952), *passim*. We are however unable to agree with Rümke (or his translator) when we read that for a religious attitude "Sacrifice of individuality must be made. There lies the strongest obstacle to belief" (p. 44). On the contrary we would maintain that an adult person's surrender to the service of God requires a strong individuality (not to be confused with individualism), and that it is in his subordination to God that individuality is fully established.

39. See above, pp. 76ff.

40. *Psychological Types*, pp. 616f.

41. Ibid., pp. 554ff., 601ff.

42. Cf. V. White, *God and the Unconscious*, pp. 38f.

43. "Amplification" is the therapeutic method of comparing a patient's dreams, phantasies, etc., with data provided by mythology, archaeology and comparative religion. It is employed, Jung explains, because "these fields offer me invaluable analogies with which to enrich the associations of my patients" (*CW*, XVI, p. 170).

44. Cf. V. White, "Incarnations and the Incarnation," *God the Unknown*, pp. 75ff.

45. "The human imagination has always been controlled by certain basic images, in which man's own nature, his relation to his fellows, and his dependence upon the divine power find expression.... In ages for which religion and poetry were a common possession, the basic images lived in the conscious mind; men saw their place and destiny, their worth and guilt, and the process of their existence, in terms of them. Being externalized, the images taken for the reality of the divine became idolatry, and taken for the reality of nature became a false science. The rejection of idolatry meant not the destruction but the liberation of the images. Nowhere are the images in more vigour than in the Old Testament, where they speak of God, but are not he. The images are not through all ages absolutely invariable, and there is no historical study more significant than the study of their transformations. Such a transformation finds expression in the birth of Christianity; it is a visible rebirth of images. This should be common ground to believers and unbelievers.... The historian will see the transformation as gradual, prepared within Judaism and outside it: but it precipitated itself in the thought and action of Jesus Christ." Austin Farrer, *A Rebirth of Images* (1949), pp. 13f. See also the same author's Bampton Lectures, *The Glass of Vision* (1948), especially the lectures on

"Images and Inspiration" and "Archetypes and Incarnation." The archetypes in Christianity are also studied in some detail in F. W. Dillingstone,
Christianity and Symbolism (1955).

46. Notably in his *Griechische Mythen in christlicher Deutung* (Zürich, 1945),
"Der Spielende Mensch," *Eranos Jahrbuch XVI* (1948), pp. 11ff.

47. Justin Martyr, *Apologia*, I, 46.

48. Clement Alex, *Protreplikos*, XII, 119.

49. See Michael Fordham, *New Developments in Analytical Psychology* (1958),
chapters V–VIII; also Eve Lewis, "The Development of the Religious
Attitude in Children."

50. M. Eliade, *Das Heilige und das Profanes* (1957); *The Myth of the Eternal
Return* (1955). Eliade recognizes of course that "the great majority of
so-called Christian populations continue, down to our own day, to preserve themselves from history by ignoring it and tolerating it rather than
by giving it the meaning of a negative or positive theophany" (ibid., p.
111).

51. *Summa*, I-II, 106, 1.

52. Ibid., 107, 1 ad 2.

53. Augustine, *ad Inquisitiones Ianuarii* (Ep. 55.19), quoted *Summa*, 107,
4.

54. Jean Daniélou, summarizing Origen's doctrine, in *Origen*, trans. W.
Mitchell (1955), pp. 259ff. See also J. D. N. Kelly, *Early Christian
Doctrines* (1958), p. 128.

55. Jung nevertheless suggests that the youthful, childless "mariophanies" of
our time are truly archetypal manifestations, akin to the Kore (as distinct
from Demeter) figures in ancient Greece (cf. "The Psychological Aspects
of the Kore," in Jung–Kerenyi, *Essays on a Science of Mythology* [1949]).
This spontaneous appearance in the visions and imagery associated with
Lourdes, Fatima, Beauraing, etc., of a childless, nubile maiden expresses,
according to this view, the deep unconscious hopes of the masses for the
birth of a new Saviour: we might prefer to say, the eschatological hope
for a second coming. Bulgakov (*The Wisdom of God*) interprets the ikon
of Mary in Kiev as the young "unwedded Bride" somewhat similarly.

56. See above, Chapters IV and V.

57. *Summa*, II-II, 82, 3 ad 2.

58. See *Summa*, I, 8, 1, 3; 43, 3.

59. See *CW*, XI, p. 248ff.

60. See above, pp. 199ff.
61. Cf. 2 Corinthians 3:6.
62. See Anthony Storr, "The Religious Development of the Individual," *Christian Essays in Psychiatry*, pp. 73ff.
63. Thomas Carlyle, "Hudson's Statue," *Latter-Day Pamphlets*, No. 7 (1850).

APPENDIX I

1. *Christian Essays in Psychiatry*, ed. P. Mairet (S.C.M. Press, 1956), p. 20.
2. *Life of the Spirit* (October 1957), pp. 158ff.
3. Ibid., p. 159.
4. Ibid., p. 162.
5. See our *God and the Unconscious*, pp. 53ff., 151ff.
6. Ibid.

APPENDIX II

1. To quote a verse attributed to Lillian Smith, *The Family of Man* (Museum of Modern Art, New York, 1955), p. 49.
2. *De Trin.*, 14. 7, cf. Aquinas, *De Veritate*, 10. 3)
3. *De Trin.*, 10. 11.
4. "Vita qua vivimus anima dicitur," *Ennarratio in Ps.* 137, 4.

APPENDIX III

1. For most of the above, see especially Jung's *Psychological Types*, pp. 544ff., 601ff.).
2. See especially, Michael Fordham, *The Life of Childhood* (1944).
3. For the preceding, see Michael Fordham, *New Developments in Analytical Psychology*, pp. 4ff.
4. "The Spirit of Psychology," *Spirit and Nature*, pp. 414f. This essay is Jung's most articulated statement of his developed conception of archetypes, and should be studied by any reader who wishes to pursue the matter.
5. For example, *CW*, VII, p. 238.

6. See L. Stein, "Analytical Psychology: A 'Modern; Science," *Journal of Analytical Psychology*, III (January 1958), pp. 43ff.
7. Fordham, *New Developments in Analytical Psychology*, pp. 8ff.
8. Ibid.
9. See Jung, "Spirit of Psychology," pp. 410ff.
10. *The Objective Psyche*, p. 34.
11. See Leslie Paul, *Nature into History* (1957), *passim.*

APPENDIX VI

1. Quoted. J. Jacobi, *Psychological Reflections*, p. 96f.
2. Margaret Mead, *Male and Female* (1949), p. 8.
3. Ibid., p. 148f.
4. *The Origins and History of Consciousness*, p. 112.
5. Gerhard Clostermann, *Das weibliche Gewissen* (1953), with its copious bibliography.
6. *Psychological Types*, p. 597.
7. Quoted J. Jacobi, *Psychological Reflections*, p. 100.
8. Ibid., p. 94.
9. Neumann, *The Origins and History of Consciousness*, p. xxii.

APPENDIX VII

1. This fact should not invalidate the application of a similar method to other sources. The Epistle itself refers not only to the Mosaic ordinance, but also to the sacrifices of Abel, Abraham and even (*par excellence*) of the "pagan" Melchisedech. It is just these three non-Levitical sacrifices which are mentioned in the Canon of the Mass.
2. This is now authoritatively made clear in the encyclical *Mediator Dei* (Pius XII, 1947), para 74: "The divine wisdom has devised a way in which our Redeemer's sacrifice is marvellously shown forth by *external signs symbolic* of death. By the "transubstantiation," both his body and blood are rendered really present; but the eucharistic species under which he is present *symbolize* the violent separation of his body and blood, and so a *commemorative showing forth of* the death which took place in reality

on Calvary is repeated in each Mass, *because* by distinct *representations* Christ Jesus is *signified and shown forth in his state of victim*" (italics ours).

3. *De Trinitate*, IV, 14.

4. G. R. Levy, *The Gate of Horn* (1948), p. 207.

5. Mircea Eliade, *The Myth of the Eternal Return* (1955), p. 36.

6. C. G. Jung, "Transformation Symbolism in the Mass," in *The Mysteries: Papers from the Eranos Yearbooks* (Routledge, 1955), p. 321.

7. Ibid., p. 320.

8. G. R. Levy, *The Gate of Horn*, pp. 205ff.

9. *Cur Deus Homo?* II, 6.

10. Jung, "Transformation Symbolism in the Mass," p. 314.

11. St. John Chrysostom, quoted by Pius XII, *Mediator Dei*, para. 73.

12. Cf. *Mediator Dei*, paras. 21, 22.

13. See Jung, "Transformation Symbolism in the Mass," pp. 322ff.

14. Ibid., p. 315.

15. Levy, *The Gate of Horn*, p. 42; cf. pp. 86, 105.

16. Jung, "Transformation Symbolism in the Mass," p. 320.

17. J. Layard in *Eranos Jahrbuch* XXIV (1955), p. 340.

18. Ibid.

19. C. G. Jung, *Psychology of the Unconscious*, trans. B. M. Hinkle (1915), pp. 475, 478f. Jung has developed, and in some respects modified, this estimate in the expanded and revised versions of this book, *CW*, V (1956), pp. 433ff.

20. See J. A. T. Robinson, *The Body* (S.C.M. Press, Studies in Biblical Theology, No. 5), pp. 58ff.

21. *Summa*, III, 73, 1.

22. *Summa*, II-II, 85, 1.

23. *Mediator Dei*, paras. 89, 97, 103, 110; cf. 24, 28.

24. *Summa*, III, 79, 5.

25. *Summa*, II-II, 82, 2.

Designed by Fiona Cecile Clarke, the CLUNY MEDIA *logo
depicts a monk at work in the scriptorium,
with a cat sitting at his feet.*

*The monk represents our mission to emulate
the invaluable contributions of the monks
of Cluny in preserving the libraries of the West,
our strivings to know and love the truth.*

*The cat at the monk's feet is Pangur Bán, from the
eponymous Irish poem of the 9th century.
The anonymous poet compares his scholarly
pursuit of truth with the cat's happy hunting of mice.
The depiction of Pangur Bán is an homage to the work
of the monks of Irish monasteries and a sign
of the joy we at Cluny take in our trade.*

"Messe ocus Pangur Bán,
cechtar nathar fria saindan:
bíth a menmasam fri seilgg,
mu memna céin im saincheirdd."

Made in the USA
Middletown, DE
25 August 2023